grzimek's
Student Animal Life Resource

• • • •

grzimek's
Student Animal Life Resource

• • • •

Crustaceans, Mollusks, and Segmented Worms

Arthur V. Evans, D.Sc., author

Madeline S. Harris, project editor
Neil Schlager and Jayne Weisblatt, editors

THOMSON

GALE

Detroit • New York • San Francisco • San Diego • New Haven, Conn. • Waterville, Maine • London • Munich

THOMSON

GALE

Grzimek's Student Animal Life Resource: Crustaceans, Mollusks, and Segmented Worms

Arthur V. Evans, D.Sc

Project Editor
Madeline S. Harris

Editorial
Melissa Hill, Heather Price, Lemma Shomali

Indexing Services
Synapse, the Knowledge Link Corporation

Rights and Acquisitions
Margaret Abendroth, Timothy Sisler

Imaging and Multimedia
Randy Bassett, Michael Logusz, Dan Newell, Chris O'Bryan, Robyn Young

Product Design
Tracey Rowens, Jennifer Wahi

Composition
Evi Seoud, Mary Beth Trimper

Manufacturing
Wendy Blurton, Dorothy Maki

LIBRARY OF CONGRESS CATALOGING-IN-PUBLICATION DATA

Evans, Arthur V.
Grzimek's student animal life resource. Crustaceans, mollusks, and segmented worms /
Arthur V. Evans ; Neil Schlager and Jayne Weisblatt, editors.
    p. cm.
  Includes bibliographical references and index.
  ISBN 0-7876-9411-8 (hardcover : alk. paper)
  1. Crustacea—Juvenile literature. 2. Mollusks—Juvenile literature.
  3. Annelida—Juvenile literature. I. Schlager, Neil, 1966- II. Weisblatt, Jayne.
III. Title.
  QL437.2.E93 2005
  595.3—dc22   2005015905

ISBN 0-7876-9402-9 (21-vol set), ISBN 0-7876-9411-8

This title is also available as an e-book
Contact your Thomson Gale sales representative for ordering information.

Printed in Canada
10 9 8 7 6 5 4 3 2 1

Contents

Reader's Guide

Grzimek's Student Animal Life Resource: Crustaceans, Mollusks, and Segmented Worms offers readers comprehensive and easy-to-use information on Earth's crustaceans, mollusks, and segmented worms. Entries are arranged by taxonomy, the science through which living things are classified into related groups. Each entry includes sections on physical characteristics; geographic range; habitat; diet; behavior and reproduction; animals and people; and conservation status. All entries are followed by one or more species accounts with the same information as well as a range map and photo or illustration for each species. Entries conclude with a list of books, periodicals, and Web sites that may be used for further research.

ADDITIONAL FEATURES

Grzimek's Student Animal Life Resource: Crustaceans, Mollusks, and Segmented Worms includes a pronunciation guide for scientific names; a glossary; an overview of Segmented Worms, Crustaceans, Mollusks, and their relatives; a list of species in the volume by biome; a list of species by geographic range; and an index. The volume has 159 full-color maps, photos, and illustrations to enliven the text, and sidebars provide additional facts and related information.

NOTE

Grzimek's Student Animal Life Resource: Crustaceans, Mollusks, and Segmented Worms has standardized information in the Conservation Status section. The World Conservation

Union (IUCN) Red List provides the world's most comprehensive inventory of the global conservation status of plants and animals. Using a set of criteria to evaluate extinction risk, the IUCN recognizes the following categories: Extinct, Extinct in the Wild, Critically Endangered, Endangered, Vulnerable, Conservation Dependent, Near Threatened, Least Concern, and Data Deficient. These terms are defined where they are used in the text, but for a complete explanation of each category, visit the IUCN web page at http://www.iucn.org/themes/ssc/redlists/RLcats2001booklet.html.

ACKNOWLEDGEMENTS

Gale would like to thank several individuals for their assistance with this volume. Arthur V. Evans, D.Sc., wrote the text. At Schlager Group Inc., Neil Schlager and Jayne Weisblatt coordinated the writing and editing of the volume.

Special thanks are also due for the invaluable comments and suggestions provided by the *Grzimek's Student Animal Life Resource: Crustaceans, Mollusks, and Segmented Worms* advisors:

- Mary Alice Anderson, Media Specialist, Winona Middle School, Winona, Minnesota
- Thane Johnson, Librarian, Oklahoma City Zoo, Oklahoma City, Oklahoma
- Debra Kachel, Media Specialist, Ephrata Senior High School, Ephrata, Pennsylvania
- Nina Levine, Media Specialist, Blue Mountain Middle School, Courtlandt Manor, New York
- Ruth Mormon, Media Specialist, The Meadows School, Las Vegas, Nevada

COMMENTS AND SUGGESTIONS

We welcome your comments on *Grzimek's Student Animal Life Resource: Crustaceans, Mollusks, and Segmented Worms* and suggestions for future editions of this work. Please write: Editors, *Grzimek's Student Animal Life Resource: Crustaceans, Mollusks, and Segmented Worms*, U•X•L, 27500 Drake Rd., Farmington Hills, Michigan 48331-3535; call toll free: 1-800-877-4253; fax: 248-699-8097; or send e-mail via www.gale.com.

Pronunciation Guide for Scientific Names

Amphionidacea am-fee-oh-nih-DAY-see-ay

Amphionides reynaudii am-fee-OH-nih-deez ray-NOH-dee-eye

Amphipoda am-fee-POH-day

Anaspidacea an-ah-spih-DAY-see-ay

Anaspides tasmaniae an-ah-SPIH-dayz taz-MAY-nee-ee

Antalis entalis an-TAL-is en-TAL-is

Antrobathynella stammeri an-troh-bath-EE-nel-lay STAM-mer-eye

Aplacophora ah-plak-oh-FOR-ay

Apseudes intermedius ap-SEE-oo-dez in-ter-MEE-dee-us

Argulus foliaceus AR-gyu-lus foh-lee-AY-see-us

Armadillidium vulgare ar-mah-dil-LID-ee-um vul-GAR-ee

Bathynellacea bath-ee-nel-AYS-see-ay

Bivalvia bi-VAL-vee-ay

Bonellia viridis bon-NEL-lee-ay vih-RID-iss

Brachipoda brah-kee-POE-day

Branchiura bran-chee-YUR-ray

Branchiopoda bran-kee-oh-POE-day

Caprella californica kap-REL-lay kal-ih-FOR-nih-kay

Cephalocarida sef-fal-oh-KAR-ee-day

Cephalopoda sef-fal-oh-POE-day

Chiridotea caeca kih-ree-DOE-tee-ay SEE-kay

Chiton KI-ton

Chlamys opercularis KLAM-iss ah-per-kyu-LAH-ris

Conax variabilis KON-acks var-ee-AH-bih-lis

Conus geographus KON-us jee-oh-GRAF-us

Copepoda koh-pee-POE-day

Corolla spectabilis kuh-ROE-lay spek-TAH-bih-lis

Cryptochiton stelleri krip-toh-KEE-ton STEL-ler-eye

Cumacea koo-MAY-see-ay

Cyclaspis longicaudata sy-KLAS-pis lawn-jih-kaw-DAY-tay

Dahlella caldariensis dah-LEH-lay kal-dah-ree-EN-sis

Daphnia pulex daf-NEE-ay PULL-ecks

Decapoda dek-ah-POE-day

Derocheilocaris typicus deh-roe-kee-eye-loh-KAY-ris TIH-pih-kus

Diplocardia riparia dihp-loh-KAR-dee-ay rih-PAH-ree-ay

Dreissena polymorpha dree-eye-SEE-nay pol-lee-MOR-fay

Echiura eh-kee-YU-ray

Ectoprocta ek-toh-PROK-tay

Electra pilosa ee-LEK-tray pih-LOH-say

Epiperipatus biolleyi eh-pee-pair-ee-PAT-us bi-oll-LEE-eye

Euphausia pacifica yu-FAH-see-ay pah-SIF-ih-kay

Euphausia superba yu-FAH-see-ay soo-PER-bay

Euphausiacea yu-fah-see-AY-see-ay

Eurythoe complanata yu-RITH-oh-ee kom-PLAH-nay-tay

Gastropoda gas-troh-POE-day

Gnathophausia ingens nath-oh-FAW-see-ay IN-jenz

Haementeria ghilianii he-MEN-teh-ree-ay jil-lee-AN-ee-eye

Helix pomatia HE-licks poh-MAH-tee-ay

Hemithyris psittacea heh-me-THY-ris sih-TEH-see-ay

Hirundinea hih-run-DIH-nee-ay

Hutchinsoniella macracantha huch-in-son-ee-EL-lay mack-rah-KAN-thay

Hymenocera picta hy-MEN-oh-seh-ray PIK-tay

Isopoda eye-so-POE-day

Itoitantulus misophricola ee-toh-ee-TAN-too-lus mih-so-FRY-koh-lay

Laevipilina antarctica lee-vih-pih-LEE-nay an-TARK-tih-kay

Lepeophtheirus salmonis leh-pee-off-thee-EYE-rus sal-MON-is

Linguatula serrata ling-gwa-TOO-lay ser-RAH-tay

Loligo pealeii LOH-lih-go pee-AH-lee-eye

Lophogastrida loh-foh-GAS-tree-day

Lottia pelta loh-TEE-ay PEL-tay

Macrobdella decora mak-robe-DEL-lay DEK-oh-ray

Megascolides australis meg-ah-SKOH-lih-deez aws-TRAH-lis

Mictacea mik-tah-SEE-ay

Mictocaris halope mik-toh-KAR-is hah-LOH-pee

Monoplacophora mon-oh-plak-oh-FOR-ay

Monstrilla grandis mon-STRIL-lay GRAN-dis

Mysida MY-sih-day

Mysis relicta MY-sis ree-LIK-tay

Mystacocarida my-stah-koh-KAR-ee-day

Myzostoma cirriferum my-zoh-STOH-may sir-rih-FAIR-um

Myzostomida my-zoh-STOH-mih-day

Nannosquilla decemspinosa nan-noh-SKWIH-lay dee-sem-
SPIH-noh-say

Nautilus pompilius NAW-til-us pom-PIL-ee-us

Neocyamus physeteris nee-oh-sy-AM-us fiz-eh-TEH-ris

Octopus vulgaris OK-toh-pus vul-GAR-iss

Odontodactylus scyllarus oh-DON-toh-dak-til-us sky-LAR-us

Oithona plumifera oh-ith-OH-nay ploo-mih-FEH-ray

Oligochaeta oh-lih-GO-kee-tay

Oniscus asellus oh-NIS-kus ah-SEL-us

Onychophora oh-nee-KOH-feh-ray

Orchestoidea californiana or-keh-STOY-dee-ay kal-ih-FOR-
nee-an-ay

Ostracoda oh-strah-KOH-day

Paralithodes camtschaticus par-ah-lih-THO-deez kam-SHAH-
tee-kus

Penaeus monodon pen-EE-us MON-oh-don

Pentastomida pen-tah-STOH-mih-day

Phoronida for-OH-nih-day

Phoronis ijimai for-OH-nis ee-JIHM-eye

Phyllocarida fy-loh-KAR-ih-day

Pinctada margaritifera PINK-tah-day mar-gar-ee-tee-FAIR-ay

Placiphorella velata plah-see-for-EL-ay vel-AH-tay

Pogonophora poh-go-no-FOR-ay

Polychaeta pol-ee-KEE-tay

Polyplacophora pol-ee-plah-koh-FOR-ay

Procambarus clarkii pro-kam-BAR-us KLARK-ee-eye

Remipedia *reh-mih-PEE-dee-ay*

Richtersius coronifer rik-TER-see-us kor-OH-nih-fer

Riftia pachyptila RIF-tee-ay pak-ihp-TIL-ay

Sabellaria alveolata sah-bel-AIR-ee-ay al-vee-oh-LAH-tay

Scaphopoda skaf-oh-POH-day

Semibalanus balanoides sem-ee-bah-LAH-nus bah-lah-noh-EE-dez

Serpula vermicularis ser-PYU-lay ver-mih-kyu-LAH-ris

Siboglinum fiordicum sih-boh-GLIH-num fee-OR-dih-kum

Sipuncula sih-PUN-kyu-lay

Sipunculus nudus sih-PUN-kyu-lus NOO-dus

Spelaeogriphacea speh-lee-oh-grih-FAY-see-ay

Spelaeogriphus lepidops speh-lee-oh-GRIH-fus LEH-pih-dops

Speleonectes gironensis speh-lee-oh-NEK-teez jih-roh-NEN-sis

Spiomenia spiculata spee-oh-MEN-ee-ay spih-kyu LAH-tay

Stomatopoda stoh-mah-toe-POE-day

Stygiomysis cokei stij-ee-oh-MY-sis KOH-kee-eye

Tanaidacea tah-nah-ee-DAY-see-ay

Tantulocarida tan-too-loh-KAR-ee-day

Tardigrada tar-dih-GRAH-day

Thecostraca thee-koh-STRAH-kay

Thermosbaena mirabilis ther-mohs-BEE-nay mih-RAH-bih-lis

Thermosbaenacea ther-mohs-bee-NAY-see-ay

Tridacna gigas trih-DAK-nay gig-as

Triops longicaudatus TREE-ops lon-jee-kaw-DAY-tus

Trochus niloticus TROH-kus nye-LAW-tee-kus

Trypetesa lampas trip-ee-TEH-say LAM-pas

Uca pugilator YU-kay PYU-jil-ay-tor

Vampyroteuthis infernalis vam-py-roh-TOO-this in-fer-NAH-lis

Vargula hilgendorfii VAR-gyu-lay hil-gen-DORF-ee-eye

Vestimentifera ves-tee-men-TIH-fer-ay

Words to Know

A

Anchialine caves Underground caves filled with sea water without a surface connection to the ocean.

Anus Opening at the end of the digestive system where solid waste leaves the body.

Asexual In animals, describing reproduction without eggs or sperm.

Asexual reproduction Producing young without mating.

B

Bacteria One-celled organisms that break down the wastes and dead bodies of other organisms.

Benthic Living on the bottom of a body of water.

Bilateral symmetry Can be divided into equal halves only along one plane.

Biramous Having two branches as on a crustacean leg.

Bivalve Clam, mussel, oyster, or other aquatic or marine animal that lives in a shell with two plates.

Buoyancy The ability to float or rise up in the water.

Byssus Bundle of tough fibers that attaches some bivalves to rocks, wood, and other hard surfaces.

C

Carapace A shieldlike structure that protects the body.

Carnivore An animal that eats other animals.

Carnivorous Flesh-eating.

Cephalothorax The tightly joined head and thorax of some arachnids and crustaceans.

Chaetae Small, stiff bristles.

Chelate Thoracic limb of a crustacean with pincher-like claw.

Chemosynthesis Conversion of chemical reactions to simple sugars and other compounds that can be used as food.

Cilia Fine, stiff hairlike structures.

Cirri Small, flexible, tentaclelike structures.

Clitellum A swollen, collarlike band toward the front of earthworms.

Coelom The body cavity.

Columella The central column inside a snail shell.

Commensals Organisms that live with other organisms, but neither help nor harm them.

Crepuscular Active at dusk or at dawn.

Cryptobiosis The ability to stop all life processes without being dead.

Cuticle Body covering without individual cells.

Cyrtopia Fifth larval stage of krill in which the antennae are no longer used for swimming.

Cyst Non-living, protective membrane surrounding a dormant cell or cells.

D

Dehydration Loss of water.

Denticles Very small teeth.

Detritus Bits of plant and animal tissues.

Diapause A resting state usually associated with harsh seasonal or environmental conditions.

Diurnal Active during the day.

E

Embryo A developing egg.

Endemic Describing something found in only one place or habitat.

Endopod The inner branch of the biramous crustacean leg.

Exopod The outer branch of the biramous crustacean leg.

Exoskeleton Outer skeleton.

Eukaryote Organism with cells that have a membrane and nucleus.

F

Flagship species A species that has special appeal to the public and therefore is used to convey conservation concerns.

Foraminiferans Single-celled organisms that have a nucleus.

Fossil Remains of ancient organisms preserved in stone and other materials.

H

Hemoglobin A red-colored protein that carries oxygen in the blood of many animals.

Herbivore An animal that eats plants.

Hermaphrodite An individual animal that can produce both sperm and eggs.

I

Introvert Slender part of the sipunculan body that is extended or withdrawn into the body.

Invertebrate Animal without a backbone.

L

Larva (pl. larvae) An immature animal that cannot reproduce.

Ligament Fiberlike tissue that connects valves and bones or supports organs.

Lophophore A feeding structure with tentacles found in phoronids, ectoprocts, and brachiopods.

Lymph A yellowish body fluid of mammals filled with white blood cells.

M

Mandibles The first pair of jawlike appendages.

Mantle A special structure that makes a hard shell.

Marsupium A special pouch used by female animals to carry their young.

Maxillae The second pair of jawlike appendages behind the mandibles.

Maxillipeds Leglike appendages behind the maxillae in crustaceans.

Metanauplius A late crustacean larval stage with only three pairs of functional limbs on the head only.

N

Nocturnal Active at night.

Nucleus A central cell structure surrounded by a double membrane that contains genetic information.

O

Omnivore An animal that eats both plants and other animals.

Operculum A flaplike cover.

Ovaries Female reproductive organs that produce eggs.

Oviparous Egg-laying

Oviviparous Having young that are produced by eggs hatching inside the body of the mother.

P

Papillae Small bumps on the body surface.

Parasite An organism that lives in or on another and does not benefit its host.

Parthenogenesis Egg development without fertilization.

Pedicel A stalklike support.

Pelagic Living in or on the open sea.

Pereopods The thoracic limbs of crustaceans.

Pheromones Chemicals produced by animals to bring out a certain behavior in members of the same species.

Photosynthesis Conversion of sunlight to simple sugars and other compounds that can be used as food.

Phytoplankton Microscopic plants free-floating in water.

Plankton Microscopic plants and animals floating in water and carried on ocean currents.

Pleopods Paired limbs of crustaceans found underneath the abdomen.

Proboscis Long, flexible mouthparts.

Prokaryote Organism with cells that have no membranes or nucleus.

Protostome Animal that starts as an embryo in which the mouth develops before the anus.

Protozoea First of two stages of free-swimming crustacean larva with thoracic limbs for swimming.

R

Radula In mollusks, a usually ribbonlike mouthpart covered with rows of scraping teeth.

Raptorial Adapted for grabbing or seizing prey.

Rostrum Narrow, beaklike projection.

S

Sessile Describing an animal permanently attached and unable to move.

Seston Food materials found floating in the ocean.

Sexual In animals, reproduction that requires eggs and sperm.

Sinuses Openings, cavities, or channels inside the body.

Siphons Tubelike structures of mollusks that take in or expel water.

Spiracles Air-breathing holes connected to the trachea or windpipe.

Stylet A small bristle- or needle-like structure.

Swimmerets Abdominal appendages (pleopods) of crustaceans used for swimming.

T

Telson Last segment of a crustacean's body.

Terrestrial Living on land.

Torsion The act of twisting or being twisted.

Troglodytic Living in a cave.

Tun In water bears, the stage in which all life processes are shut down.

U

Umbo A bulge.

Uropods A pair of fanlike appendages on the tail of a crustacean.

V

Vertebrate An animal with a backbone.

Viviparous Describing an animal that produces young by live birth instead of eggs.

W

Whorl Single coil or spiral of a snail shell.

Z

Zoea Second of two stages of free-swimming crustacean larva with thoracic limbs for swimming.

Zooplankton Microscopic animals free-floating in water and carried on ocean currents.

Getting to Know Crustaceans, Mollusks, Segmented Worms, and Their Relatives

TYING IT ALL TOGETHER

Crustaceans, mollusks, segmented worms, and their relatives are incredibly different from each other. They differ in the shapes and makeup of their bodies, methods of reproduction and development, and in the ways they go about their lives. But they are related to one another based on a set of unique characteristics or features that they all have in common.

To understand these features, it is useful to know what makes up the bodies of all living things. The tissues of animals, plants, and other organisms are made up of cells. Cells are tiny units of life that are often surrounded by a skin-like covering called a membrane and have a nucleus (NU-klee-us) inside. The nucleus is the part of the cell that controls growth and reproduction.

All living things are divided into two major groups based on the structure of their cells. The first group includes bacteria and their relatives. These organisms have cells with no membranes and no nuclei (NU-klee-eye; the plural of nucleus). All remaining groups of organisms, including plants and animals, have cells with a nucleus and a membrane. These organisms include animals both with and without backbones. Those with backbones are called vertebrates (VER-teh-brehts), while those without are called invertebrates (in-VER-teh-brehts).

None of the animals included in this volume have backbones, but that is not why they are related. Instead, they are grouped together because they have other special features not found in other animals. Most of the features that unite these animals are seen only during the development of their eggs.

A developing animal egg is called an embryo (EM-bree-yo). Each embryo starts out as a single cell. Embryos develop and grow as the cell divides, doubling first into two cells, then four, then eight, and so on. They continue to divide until they form a hollow, ball-like mass of cells. By this time the cells are arranged into three distinct layers. Each layer is destined to become specific tissues and organs of the adult animal's body.

Cell division and tissue development in the embryo occurs in regular, predictable patterns. The animals included in this book, along with insects, spiders, and their relatives, undergo a special pattern of egg development. For example, in the tissues that eventually become the digestive system, the mouth develops first. Invertebrate animal embryos with mouths that develop first are called protostomes (PRO-toe-stomz). Protostome is based on the Greek words *protos*, meaning "first," and *stoma*, or "mouth."

IN THE BEGINNING

Protostomes were here long before the dinosaurs. Ancient protostomes with shells, or hard external skeletons called exoskeletons, were the most likely to become fossils. Fossils are the remains of plants, animals, and other organisms that lived a long time ago. The remains are found in rocks and other materials. The earliest relatives of arthropods (crustaceans, insects, arachnids, and relatives) probably lived in ancient seas more

An illustration depicting what the ocean may have looked like during the Jurassic Period; present are ammonite (Titanites anguiformis) *based on fossils from Portland, Dorset, England and ichthyosaurs* (Stenopterygius sp.) *based on fossils from Holzmanaden, Germany. (© Chase Studios, Inc./Photo Researchers, Inc.)*

than 600 million years ago. Based on fossil evidence, velvet worms and mollusks are between 570 to 580 million years old. The oldest fossils that are definitely identified as crustaceans are about 530 million years old. The oldest fossils of water bears and segmented worms belong to species that lived in the oceans and are about 520 million years old. The first protostomes to leave the sea, including scorpions, centipedes, and millipedes, did so about 415 million years ago. The first insect fossils are about 400 million years old.

BUILT FOR SUCCESS

The ancient ancestors of protostomes probably had soft, wormlike bodies similar to today's sipunculans (phylum Sipuncula) and echiurans (phylum Echiura). These animals burrow in mud and sand on the ocean floor. But most protostomes have tough exoskeletons that support and protect their bodies. Having an exoskeleton allows these species to get out of the mud and sand and live in a wider variety of habitats, including land.

Like segmented worms, the bodies of arthropods are made up of repeating segments. Unlike worms, the exoskeletons of arthropods are hard and include jointed antennae, mouthparts, and legs. The body segments of arthropods are joined together to form specialized body regions, like a head and body trunk. In some groups of arthropods, the body trunk is divided into a thorax and abdomen. In crustaceans, the head and thorax are joined as one body region.

Having a tough exoskeleton puts limits on flexibility and growth. Crustaceans and other arthropods have solved these problems by having jointed limbs and other appendages to allow flexibility and by molting. Molting is when the animal grows a new exoskeleton and sheds the old one. Water bears (phylum Tardigrada) and velvet worms (phylum Onychophora) also molt.

Like exoskeletons, the shells of mollusks also provide support and protection. A thick sheet of skin called the mantle covers their soft bodies. The mantle has special tissues that make the shell or shell plates, forming a hard, protective shelter. Instead of limbs, a mollusk uses a powerful, muscular foot to get around.

BEHAVIOR

Protostomes fly, swim, burrow, forage, and hunt to find food and mates, to reproduce, and to defend themselves. Most

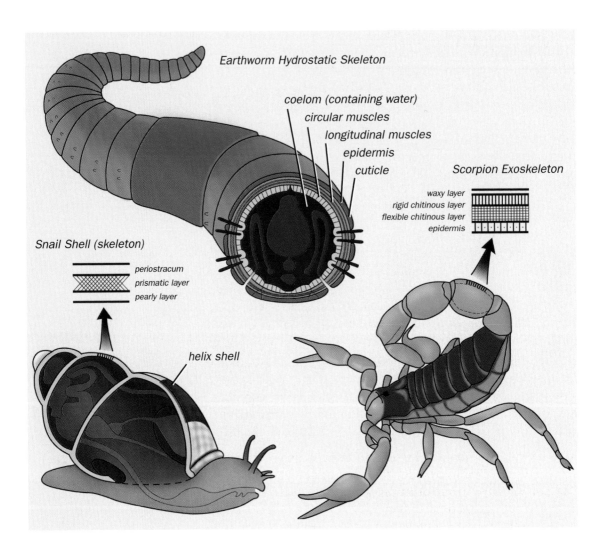

Earthworm Hydrostatic Skeleton

coelom (containing water)
circular muscles
longitudinal muscles
epidermis
cuticle

Scorpion Exoskeleton

waxy layer
rigid chitinous layer
flexible chitinous layer
epidermis

Snail Shell (skeleton)

periostracum
prismatic layer
pearly layer

helix shell

Different types of skeletons: external (snail), hydrostatic (earthworm), and jointed (scorpion). (Illustration by Kristen Workman. Reproduced by permission.)

species live alone and come together only to mate. But some, like bryozoans (phylum Ectoprocta), are permanently connected to their neighbors. They live in branching masses that sometimes resemble plants. In some species, groups of individual bryozoans have special jobs, such as gathering food or forming a skeleton-like frame to support the colony.

Defensive behavior

Some protostomes defend themselves by standing their ground and flashing bright colors, waving menacing claws, or displaying sharp fangs. Others avoid danger by retreating into burrows or running, jumping, flying, or swimming away. Still

others rely on armored defenses and depend on hard, bristly, spiny, or slimy bodies to repel hungry predators. Some species smell or taste bad, while others spray or squirt nasty chemicals at their enemies. Octopuses, cuttlefishes, and squids release a cloud of inky fluid to confuse and hide from predators.

Many protostomes avoid danger by using camouflage to blend in with their backgrounds. Others resemble objects that predators do not find appetizing, such as rocks, leaves, sticks, or bird droppings. Many biting, stinging, bad-tasting, and foul-smelling species do not hide at all. They are brightly marked or distinctively colored as a warning to potential predators. Species that do not bite or sting sometimes copy, or mimic, the colors, patterns, and body shapes of those that do in order to fool predators.

FEEDING STRATEGIES

Herbivores (HER-bih-vorz) prefer to eat living plants. For example, many snails living on land and in the ocean use their

rough, tonguelike mouthparts, or radula (RAE-juh-luh), to scrape up living plant tissues. But the sea snail known as the cone shell (*Conus geographus*) is a carnivore (KAR-nih-vor). It uses the teeth on its radula to harpoon marine worms and fish. Omnivores (am-nih-vorz) eat both plants and animals. Crayfish, shrimps, and octopuses are all omnivores. They, and other species of protostomes, will eat whatever they find. Blood-feeding leeches even become scavengers if a blood meal is not available.

Many marine and freshwater protostomes are filter feeders. They use special feeding structures to strain out or trap tiny bits of plants, animals, and other food floating in the water, or that has settled on the bottom. For example, brachiopods (phylum Brachiopoda) and bryozoans (phylum Ectoprocta) have special organs ringed with sticky tentacles that help them to catch tiny bits of food carried in the water.

REPRODUCTION

Temperature, amount of daylight, moon cycle, seasonal rainfall, and tidal patterns are all signals that trigger reproduction. The rhythm of these natural events helps to coordinate the production of eggs and sperm so that they are ready at the same time, increasing the likelihood of fertilization.

Most species require males and females to reproduce. Ocean-dwelling species usually release their eggs and sperm into the

water. But in others, the female keeps the eggs inside her body and takes in sperm that has been released in the water. In the majority of species, males and females actually come into contact and mate. Males place their sperm, or sperm packets, directly on or inside the female's body. Hermaphrodites (her-MAE-fro-daits) are individual organisms that are able to make both eggs and sperm. In some hermaphrodites, male and female organs are present at the same time. However, in others, the adults start out as males and then become females. Sometimes the eggs develop without fertilization. This type of reproduction is called parthenogenesis (PAR-thih-no-JEH-ne-sis).

A few protostomes reproduce without any sperm or eggs at all. Instead, pieces of their bodies simply break off and the missing parts grow back. This process is called budding. Some protostomes use more than one means of reproduction.

LARVAL DEVELOPMENT

The protostome embryo develops rapidly into a fully functional juvenile, or larva (LAR-vuh). The plural of larva is larvae (LAR-vee). The larvae have greater mobility than the adults. They often spend part of their lives floating around on ocean currents with other plankton. Plankton includes plants, animals, and other mostly tiny organisms. It is during the larval stages that many protostomes, such as segmented worms, mollusks, and crustaceans, move and settle into new habitats. In some groups, the larvae resemble small adults and reach adulthood directly by simply growing larger and gaining the ability to reproduce. Larvae that do not resemble the adults at all develop indirectly. They must go through several distinct stages before they acquire adult features.

PROTOSTOMES AND HUMANS

Protostomes have long provided people with food, medicine, materials, and services. For centuries, clams, mussels, oysters, snails, and other mollusks have been an important part of the human diet throughout the world. Crustaceans, such as shrimps, lobsters, and crabs are also important sources of food. Since medieval times, leeches (phylum Annelida) have been

The burrowing activities of earthworms enrich the soil, providing water, plant material and other nutrients. (© Holt Studios/Bob Gibbons/Photo Researchers, Inc.)

used in various medical treatments. Today they are used to keep blood flowing into tissues after surgery, or to obtain other substances that are useful for treating disease. Other species of protostomes produce chemicals that are used as painkillers or show promise for treating cancer. Seashells are worn as jewelry and are also used as materials for making crafts and furniture. The shells of the cowry, a sea snail, were once used as money in parts of Asia, Africa, and elsewhere.

Protostomes are especially valuable for the services they provide. The burrowing activities of earthworms enrich the soil by mixing it with plant materials and other nutrients. Mussels, oysters, and barnacles keep oceans, bays, and estuaries clean and clear by filtering out huge amounts of plant, animal, and other tissues. For example, the oysters in the Chesapeake Bay once filtered the entire volume of water in the bay every three to four days. But today, after years of harvesting, there are only enough oysters left to filter the entire bay once a year. As a result, the water quality of the bay is very poor.

Some protostomes are harmful or are considered pests. For example, mollusks sometimes have other organisms living inside their bodies. These organisms can be dangerous to people who eat the mollusks. Bryozoans, earthworms, marine worms, crustaceans, insects, and mollusks sometimes become pests when they are accidentally introduced into a habitat outside of their normal distribution. Their presence can cause major changes in natural environments and can harm native species by competing with them for food and space.

PROTECTING PROTOSTOMES

Habitat destruction is the number one threat to protostomes, followed by over-harvesting, pollution, and the introduction of non-native species. Yet, people depend on them for food, pollination, and healthy habitats. Many governments recognize the importance of protostomes and have created laws that preserve habitats, limit hunting and fishing, and protect against the introduction of potentially harmful species.

To identify species in need of protection, the World Conservation Union (IUCN) publishes a list of species threatened by extinction called the Red List. Extinct species have completely died out and will never again appear on Earth. The IUCN

Over-harvesting is a threat to many species that humans eat, yet many people depend on them for food. (© Vanessa Vick/Photo Researchers, Inc.)

places species in the categories Extinct, Extinct in the Wild, Critically Endangered, Endangered, Vulnerable, Lower Risk, Near Threatened, Data Deficient, or Least Concern. The 2004 Red List includes 3,835 species of protostomes. Unfortunately, scientists may never know just how many species need protection. Their habitats are disappearing so quickly that scientists do not have enough time to study all of the species before they and their habitats are gone and lost forever.

FOR MORE INFORMATION

Books:

Amos, W. H., and S. H. Amos. *Atlantic & Gulf Coasts. National Audubon Society Nature Guides*. New York: Alfred A. Knopf, 1997.

Brusca, R. C., and G. J. Brusca. *Invertebrates*. Second edition. Sunderland, MA: Sinauer Associates, Inc., 2003.

McConnaughey, B. H., and E. McConnaughey. *Pacific Coasts. National Audubon Society Nature Guides*. New York: Alfred A. Knopf, 1998.

Meinkoth, N. A. *National Audubon Society Field Guide to North American Sea Shore Creatures*. New York: Alfred A. Knopf, 1981.

Rehder, H. A. *National Audubon Society Field Guide to North American Seashells*. New York: Alfred A. Knopf, 1997.

Web sites:

2004 IUCN Red List of Threatened Species. http://www.iucnredlist
.org/ (accessed on May 8, 2005).

BioKIDS: Critter Catalog. http://www.biokids.umich.edu/critters/
index.html (accessed on May 8, 2005).

Crustacea.net. http://www.crustacea.net/index.htm (accessed on
May 8, 2005).

Ecowatch. http://www.ento.csiro.au/Ecowatch/index.htm (accessed on May 8, 2005).

Endangered Species Program. U.S. Fish & Wildlife Service. http://
endangered.fws.gov/ (accessed on May 8, 2005).

Invertebrate Zoology. http://www.austmus.gov.au/invertebrates/
index.htm (accessed on May 8, 2005).

Tree of Life Web Project. http://tolweb.org/tree/phylogeny.html
(accessed on May 8, 2005).

Class: Polychaeta
Number of families: 86 families

class

CHAPTER

phylum
◉ **class**
subclass
order
monotypic order
suborder
family

PHYSICAL CHARACTERISTICS

Clam worms, sand worms, and tubeworms range in length from 0.078 inches to 9.8 feet (2 to 300 millimeters). Their bodies consist of a head, body trunk, and tail. Most species have long, segmented bodies that are tubelike and covered with bristles. Along the sides of their bodies are flaps that help them to swim, burrow, draw bits of food suspended in the water to their mouths, and grip surrounding rocks, sand, or mud. The side flaps are also used like gills to help them breathe underwater.

Clam worms, sand worms, and tubeworms vary in color, ranging from clear to light tan, red, pink, green, yellow, or a combination of these and other colors. The bodies of some species are shiny and reflect rainbowlike patterns. Their body shapes also vary and usually reflect their lifestyles. Active species, such as those that hunt for their food and some burrowers, have bodies with segments that are all very similar in appearance to one another. They have well-developed flaplike appendages, eyes, and other sensory organs. Some of these species have a mouth with tough jaws and the ability to extend part of their digestive tract outside the body to feed. Less active species, such as those living in tubes in sand or mud or in permanent burrows, have distinct body regions, each specialized to perform a certain job. Their fleshy side flaps are sometimes greatly reduced, even absent. Their mouths have tubes with special tentacles that help them to gather food.

GEOGRAPHIC RANGE

Clam worms, sand worms, and tubeworms are found in oceans and seas worldwide.

HABITAT

Clam worms, sand worms, and tubeworms are found in every ocean habitat from warm tropical seas to cold polar waters. They swim in open water or crawl along the seashore or sea bottom. Many species dig in muddy or sandy ocean bottoms to establish temporary or permanent burrows and tubes. Others are found among mussel beds on rocks or pilings, rocky reefs, or on corals. Some of these species live under rocks. Others live inside tubes made of sand or lime attached to rocks and corals. Some species are able to live in water that is less salty than the ocean. They live in estuaries (EHS-chew-AIR-eez), or areas where rivers meet the sea, and even in some freshwater habitats.

Some species live on the bodies of crustaceans (krus-TAY-shuns), or water-dwelling animals that have jointed legs and a hard shell but no backbone. The worms do not harm the crustaceans, but actually help them by keeping their breathing organs clean of organisms. Other species live inside the bodies of mussels, clams, oysters, and unsegmented worms as parasites (PAIR-uh-sites). Parasites live on or inside another animal and depend on them for food for their entire lives.

DIET

As a group, clam worms, sand worms, and tubeworms eat virtually all food resources in the ocean. Carnivores (KAR-nih-vorz) eat all kinds of small marine animals. Herbivores (URH-bih-vorz) feed on plant tissues. Omnivores (AM-nih-vroz) eat both plants and animals, dead or alive. These worms are raptorial, deposit, or suspension feeders. Raptorial (rap-TORE-ee-uhl) feeders are predators that actively hunt for their food. They extend part of their digestive tract out of the mouth and grab their prey with their hard jaws. Some species inject paralyzing venom into their prey.

Deposit feeders eat the surrounding sand or mud and digest whatever food in the form of detritus (dih-TRY-tuhs), bits of plants, animals, and animal waste, it contains. Selective deposit feeders use their sticky mouthparts or tentacles to capture and eat bits of food without having to swallow lots of mud and sand.

Suspension feeders either use their tentacles to stir up food into the water or sift food particles from water currents. Some burrowing species use their tentacles to pull water that carries floating food particles into their burrows.

BEHAVIOR AND REPRODUCTION

Some clam worms, sand worms, and tubeworms live in dense groups. Others live alone. Many species avoid light. They quickly take shelter under rocks or retreat inside their tubes or burrows when disturbed.

Most species of these worms require males and females to reproduce. Some will form temporary pairs during the breeding season. Males and females release their sperm and eggs into the water where fertilization takes place. Fertilization (FUR-tih-lih-ZAY-shun) is the joining of the egg and sperm to start development. After the eggs are fertilized, the pairs will become very aggressive and may eat each other. In other species, fertilization happens inside the body. The eggs are then released into the water, attached to some object, or kept inside the body until they hatch.

The larvae (LAR-vee), or animals in an early stage that change form before becoming adults, usually develop in open water. As they develop, additional segments are formed behind a special growth zone. Their lifespan can range from a few weeks to several years.

CLAM WORMS, SAND WORMS, TUBEWORMS, AND PEOPLE

Species of these worms respond quickly to increased amounts of pollution in the water and on the ocean bottom. Their presence or absence may indicate important changes in the marine environment. Some also harm oyster beds managed for harvesting.

CONSERVATION STATUS

Three species of clam worms, sand worms, and tubeworms are listed by the World Conservation Union (IUCN). *Mesonerilla*

YOU WANT A PIECE OF ME?

As clam worms, sand worms, and tubeworms grow, they can replace various body parts and even make new worms from broken bits of their own bodies. They can even replace the rear body segments if they are bitten or pulled off by a predator. Rear body segments are usually easy to replace, but a lost head is replaced only rarely. Some species use this ability as a means of reproducing without first having to find a mate. This is called asexual (ay-SEK-shuh-wuhl) reproduction.

prospera is listed as Critically Endangered, or facing an extremely high risk of extinction in the wild. *Erythrina polychaeta* is Vulnerable, or facing a high risk of extinction in the wild. The Palolo worm, *Eunice viridis*, is also listed, but there is not enough information to determine if it is threatened.

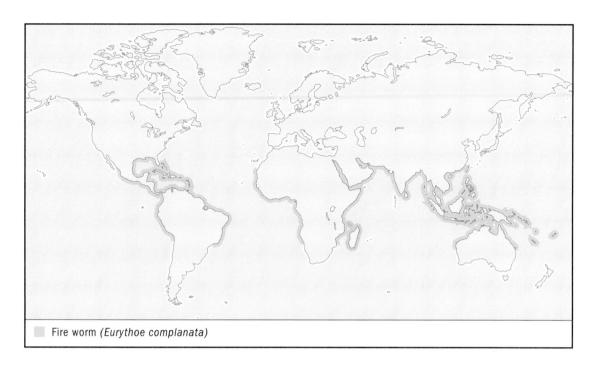

Fire worm (*Eurythoe complanata*)

FIRE WORM
Eurythoe complanata

Physical characteristics: The body of a fire worm is flat and long, measuring up to 4.7 to 5.5 inches (120 to 140 millimeters). The head has one pair of eyes, tentacles, and a pair of fleshy lobes associated with the mouth. The fleshy side flaps are well developed and have stiff, hollow bristles filled with defensive toxins. The bristles easily break off and cause a burning, stinging sensation when they come into contact with human skin. The fire worm also has blood red gill tufts, a part of the breathing system.

Geographic range: Fire worms live in all tropical seas.

Habitat: Fire worms live in crevices under and between rocks or in dead coral. They are also found in sand and mud.

Diet: Fire worms are omnivorous and will scavenge both dead plants and animals. They use their mouthparts to scrape and squeeze bits of food into their mouths. Prey is located by touch and also by special sensors that detect chemicals produced by other animals.

Fire worms have venomous bristles that cause swelling and burning if touched. (Photograph by Leslie Newman and Andrew Flowers. Reproduced by permission.)

Behavior and reproduction: Males and females are not always required for reproduction. Some individuals may break up into one or more parts, with each part growing into a new individual.

Fire worms and people: Fire worms get their name because of their stings that cause burning and swelling.

Conservation status: Fire worms are not considered endangered or threatened. ■

Tubeworm (*Serpula vermicularis*)

TUBEWORM
Serpula vermicularis

Physical characteristics: The body of a tubeworm is pale yellow to red and has up to 200 segments. It measures up to 1.9 to 2.7 inches (50 to 70 millimeters) long. The head is crowned with numerous tentacles that spread out into circular, feathery fans when extended outside the tube. The head also has a pinkish white, funnel-shaped cover. The cover acts as a cork when the worm withdraws inside its tube. The hard tube is made of calcium carbonate and has a few irregular ridges.

Geographic range: Tubeworms live in the northeast Atlantic Ocean and the Mediterranean Sea.

Habitat: Tubeworms live in depths to 820 feet (250 meters). They live in hard tubes attached to hard surfaces, such as rocks, stones,

and bivalves. Bivalves are clams, mussels, oysters, and other aquatic animals with shells made up of two parts or halves.

Diet: They use their fanlike tentacles to create currents that draw in water carrying bits of floating food.

Behavior and reproduction: Tubeworms are usually solitary in open waters, but in sheltered habitats dense populations of tubes, they may form small reefs.

Every summer males and females release sperm and eggs into the water where fertilization takes place. The larvae reach adulthood in less than one year. Their entire life cycle takes anywhere from two to five years.

Tubeworms and people: The tubeworms' permanent tubes help to create habitats for other marine species.

Conservation status: Tubeworms are not considered endangered or threatened. ■

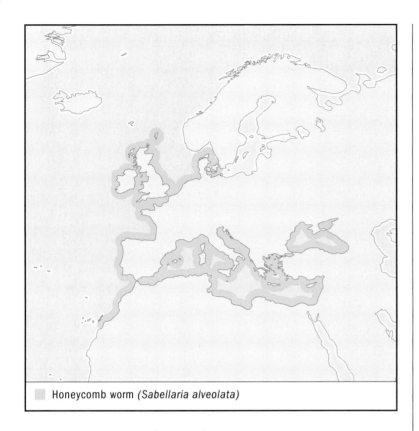

Honeycomb worm *(Sabellaria alveolata)*

HONEYCOMB WORM
Sabellaria alveolata

Physical characteristics: Honeycomb worm adults measure 1.1 to 1.5 inches (30 to 40 millimeters) long. The body trunk has three pairs of flattened bristles that form a cover to close the tube opening. The colors of the tubes are determined by the sand and other materials used to construct them.

Geographic range: Honeycomb worms are found in the Mediterranean Sea and north Atlantic to south Morocco. They are also found in the British Isles to its northern limit in the northeast Atlantic.

Habitat: Honeycomb worms are found along open coasts. They need hard surfaces to attach their tubes, but require sand and shell fragments to make their tubes.

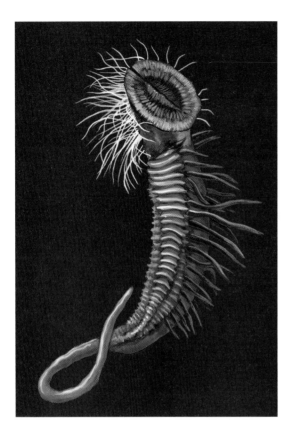

The reefs created by honeycomb worm tubes help to create habitats for other marine species. (Illustration by Amanda Humphrey. Reproduced by permission.)

Diet: They eat seston (SEHS-tun), bits of plant and animal materials that float by in the water during high tide.

Behavior and reproduction: The honeycomb worm lives in dense colonies and builds tubes that are permanently attached to hard surfaces. The tubes are made using coarse sand and/or bits of shells. The openings to the tubes are so tightly packed together they resemble a honeycomb. The tubes are up to 7.8 inches (20 centimeters) in length, with openings up to 0.19 inches (5 millimeters) in diameter. If the tubes are exposed during low tide, the worms will survive by plugging the entrance with a cover to avoid drying out or being eaten by other animals.

Males and females reproduce every year. The female produces from one hundred thousand to one million eggs at a time. The larvae eat plankton, or microscopic plants and animals drifting in water. Larvae may drift up to 6.2 miles (10 kilometers) from where they hatched.

Honeycomb worms and people: The reefs created by honeycomb worm tubes help to create habitats for other marine species. Fishermen collect and use honeycomb worms as bait.

Conservation status: The honeycomb worm is not considered endangered or threatened. ■

FOR MORE INFORMATION

Books:

Blaxland, B. *Earthworms, Leeches, and Sea Worms.* New York: Chelsea House Publications, 2002.

Brusca, N. C., and G. J. Brusca. *Invertebrates.* 2nd edition. Sunderland, MA: Sinauer Associates, 2003.

Periodicals:

MacDonald, I. R., and C. Fisher. "Life without Light." *National Geographic* 190, no. 4 (October 1996): 86-97.

Web sites:

"Annelids." *Encyclopedia Britannica.* http://www.britannica.com/eb/print?tocId=9110238&fullArticle=true (accessed on December 21, 2004).

"Introduction to Polychaetes." http://www.ucmp.berkeley.edu/annelida/polyintro.html (accessed on December 20, 2004).

"Reefkeeper's Guide to Invertebrates. Part 11: Potentially Dangerous Polychaetes." Aquarium Net. http://www.reefs.org/library/aquarium_net/0198/0198_2.html (accessed on December 21, 2004).

Videos:

The Biology of Annelids. Beaufort, SC: BioMedia Associates, 2000.

MYZOSTOMIDS

Myzostomida

Class: Myzostomida
Number of families: 8 families

phylum

● **class**

subclass

order

monotypic order

suborder

family

PHYSICAL CHARACTERISTICS

Myzostomids are typically round in outline and flat. Their bodies measure 0.118 to 1.181 inches (3 to 30 millimeters) in length and are fringed with flexible, needle-thin projections called cirri (si-ri). The upper body surface is smooth, but the lower surface usually has five pairs of flaps used for moving around. Each flap is armed with small hooks to help them attach to their hosts, sea lilies. There are also four pairs of slit-like or suckerlike organs on the underside that probably act as sensory organs. In some species, these organs are greatly reduced in size or absent. Myzostomids feed by extending their throats forward out of the mouth inside out.

GEOGRAPHIC RANGE

Myzostomids are found in all oceans.

HABITAT

Most myzostomids live in warm tropical waters on the bodies of sea lilies, sea stars, and their relatives. A few species are found in the Arctic and Antarctic oceans. They live in shallow waters to depths of over 9,840 feet (3,000 meters).

DIET

Most species use their extended mouthparts to suck up food particles floating in the water around them. A few myzostomid parasites eat the tissues or bodily fluids of sea lilies, sea stars, and brittle stars. Parasites (PAIR-uh-sites) are animals that live in and feed off of the bodies of other animals, often harming the host.

BEHAVIOR AND REPRODUCTION

All myzostomids live on the bodies of sea lilies, sea stars, and brittle stars. Most species live as commensals on the outside of the bodies of sea lilies. Commensals (kuh-MEHN-suhls) are animals that live on or with other animals without harm to either one. Sea lilies and their relatives obtain food by catching floating food particles with short tentacles located along grooves on their arms lined with small hairlike structures called cilia (SIH-lee-uh). When myzostomids want to eat, they simply extend their mouthparts into this groove and suck up water and bits of food into their mouths.

A few species of myzostomids are parasites on sea lilies, sea stars, or brittle stars. They live inside the outer tissues of their hosts, or infest the body cavities, reproductive organs, or digestive systems.

LOOKING FOR A HOME

The strange bodies of myzostomids make them difficult to classify. When they were discovered in 1827, myzostomids were placed with flukes, a kind of flatworm. Later they were classified with a group that contained water bears and crustaceans (krus-TAY-shuns), water-dwelling animals that have jointed legs and a hard shell but no backbone. Today most scientists consider them with the group that includes sand worms, earthworms, and leeches. Studies, including DNA analysis, show that they are most closely related to flat worms.

Most species of myzostomids can function as both male and female. Smaller individuals function as males, but as they become larger, they also have female reproductive organs. Later, some older individuals may have only female reproductive organs. Reproduction takes place when one individual briefly comes into contact with another and attaches a sperm packet. Sperm from the packets penetrate the skin and fertilize mature eggs inside the body. The fertilized (FUR-teh-lyzed) eggs are later released into the water. The eggs hatch into free-swimming, unsegmented larvae (LAR-vee) with bands of cilia. Larvae are animals in an early stage that change form before becoming adults.

MYZOSTOMIDS AND PEOPLE

Myzostomids have no direct impact on humans or their activities.

CONSERVATION STATUS

Myzostomids are not considered endangered or threatened.

Myzostoma cirriferum

SPECIES ACCOUNT

NO COMMON NAME
Myzostoma cirriferum

Physical characteristics: The body of *Myzostoma cirriferum* is egg-shaped and flat, measuring up to 0.09 inches (2.4 millimeters) in length with ten pairs of cirri around the edge. The tubelike mouthparts reach up to 0.04 inches (1 millimeter) when fully extended. The flaps and other organs are well developed and are located underneath the body.

Geographic range: They are found in the Mediterranean Sea and along the northeastern Atlantic coasts of Europe.

Habitat: This species lives on shallow-water sea lilies.

Diet: *Myzostoma cirriferum* eats floating particles of food diverted from the food grooves on the arms of the sea lilies.

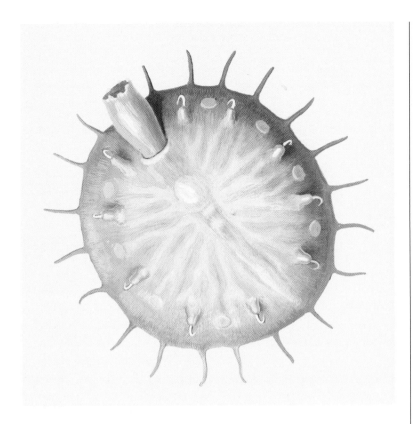

Myzostoma cirriferum *eat floating particles of food diverted from the food grooves on the arms of the sea lilies. (Illustration by John Megahan. Reproduced by permission.)*

Behavior and reproduction: Several hundred of these myzostomids may infest a single sea lily.

Mature individuals reproduce year round by attaching sperm packets to one another. Sperm from the packets penetrates the skin and fertilizes eggs inside the body.

***Myzostoma cirriferum* and people:** This species does not directly impact people or their activities.

Conservation status: This species is not considered endangered or threatened. ■

FOR MORE INFORMATION

Books:

Grygier, M. J. "Class Myzostomida." In *Polychaetes and Allies: The Southern Synthesis. Fauna of Australia.* Vol. 4A, *Polychaeta, Myzostomida, Pogonophora, Echiura, Sipuncula,* edited by Pamela L. Beesley, Graham J. B. Ross, and Christopher J. Glasby. Melbourne, Australia: CSIRO, 2000.

Periodicals:

Eeckhaut, I., and M. Jangoux. "Life Cycle and Mode of Infestation of *Myzostoma cirriferum* (Annelida)." *Diseases of Aquatic Organisms* 15 (1993): 207-217.

Eeckhaut, I., D. McHugh, P. Mardulyn, R. Tiedemann, D. Monteyne, M. Jangoux, and M. C. Milinkovitch. "Myzostomida: A Link between Trochozoans and Flatworms?" *Proceedings of the Royal Society, London, Series B,* 267 (2000): 1383-1392.

class
CHAPTER

PHYSICAL CHARACTERISTICS

The segmented bodies of earthworms measure up to 19.68 feet (6 meters) and resemble a tube within a tube. The outer body wall is made up of two muscle layers. The outer layer is made up of a series of circles wrapped around the body, while the inner layer of muscle runs along the length of the body. This inner layer shortens or extends the length of the body. Inside the body is the digestive tract, a tube that runs from the mouth, where food is taken in, to the anus (AY-nuhs), where waste, undigested food, and other particles leave the body. Between the muscular body wall and the digestive tract is the body cavity, where all the other organs are located. These organs are usually organized into body segments, just like the outer body. Earthworms do not have flaplike structures to help them move. All but the first body segment is covered with small, stiff bristles, or chaetae (KEY-tee), that help earthworms to hold position as they burrow through the soil. Toward the front of the body is a swollen, collarlike band called the clitellum (KLAI-teh-lum). Special tissues in the clitellum produce a collarlike egg case called a cocoon. These tissues also produce food for the eggs as they develop.

GEOGRAPHIC RANGE

Earthworms are found worldwide. They do not occur in deserts, polar regions, or in strongly acid soils. A few species have been widely distributed by humans.

phylum
◆ **class**
subclass
order
monotypic order
suborder
family

HABITAT

Most earthworms live in the soil, but some prefer the mud along the shores of fresh or salty bodies of water. Depending on species, many earthworms live in the upper leaf litter layer, topsoil, or in deeper layers in the soil. Others live high above the forest floor in soils that accumulate among the branches of tree canopies in tropical rainforests.

DIET

Earthworms eat dead and decomposing leaves, decaying roots, and other bits of plant material, or detritus (dih-TRY-tuhs), in the soil. Worms living in leaf litter layer, upper soil, or in soils in tree canopies eat freshly dead plant materials. Other species, such as the European night crawler, always live in deep burrows. They come up to the surface to also eat freshly dead plant tissues. Still other species remain deep in the soil, where they eat long-buried bits of detritus.

BEHAVIOR AND REPRODUCTION

Earthworms defend themselves in a variety of ways. Those living in tunnels escape danger by quickly withdrawing into their burrows. Those living near or on the surface have the ability to move quickly. They jump and thrash wildly about and will even purposely break off a few tail segments when threatened by a predator. Species living deep in the soil have few defensive behaviors. Some will twist and coil their bodies or produce bad smelling or tasting fluids.

Earthworms have both male and female reproductive organs. Individuals in cooler climates mate in spring or fall to exchange sperm. Many tropical species are active during the rainy season. Worms align themselves in opposite directions and place sperm directly into the other's body. The collarlike cocoon produced by the clitellum passes over the female reproductive openings to receive one or more eggs, and then over the male openings to receive sperm. Fertilization takes place inside the cocoon.

Cocoons are deposited in the soil soon after mating. The developing eggs are nourished inside the case with materials also produced by the clitellum. The young earthworm passes through several stages before emerging from the cocoon as a small earthworm. Depending on the species, young earthworms may take several months or years to reach adulthood.

EARTHWORMS AND PEOPLE

Earthworms are very important because they improve and maintain soils, helping plants to grow. Their burrowing activities not only allow air into the soil, but also provide food for growing plants by mixing soil with bits of plant materials. Several species of earthworms are raised to collect their waste for use as a high-quality compost for gardening. Others species are raised and sold as fish bait.

CONSERVATION STATUS

Seven species of earthworms are listed by the World Conservation Union (IUCN). The Australian Lake Pedder earthworm is listed as Extinct, or no longer living. *Phallodrilus macmasterae* from Bermuda is listed as Critically Endangered, or facing an extremely high risk of extinction in the wild. Three of the four species considered Vulnerable live in the United States. Vulnerable means the species are facing a high risk of extinction in the wild. These include the American giant Palouse earthworm from Oregon, the Washington giant earthworm from Washington state, and *Komarekiona eatoni* that lives in the Midwest. The fourth species is the Gippsland giant worm of Australia. It is the only species that is clearly protected.

Another American species from Louisiana, *Lutrodrilus multivesiculatus*, is listed as Lower Risk, or at risk of becoming threatened with extinction in the future. These and other earthworms are threatened by loss of habitat and by the fact that many live only in a few places. For example, the grassland habitats of many species have been converted into farmland.

MR. DARWIN'S CAN OF WORMS

The famous scientist Charles Darwin (1812-1882) spent 40 years observing and studying the behavior of earthworms, mostly in his garden. He was the first to see their role in making soil more fertile. He estimated that in a single acre every year the worms could haul up 7 to 18 tons of soil to the surface as body waste, or castings. Darwin's last book, *The Formation of Vegetable Mould through the Action of Worms with Observations on Their Habits,* was published in 1881, just six months before his death.

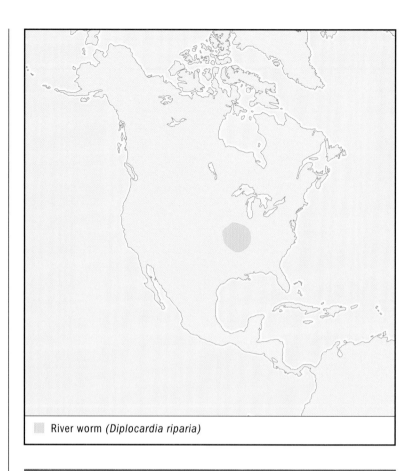

River worm (*Diplocardia riparia*)

RIVER WORM
Diplocardia riparia

Physical characteristics: The river worm has a dark brown body 4.7 to 7.8 inches (120 to 200 millimeters) in length. It has small pairs of lengthwise grooves underneath the body.

Geographic range: The river worm is found in the Central United States, including Iowa, Illinois, Missouri, Kansas, and Nebraska.

Habitat: River worms live in fine soils washed up along river banks and beneath stands of silver maples.

Diet: They burrow through leaf litter and just below the soil surface, eating detritus buried in river mud.

River worms live in fine soils washed up along river banks and beneath stands of silver maples. (Illustration by Bruce Worden. Reproduced by permission.)

Behavior and reproduction: Nothing has been written about their behavior. River worms have both male and female reproductive organs.

River worms and people: River worms are collected and sold for fish bait. This species is more tolerant of summer heat than other bait species.

Conservation status: This species is not considered endangered or threatened. However, exotic species brought in as fish bait have become established along some rivers and streams, crowding out the river worm. ■

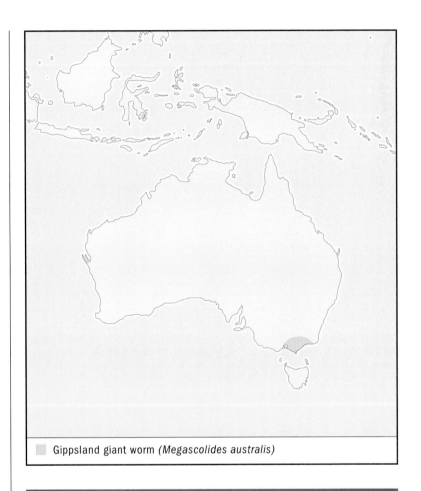

Gippsland giant worm (Megascolides australis)

GIPPSLAND GIANT WORM
Megascolides australis

Physical characteristics: The head of the Gippsland giant worm is dark purple. The rest of the body is pinkish gray. They measure up to 31.5 to 39.3 inches (80 to 100 centimeters) in length and have small pairs of markings underneath the body.

Geographic range: The Gippsland giant worm lives only in the Bass River Valley of Victoria, Australia.

Habitat: This species burrows in clay soils along streams and in other moist, but not too wet, habitats.

Diet: This species eats detritus in soil.

Behavior and reproduction: The giant worm's entire life, including feeding, mating, and waste deposition, occurs underground. They burrow down to the layer of soil that is soaked with water.

Cocoons are deposited underground, and eggs develop for 12 to 14 months. The larvae (LAR-vee), or animals in an early stage that change form before becoming adults, emerge from the cocoons measuring 7.8 inches (20 centimeters) in length.

Gippsland giant worms and people: The Gippsland giant worm is one of the largest earthworms in the world and a wonder of nature. Tourists flock to the Giant Worm Museum in Bass and to the worm festival in the town of Koramburra.

Conservation status: This species is listed as Vulnerable by the World Conservation Union (IUCN). This means that the Gippsland giant worm faces a high risk of extinction in the wild. It lives only in a very small area and is threatened by land development for farming and reduced water levels in the soil.   ■

FOR MORE INFORMATION

Books:

Blaxland, B. *Earthworms, Leeches, and Sea Worms.* New York: Chelsea House, 2002.

Edwards, C. A., and P. J. Bohlen. *Biology and Ecology of Earthworms.* 3rd edition. New York: Chapman and Hall, 1996.

Wells, S. M., R. M. Pyle, and N. M. Collins. *The IUCN Invertebrate Red Data Book.* Gland, Switzerland: IUCN, 1983.

Web sites:

About Earthworms. *Worm Watch.* http://www.naturewatch.ca/english/wormwatch/about/guide/intro.html (accessed on December 23, 2004).

Annelids. *Encyclopedia Brittanica.* http://www.britannica.com/eb/print?tocId=9110238&fullArticle=true (accessed on December 21, 2004).

Careful! Worms Underfoot. http://www.ars.usda.gov/is/kids/soil/story2/goodworm.htm (accessed on December 23, 2004).

Earthworm. *Fact Monster.* http://www.factmonster.com/ce6/sci/A0816562.html (accessed on December 23, 2004).

Earthworms and Redworms. http://www.lawrencehallofscience.org/foss/fossweb/teachers/materials/plantanimal/earthworms.html (accessed on December 23, 2004).

Videos:

The Biology of Annelids. Beaufort, SC: BioMedia Associates, 2000.

class
CHAPTER

phylum
● **class**
subclass
order
monotypic order
suborder
family

PHYSICAL CHARACTERISTICS

Most leeches are flattened from top to bottom and measure 0.196 to 0.787 inches (5 to 20 millimeters) in length. The longest species may reach 17.72 inches (450 millimeters). Leeches have eyespots on the head that are able to detect movement from contrasting patterns of light and shadow. The mouth is located underneath the head and is surrounded by a sucker. The sucker helps draw blood and other bodily fluids into the mouth. Like earthworms, leeches have a clitellum (KLAI-teh-lum), a specialized collarlike band behind the head. The clitellum is filled with special tissues that secrete a protective covering, or case, for the eggs. Leeches are not covered with stiff bristles nor do they have paddlelike flaps. To gain traction, leeches have suckers at the front and rear of their bodies. The tail sucker is used for swimming, getting around, or remaining attached to a host. Blood-feeding species have special pouches that allow them to increase their intake of fluid. They can expand up to six times their normal weight.

GEOGRAPHIC RANGE

Leeches live on all continents except Antarctica.

HABITAT

Leeches are found in a wide variety of habitats. Those living in the ocean and estuaries (EHS-chew-air-eez), or wide areas where rivers join the sea, are found on rocks, plants, or attached to fish or other sea animals. Species living on land are found in moist habitats, such as rainforests or wet coastal forests. They are usually found clinging to plants or under rocks. Freshwater species live in swamps, ponds, streams, and rivers where they are live on wood, rocks, vegetation, or on other animals.

DIET

Leeches are all carnivores (KAR-nih-vorz) and feed on the flesh or fluids of other animals. Some species feed only on the blood of their prey. Many leeches are predators that ambush a wide variety of invertebrates (in-VER-teh-brehts), animals without backbones. Prey includes insects, earthworms and their relatives, beach hoppers, snails, and freshwater clams. Predatory leeches swallow their prey whole or pierce the bodies of their victims with their retractable, needlelike mouthparts, or proboscis (pruh-BAH-suhs). These mouthparts are then used like a soda straw to suck out bodily fluids.

Blood-feeding leeches attack fishes, turtles, crocodiles and their relatives, frogs, ducks, geese, other water birds, and mammals, including humans. Some leeches feed on only one kind of animal. Others will feed on anything. If larger prey is not available, these leeches will survive on worms, insects, and other invertebrates. Although some blood-sucking species use a proboscis, most use their jaws to pierce the skin of their victims. They have two or three razor-sharp jaws, each shaped like half of a circular saw blade. Two-jawed leeches leave a V-shaped mark. Those with three jaws leave a Y-shaped wound. These leeches have chemicals in their saliva that prevent the blood of mammals from clotting, either at the wound or inside their own bodies.

BEHAVIOR AND REPRODUCTION

Many leeches swim through the water with snakelike motions. They release their grip with the tail sucker and push off from a rock or plant, before wriggling their body back and forth. Species living on land move along the ground like an inchworm, stretching and shortening their bodies by using the suckers on both ends.

Leeches must mate to reproduce. Mating occurs when a leech attaches a sperm packet in the body of its mate. Some species have corresponding male and female organs that allow the placement of sperm directly into their mate's female reproductive organs. Fertilization (FUR-teh-lih-ZAY-shun) occurs inside the female's body. As the cocoon passes over the female reproductive organs, the developing eggs, or embryos (EHM-bree-ohz), are deposited inside.

The cocoons are either left in the soil, or attached to the bodies of other animals. Young leeches resemble the adult when they hatch. Fish leeches attach their egg cases to the bodies of crustaceans (krus-TAY-shuns), or water-dwelling animals with soft bodies covered by hard shells, such as shrimp or lobster. When fishes eat infested crustaceans, the young leeches attach themselves inside the fishes' mouth cavity. Some leeches carry their eggs in a clear sack under their body. When the adult finds a host, like a turtle or frog, the young hatch and also attach themselves to the host.

TAKE TWO LEECHES AND CALL ME IN THE MORNING

Doctors use farm-raised leeches for several kinds of medical treatments. They are used to remove pools of thickened blood under the skin grafts of burn patients. A hungry leech can restore the circulation in clogged veins by sucking out blood clots. They are especially useful for improving the circulation in reattached body parts, such as fingers and ears, by helping to restore blood flow through reconnected veins.

LEECHES AND PEOPLE

Leeches were used in the 1700s and 1800s to treat all kinds of ailments, from headaches to being overweight. It was highly unlikely that any of these uses was successful. Today, leeches are used to treat tiny blood clots that form after surgery. The anti-clotting properties of their saliva may also be useful for treating heart disease, possibly even cancer. Aquatic leeches are used to measure environmental health because they are sensitive to heavy metal pollution and low oxygen content in freshwater habitats.

CONSERVATION STATUS

One species of leech, the European medicinal leech, is listed by the World Conservation Union (IUCN) as Lower Risk, or at risk of becoming threatened with extinction in the future. They are threatened due to habitat loss and over-collecting. Other species with limited distributions may also be threatened.

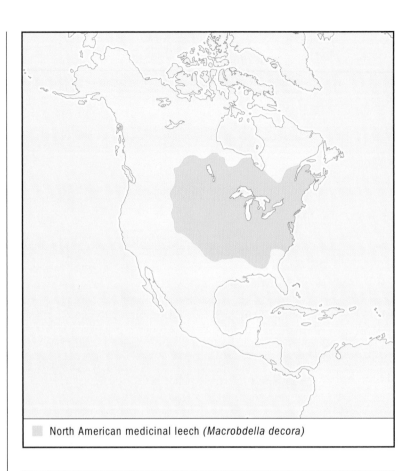

North American medicinal leech (*Macrobdella decora*)

NORTH AMERICAN MEDICINAL LEECH
Macrobdella decora

Physical characteristics: The North American medicinal leech grows up to 3.9 inches (100 millimeters) long and 0.39 inches (10 millimeters) wide. The upper surface of the body is olive with a row of orange spots down the middle. The underside is orange. An arch of ten eyes is arranged in five pairs. Each of the three jaws has very fine small teeth.

Geographic range: This species is found in Eastern North America, from southern Canada to the Carolinas and along the Mississippi River drainages.

Habitat: This leech is found in naturally occurring freshwater lakes, ponds, streams, and marshes. It is usually found at the water surface near shore when at rest.

Diet: The North American medicinal leech feeds mostly on amphibian and fish blood, but occasionally attacks mammals. Blood meals are stored in the body up to several months.

Behavior and reproduction: This species is an excellent swimmer. They can detect prey up to several yards (meters) away by following waves in the water.

Sperm is deposited directly into the female reproductive organs of the mate. Up to ten or more eggs are laid in the cocoon. The cocoons are deposited on land near the edge of a body of water.

North American medicinal leeches and people: The North American medicinal leech was used in creation mythology of the Osage tribe of Native Americans. It was not widely used for blood-letting. This species was also seen in the film *Stand by Me*.

Conservation status: The North American medicinal leech is not considered threatened or endangered. ■

Giant Amazonian leech *(Haementeria ghilianii)*

GIANT AMAZONIAN LEECH
Haementeria ghilianii

Physical characteristics: Possibly the largest freshwater leech, the giant Amazonian leech can grow up to 17.72 inches (450 millimeters) long and 3.93 inches (100 millimeters) wide. Adults are dark gray-brown. Younger individuals have a broken stripe down their backs and patches of color on every third body segment. They have only one pair of eyes.

Geographic range: They live from the mouth of the Amazon River, north to Venezuela and the Guianas.

Habitat: The giant Amazonian leech lives in coastal wetland marshes.

Possibly the largest freshwater leech, the giant Amazonian leech can grow up to 17.72 inches (450 millimeters) long and 3.93 inches (100 millimeters) wide. (Illustration by Bruce Worden. Reproduced by permission.)

Diet: Young leeches feed on amphibians. Adults usually attack caimans, anacondas, capybaras, and domestic cattle.

Behavior and reproduction: This species is a good swimmer and is usually found under rocks or in debris in the water while they digest their meals and carry their cocoons.

Sperm packets are attached to the body of the mate. Eggs are kept in a sac underneath the parent's body until they hatch and are carried to their first blood meal by the parent.

Giant Amazonian leeches and people: A special chemical isolated from the saliva of the giant Amazonian leech is sometimes used as a medical treatment to break down blood clots in humans.

Conservation status: The giant Amazonian leech is not considered endangered or threatened. ■

FOR MORE INFORMATION

Books:

Blaxland, B. *Earthworms, Leeches, and Sea Worms.* New York: Chelsea House, 2002.

Sawyer, R. T. *Leech Biology and Behaviour.* Oxford, U.K.: The Clarendon Press, 1986.

Periodicals:

Elliott, J. M., and P. A. Tullett. "The Status of the Medicinal Leech *Hirudo medicinalis* in Europe and Especially in the British Isles." *Biological Conservation* 29 (1984): 15-26.

Wells, S., and W. Coombes. "The Status of and Trade in the Medicinal Leech." *Traffic Bulletin* 8 (1987): 64-69.

Web sites:

All About Leeches Web Page. http://www.invertebrate.ws/leech/index .htm (accessed on December 26, 2004).

Class Hirudinea. *Leeches.* http://lakes.chebucto.org/ZOOBENTH/ BENTHOS/xxvi.html (accessed on December 26, 2004).

Leeches. Biological Indicators of Watershed Health. http://www .epa.gov/bioindicators/html/leeches.html (accessed on December 26, 2004).

Lovable Leeches. http://www.accessexcellence.org/LC/SS/leechlove .html (accessed on December 24, 2004).

Videos:

The Biology of Annelids. Beaufort, SC: BioMedia Associates, 2000.

phylum
CHAPTER

PHYSICAL CHARACTERISTICS

Beard worms live in tubes made out of chitin (KYE-tehn) and protein. Chitin is a substance similar to fingernails that makes up the outer skeleton of some animals. The tubes are mostly below the surface of the ocean bottom, with just the upper end exposed. The yellowish, brownish, or black tubes are not branched. They are sometimes distinctly fringed, flared, segmented, or have a ringed pattern.

Most beard worm species are 3.94 to 29.53 inches (100 to 750 millimeters) in length, but are less than 0.039 inches (1 millimeter) thick. Their bodies have up to 200 tentacles on the head region. Each tentacle has tiny branches. The long, slender body trunk is followed by a small, segmented tail. The body is covered with a flexible, skinlike cuticle (KYU-tih-kuhl) that is covered with thick parts that create various patterns. Cuticle, unlike skin, is a body covering that is not made up of individual cells. Some beard worms have a collarlike ridge that rests on the rim of the tube when the worm's body is extended beyond the tube opening.

The nervous system includes a mass of nerves toward the head, a nerve cord running along the underside of the body, and a network of small nerve fibers. All of these are completely inside the skin. Under the skin is a thick layer of muscles that runs along the length of the body. The coelom (SIGH-lum), or main body cavity, is made up of a small cavity in the head region that connects to cavities inside each of the tentacles. A pair of cavities is found inside the body trunk. The segments

■ phylum

class

subclass

order

monotypic order

suborder

family

of the tail also have a series of cavities inside, each separated by a layer of muscles.

Adults do not have a mouth or digestive system. Instead, they absorb bits of food from the water and mud directly through their tentacles and body trunk. They also have special tissues on their body trunk that contain bacteria that help to process food. The circulatory system is made up of parallel blood vessels along both their upper and undersides that run nearly the entire length of the body. The circulatory system is closed, with blood moving throughout the body inside the vessels.

GEOGRAPHIC RANGE

Beard worms live on the bottom of the Norwegian fjords and in the Atlantic, Caribbean, Pacific, Indian, Arctic, and Antarctic oceans.

HABITAT

Beard worms live on the ocean floor on continental slopes and in deep ocean trenches. Some species are found only on decaying wood near deep sea geysers at depths of 328 to 32,808 feet (100 to 10,000 meters). These deep sea geysers are called hydrothermal vents.

DIET

Most organisms depend on sunlight to produce or acquire food. The conversion of sunlight to simple sugars and other compounds that can be used as food is called photosynthesis (FO-to-SIN-thuh-sihs). Beard worms, especially those living in total darkness, must rely on billions of bacteria living in them to make food. The worms provide the bacteria with carbon dioxide produced by their own bodies and hydrogen sulfide collected from water coming through the hydrothermal vents. As the bacteria convert these chemicals into energy for themselves, they produce simple sugars and other compounds that the worms can absorb as food. The conversion of chemical reactions into food is called chemosynthesis (KEY-moh-SIN-thuh-sihs).

BEHAVIOR AND REPRODUCTION

The tentacles of the beard worm are extended from their tube opening, but the worms can withdraw quickly into their tubes when threatened by crabs or other predators.

Males and females must mate to reproduce. The males of some species release sperm packets into the water. They eventually settle on or near the tube openings of female worms. The packets break down, and sperm is released. The sperm find their way into the reproductive ducts of the females, and the eggs are fertilized inside their bodies. The eggs apparently develop inside the tube. The larvae (LAR-vee), or early stage of the animal, are free-swimming, but eventually settle into the mud and begin producing their own tubes and acquiring bacteria.

BEARD WORMS AND PEOPLE

Beard worms are of great scientific interest because some species live in extreme environments.

CONSERVATION STATUS

No beard worms are considered endangered or threatened.

STAY TUNED!

The classification of beard worms has been debated by scientists for years. Although treated here as a separate phylum, many scientists consider them to be a group within the phylum Annelida. Certain physical features, plus analysis of their DNA, support this relationship. Some scientists, however, consider beard worms a specialized group. Views of their relationships will continue to change as scientists learn more about these unusual sea creatures.

Norwegian tubeworm (*Siboglinum fiordicum*)

NORWEGIAN TUBEWORM
Siboglinum fiordicum

Physical characteristics: The body of a Norwegian tubeworm grows up to 11.8 inches (300 millimeters) in length and 0.009 inches (0.25 millimeters) thick. The smooth tube is patterned with gray or brown rings. This tubeworm has only one tentacle.

Geographic range: The Norwegian tubeworm lives only in Norway.

Habitat: Norwegian tubeworms live on the sandy or muddy bottoms of fjords, at depths ranging from 82 to 656.7 feet (25 to 200 meters).

Diet: The Norwegian tubeworm relies mostly on bacteria to produce food.

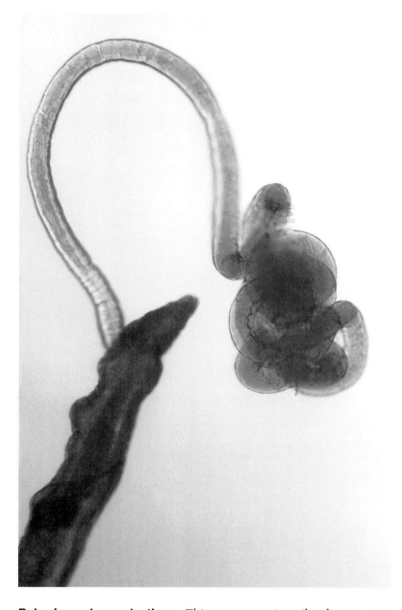

The body of a Norwegian tubeworm grows up to 11.8 inches (300 millimeters) in length and 0.009 inches (0.25 millimeters) thick. Visible here is the anterior end and tentacle. (Photograph by E. C. and A. J. Southward. Reproduced by permission.)

Behavior and reproduction: This worm uses its tail to burrow into the mud or sand.

Norwegian tubeworms and people: Norwegian tubeworms are one of the most easily studied beard worms because they live at relatively shallow depths.

Conservation status: The Norwegian tubeworm is not considered endangered or threatened. ■

FOR MORE INFORMATION

Books:

Desbruyéres, D., and M. Segonzac, eds. *Handbook of Deep-Sea Hydrothermal Vent Fauna.* Brest, France: IFREMER, 1997.

Van Dover, C. L. *The Ecology of Deep-Sea Hydrothermal Vents.* Princeton, NJ: Princeton University Press, 2000.

Periodicals:

McMullin, E. R., S. Hourdez, S. W. Schaeffer, and C. R. Fisher. "Phylogeny and Biogeography of Deep Sea Vestimentiferan Tubeworms and Their Bacterial Symbionts." *Symbiosis* 34 (2003): 1-41.

Web sites:

Introduction to the Pogonophora. http://www.ucmp.berkeley.edu/annelida/pogonophora.html (accessed on January 3, 2005).

Phylum: Vestimentifera
Number of families: 8 families

phylum
CHAPTER

PHYSICAL CHARACTERISTICS

Hydrothermal vent and cold seep worms have long, worm-like bodies reaching up to 9.8 feet (3 meters) in length. They live in whitish to gray-brown tubes at least as long as their bodies and are attached to hard surfaces on the ocean bottom. The tubes are made of chitin (KYE-tehn), a material similar to fingernails that makes up the external skeletons of insects, spiders, and their relatives. Most of the green to brown body remains inside the tube except featherlike structures, or plumes, and a pair of winglike flaps forming a collar that protects the head region. Special glands inside the flaps may produce the material used to make the tube. Bright red plumes surround the flaps. When threatened, the plumes are quickly withdrawn inside the tube. The plumes and blood vessels along the body are red because they are filled with blood containing a protein called hemoglobin (HE-meh-GLO-bihn). Hemoglobin captures oxygen from the water, helping these worms to breathe under water.

All hydrothermal vent and cold seep worms lack mouths or digestive tracts as adults. Like beard worms, they rely on the bacteria inside them for food. The body trunk is filled with reproductive organs. The segmented tail has a row of hooks that firmly anchor the body inside the tube.

GEOGRAPHIC RANGE

Hydrothermal vent and cold seep worms are found on the ocean bottom at the east Pacific Rise, mid-Atlantic Ridge,

■ **phylum**

class

subclass

order

monotypic order

suborder

family

Galápagos Rift, Okinawa Trough, Mariana Trough, and the Lau, Manus, and North Fiji Basins. They also live along the continental margins of North and South America, Spain, and in the Mediterranean Sea.

HABITAT

Hydrothermal vent and cold seep worms live mostly in deep-sea waters, usually at depths greater than 0.6 miles (1 kilometer). They live along earthquake faults, or trenches, along the ocean floor. Some species attach their tubes to the chimneylike openings around deep-sea geysers called hydrothermal vents. Relatively warm water of 68°F (20°C) bubbles up through these vents. Others build their tubes near coldwater vents known as seeps. A few species are found only on whale carcasses that have settled deep on the ocean bottom.

DIET

Hydrothermal vent and cold seep worms live in total darkness. They rely on the billions of bacteria living in their bodies to make food. The worms provide the bacteria with carbon dioxide from their own bodies and hydrogen sulfide collected from the hydrothermal vents. As the bacteria convert these chemicals into energy for themselves, they produce simple sugars and other compounds that the worms absorb as food. The conversion of chemical reactions into food is called chemosynthesis (KEY-moh-SIN-thuh-sihs).

BEHAVIOR AND REPRODUCTION

Hydrothermal vent species mature within a few years, but those living near cold seeps may take 100 years or more to reach adulthood.

There is no contact between males and females. Males release sperm or sperm packets into the water, and the sperm find their way into the tubes of the females. Large numbers of eggs are fertilized inside or just outside the female's reproductive ducts and released into the water. The young larvae (LAR-vee) swim with the help of a band of hairlike cilia (SIH-lee-uh) on the front of their bodies. In order to feed, the larvae take in bacteria that eventually settle in their bodies as they grow. These mutualistic (MYU-chu-eh-LIH-stihk) organisms benefit from their relationship with each other.

HYDROTHERMAL VENT AND COLD SEEP WORMS AND PEOPLE

Scientists refer to hydrothermal vent and cold seep worms as "flagship" animals for deep sea habitats, especially deep-sea geysers known as hydrothermal vents. This means that these species have special appeal to people because of their beauty and may convince people to save the habitats where they and other animals live.

CONSERVATION STATUS

These worms are not considered endangered or threatened.

GUTLESS WONDERS

Hydrothermal vent and cold seep worms survive in short-lived habitats that are constantly appearing and disappearing. They must settle quickly to establish themselves and build up their numbers. Yet, they must also be able to distribute themselves over considerable distances to take advantage of new tube-building sites. How they manage to achieve both goals is still a mystery!

Hydrothermal vent worm *(Riftia pachyptila)*

HYDROTHERMAL VENT WORM
Riftia pachyptila

Physical characteristics: This species is the largest of the hydrothermal vent and cold seep worms. They reach up to 9.8 feet (3 meters) long, live in white tubes, and resemble giant lipsticks with their bright red plumes. Their protective flaps are white.

Geographic range: Hydrothermal vent worms live on the East Pacific Rise, Galápagos Rift, and Guayana Basin.

Habitat: These worms are found at depths of about 1 mile (1.5 kilometers) on hydrothermal vents.

This photo of Riftia pachyptila comes from a depth of 1.5 miles (2500 meters) and was shot on a dive in the submersible Alvin. (Craig M. Young, Oregon Institute of Marine Biology. Reproduced by permission.)

Diet: Hydrothermal vent worms rely on bacteria and chemosynthesis for food.

Behavior and reproduction: These worms form dense colonies on hydrothermal vents. One of the fastest-growing marine animals, they build tubes up to 4.9 feet (1.5 meters) and reach adulthood in only 18 months.

Males release sperm into the water. Females also release fertilized eggs. The larvae are capable of spreading out to new hydrothermal vents.

Hydrothermal vent worms and people: They are "flagship" animals for hydrothermal vents and may help to conserve these habitats.

Conservation status: Hydrothermal vent worms are not considered endangered or threatened. ■

FOR MORE INFORMATION

Books:

Gage, J. *Deep-Sea Biology. A Natural History of Organisms at the Deep-Sea Floor.* Cambridge, U.K.: Cambridge University Press, 1991.

Van Dover, C. L. *The Ecology of Deep-Sea Hydrothermal Vents.* Princeton, NJ: Princeton University Press, 2000.

Periodicals:

Fisher, C. R., I. A. Urcuyo, M. A. Simpkins, and E. Nix. "Life in the Slow Lane: Growth and Longevity of Cold-seep Vestimentiferans." *Marine Ecology-Pubblicazioni della Stazione Zoologica di Napoli* 18 (1997): 83-94.

Jones, M. L. *"Riftia pachyptila* Jones: Observations on the Vestimentiferan Worm from the Galápagos Rift." *Science* 213 (1981): 333-336.

Lutz, R. A., and R. M. Haymon. "Rebirth of a Deep Sea Vent." *National Geographic* (November 1994) 186, no. 5: 114-126.

Web sites:

Tubeworm (Riftia pachyptila). http://www.ocean.udel.edu/kiosk/riftia .html (accessed on January 4, 2005).

Videos:

Scientific American Frontiers: Beneath the Sea. PBS Home Video, 2002.

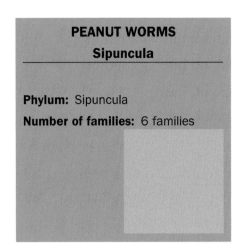

PEANUT WORMS

Sipuncula

Phylum: Sipuncula
Number of families: 6 families

phylum
C H A P T E R

PHYSICAL CHARACTERISTICS

Peanut worms are sea creatures that have bilateral symmetry (bye-LAT-er-uhl SIH-muh-tree). This means that their soft bodies can be divided into similar halves. They are sausagelike and not segmented in any way. Their bodies are gray or brown and are sometimes marked with reddish purple or green. They measure up to 11.8 inches (300 millimeters) long. The front part of the body is called the introvert (IN-treh-vuhrt). The introvert has small hooks that are used to gain traction. At the top of the introvert is the mouth. In some species, a ring of tentacles surrounds the mouth. The introvert can be pulled inside the rest of the body. Muscles pull on the mouth end, turning the introvert inward on itself, in what looks like the opposite of turning a sock inside out. Once withdrawn, the body becomes short, resembling a shelled peanut.

The thicker part of the body is called the trunk and is sometimes covered with small bumps. The soft body wall is supported by two kinds of muscles and a large body cavity filled with fluid. The body cavity is called the coelom (SIGH-lum). Ringlike circular muscles squeeze the body wall and shift fluid forward in the coelom to extend the introvert. Long muscles running the length of the body contract to move the body fluid back and pull the introvert into the trunk. Peanut worms do not have circulatory or respiratory systems. Instead, special cells floating in the fluid carry oxygen and nutrients throughout the body. A kidneylike organ inside the coelom helps filter waste from the body fluid. This waste is expelled from the body through one or two openings opposite the anus (AY-nuhs). The anus is usually located near the upper portion of the body, but in some species it is found on the introvert. The nervous system includes a bundle of nerves inside the tip of the introvert and a nerve cord that runs along the underside of the body.

GEOGRAPHIC RANGE

Peanut worms are found in all of the oceans.

HABITAT

Peanut worms are found in both cold- and warm-water habitats, at all depths between the intertidal zone and 22,510 feet (6,860 meters). Some species live in burrows in sand or mud, while others live in rock crevices, empty seashells, or tubeworm tubes. Still others bore into rock or bone. Some species make their homes in mats of algae (AL-jee) or plantlike growths that live in water, in large sponges, or among the roots of sea grasses or mangrove trees.

DIET

Peanut worms living in sand and mud swallow surrounding sediment collected with their tentacles. Those living in rocks use their introvert hooks to scrape sand, mud, and small organisms from the surfaces of surrounding rocks.

BEHAVIOR AND REPRODUCTION

Most peanut worms quickly withdraw their introverts when disturbed and avoid light by retreating into their burrows or rock crevices. They use their introvert hooks and muscles to pull their bodies forward. Swimming is not common and is accomplished by simply jerking the body trunk in all directions.

Many peanut worms can replace missing tentacles and introverts. Some species can regenerate portions of the digestive tract and body trunk. Others reproduce by purposely dividing their bodies. Each body part then develops all the necessary missing parts. This type of reproduction is called budding, or asexual (ay-SEK-shuh-wuhl) reproduction. Asexual reproduction does not involve mating or male or female reproductive systems.

Most peanut worms require both males and females to reproduce. Only one species has individuals with both male and female reproductive organs. Another species is able to reproduce without fertilization (FUR-teh-lih-ZAY-shun), or the combining of egg and sperm to start development. The sexes are identical to each other, and their reproductive organs are present only while they reproduce. Eggs and sperm are released into the coelom, where they are collected by the kidneylike organs and expelled into the water. Fertilization takes place outside of the body. Peanut worms develop in a variety of ways. Some species develop from eggs directly into miniature versions of the adults, while others must first go through various free-swimming larval stages before becoming young worms.

HOME AT LAST

Peanut worms were first illustrated in the mid-1500s and were classified with other wormlike creatures in 1767. Not until 1959 was this unique group of animals placed in their own phylum, Sipuncula. The name of the phylum comes from the Greek *siphunculus*, meaning "little tube."

PEANUT WORMS AND PEOPLE

Larger species of peanut worms are used by fishermen throughout the world as bait. In Java, the western Carolines, and parts of China, they are eaten by humans.

CONSERVATION STATUS

Peanut worms are not considered endangered or threatened.

NO COMMON NAME
Sipunculus nudus

Sipunculus nudus is often used as a research animal. They are sold as fish bait in some parts of the world. (Illustration by Bruce Worden. Reproduced by permission.)

Physical characteristics: *Sipunculus nudus* measures 6 to 10 inches (150 to 250 millimeters) long. The introvert is short, only one-third the length of the trunk, and lacks hooks. There are 24 to 34 bands of long muscles visible through the skin.

Geographic range: *Sipunculus nudus* (abbreviated as *S. nudus*) are found throughout the world in temperate, subtropical, and tropical waters. (Specific distribution map not available.)

Habitat: *S. nudus* live in burrows in the sand and are found from just below the tidal zone down to 2,953 feet (900 meters) deep.

Diet: *S. nudus* swallow the surrounding sand to digest bits of plant and animal tissues.

Behavior and reproduction: This species spends its days hidden in its burrow, extending its tentacles to feed at night.

Males and females release sperm and eggs into the water. They pass through two larval stages before becoming young worms.

***Sipunculus nudus* and people:** *S. nudus* is the best-known species of peanut worm and is often used as a research animal. They are sold as fish bait in some parts of the world.

Conservation status: *S. nudus* is not considered endangered or threatened. ■

FOR MORE INFORMATION

Books:

Cutler, Edward B. *The Sipuncula. Their Systematics, Biology, and Evolution.* Ithaca, NY: Cornell University Press, 1994.

Kozloff, E. N. *Marine Invertebrates of the Pacific Northwest.* Seattle, WA: University of Washington Press, 1996.

Ruppert, E. E., and R. S. Fox. *Seashore Animals of the Southeast.* Columbia, SC: University of South Carolina, 1988.

Web sites:

Introduction to Sipuncula. The Peanut Worms. http://www.ucmp.berkeley.edu/sipuncula/sipuncula.html (accessed on January 5, 2005).

ECHIURANS

Echiura

Phylum: Echiura

Number of families: 5 families

phylum

■ **phylum**

class

subclass

order

monotypic order

suborder

family

CHAPTER

PHYSICAL CHARACTERISTICS

Echiurans (eh-key-YUR-enz) are sea creatures sometimes known as spoon worms or fat innkeepers. They have bilateral symmetry (bye-LAT-er-uhl SIH-muh-tree) and can only be divided into similar halves along one plane. Their sausage-shaped bodies are soft, unsegmented, and have two distinct regions, the proboscis and body trunk. The proboscis (pruh-BAH-suhs) is a long, flexible, tubelike snout. The trunk may reach 15.75 inches (40 centimeters) in length, but the proboscis is much longer and can reach up to 3.28 to 6.56 feet (1 to 2 meters). The flexible and muscular proboscis is used to gather food. The lower surface is covered with hairlike cilia (SIH-lee-uh) that help move food toward the mouth located at the base of the proboscis. The proboscis can be extended or retracted, but not withdrawn inside the trunk. It is usually white, pink, green, or brown and can be short or long, scoop- or ribbonlike, and flat or fleshy and spoonlike. The tip may be squared off or notched.

The surface of the thick body trunk is smooth or rough and is gray, dark green, brown, pinkish, or reddish in color. Most species have a pair of hooks on the underside of the body, near the front of the trunk. Some also have one or two rings of bristles around the anus (AY-nuhs), or the opening of the digestive tract at the end of the body. The body wall is wrapped in layers of muscles that run around the body, along its length, or at an angle different from the other muscle groups. The body is supported from the inside by a large, fluid-filled body cavity, or coelom (SIGH-lum). A closed circulatory system may or may not be present. Pairs of kidneylike organs remove wastes from the body's fluid and expel waste from the body.

GEOGRAPHIC RANGE

Echiurans are found in all oceans.

HABITAT

Echiurans are found mostly in the ocean, but a few species live in other kinds of salty waters, such as estuaries (EHS-chew-AIR-eez), where rivers meet the sea. Most species are found in intertidal and shallow waters, but some live at depths of 32,808 feet (10,000 meters). They usually dig burrows in sand, mud, or other debris on the bottom. Some live in rock tunnels bored by other animals, or inside shells, dead corals, or under rocks. Echiurans often host crabs, mollusks, and other kinds of worms in their burrows as commensals (kuh-MEHN-suhls), where they scavenge extra food. Commensals are animals that live on or with other organisms, without harm to either one.

DIET

Echiurans eat bits of dead plants, animals, and microorganisms that live on sand, mud, and rock.

BEHAVIOR AND REPRODUCTION

To feed, some echiurans extend the sticky proboscis out of the burrow and onto the surrounding sea bottom. The tip of the proboscis gathers particles of food and covers them with a sticky coat of mucus. The cilia move the particles back toward the mouth. Other species are filter feeders. Fat innkeeper worms, *Urechis caupo*, build a sticky net of mucus and place it near the opening of their U-shaped burrow. Both ends of the burrow open to the water. As they flex their body trunks, water is drawn through the burrow, trapping bits of food and small organisms in the net. The worm eventually gathers and eats the food, net and all.

Both males and females are required for reproduction. Most species release eggs and sperm into the water. Fertilization (FUR-teh-lih-ZAY-shun) takes place in the water. In one group the eggs are fertilized inside the female's body. Developing echiurans first go through a larval stage. The unsegmented larvae (LAR-vee) are free-swimming and covered with cilia. They drift with other plankton, or microscopic water-dwelling plants and

animals, for up to three months, eventually developing into young worms and settling on the bottom.

ECHIURANS AND PEOPLE

Some echiurans are used by scientists to study how their bodies develop and function and what chemicals they produce, including a skin coloring of some females called bonellin. Bonellin is of interest to people because it may kill certain kinds of bacteria.

CONSERVATION STATUS

Echiurans are not considered endangered or threatened.

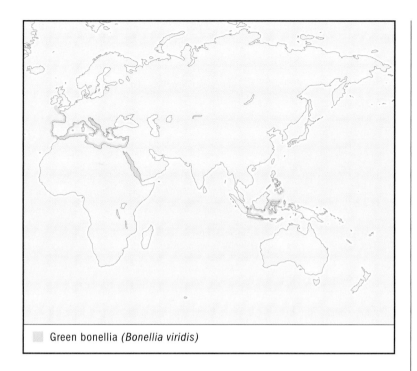

Green bonellia *(Bonellia viridis)*

GREEN BONELLIA
Bonellia viridis

Physical characteristics: The female has an egg- or sausage-shaped body measuring up to 5.9 inches (15 centimeters) long. The proboscis is long and notched at the tip and reaches up to 4.9 feet (1.5 meters). The body is dark green. Green bonellia have one pair of hooks underneath the body. The flattened, colorless males are much smaller (0.039 to 0.11 inches; 1 to 3 millimeters) and do not have a proboscis, mouth, anus, or circulatory system. Their body is made up almost entirely of reproductive organs.

Geographic range: Green bonellia are found in the northeastern Atlantic Ocean, the Mediterranean and Red seas, and the Indopacific region.

Habitat: Females live in burrows built by other animals in coarse sand, rocks, or spaces between rocks. They are found at depths of 33 to 328 feet (10 to 100 meters). They often have a variety of commensals that live with them. The male lives inside the female's body, like a parasite (PAIR-uh-site).

Diet: Green bonellia eat bits of plants, animals, and microscopic organisms found at the base of plants or in sand between rocks. Males rely on females to provide food for them.

Behavior and reproduction: Females move back and forth in their burrows with the help of their proboscis. Muscular contractions of the body wall bring fresh water in contact with the body to renew the supply of oxygen.

Sexes are separate. Fertilization occurs in the genital sac, where a male often lives. The larvae are free swimming. If the larva settles on ocean floor, it develops into a 3.9-inch (10-centimeter) long female. If the larva settles on a female's body (particularly its proboscis), it develops into a 0.039 to 0.078 inch (1 to 2 millimeter) long adult male in about 1 or 2 weeks. Males live as parasites inside the female and produce a ready supply of sperm.

Green bonellias and people: The skin-coloring chemical bonellin is of interest to scientists because it kills many different kinds of organisms, including bacteria.

Conservation status: Green bonellias are not considered endangered or threatened. ∎

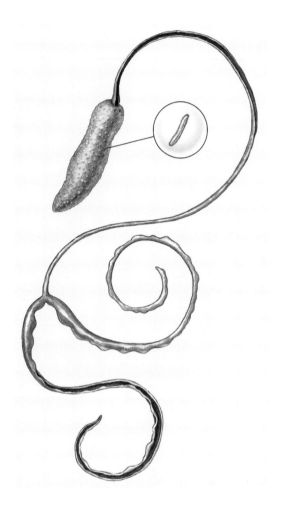

Green bonellia eat bits of plants, animals, and microscopic organisms found at the base of plants or in sand between rocks. (Illustration by Bruce Worden. Reproduced by permission.)

FOR MORE INFORMATION

Books:

Kozloff, E. N. *Marine Invertebrates of the Pacific Northwest.* Seattle, WA: University of Washington Press, 1996.

Ruppert, E. E., and R. S. Fox. *Seashore Animals of the Southeast.* Columbia: University of South Carolina, 1988.

Stephen, A. C., and S. J. Edmonds. *The Phyla Sipuncula and Echiura.* London: Trustees of the British Museum (Natural History), 1972.

Periodicals:

Agius, L. "Larval Settlement in the Echiuran Worm *Bonellia viridis*: Settlement on Both the Adult Proboscis and Body Trunk." *Marine Biology* 53 (2002): 125-129.

Web sites:

Introduction to the Echiura. http://www.ucmp.berkeley.edu/annelida/echiura.html (accessed on January 6, 2005).

Murina, V. V. *Phylum Echiura Stephen, 1965.* http://www.ibss.iuf.net/people/murina/echiura.html (accessed on January 6, 2005).

The Echiura-Spoon Worms. http://www.ldeo.columbia.edu/edu/dees/ees/life/slides/phyla/echiura.html (accessed on January 6, 2005).

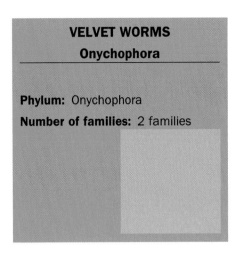

VELVET WORMS

Onychophora

Phylum: Onychophora
Number of families: 2 families

phylum

CHAPTER

■ **phylum**

class

subclass

order

monotypic order

suborder

family

PHYSICAL CHARACTERISTICS

Velvet worms have bilateral symmetry (bye-LAT-er-uhl SIH-muh-tree) and can only be divided into similar halves along one plane. They resemble caterpillars and have long, soft, and flexible bodies. Adults measure from 0.5 to 8 inches (13 to 203 millimeters) long. Most range in color from black to blue, red, brown, or gray. Some species are striped or have beautiful patterns. Their skin, or exoskeleton, is very elastic and covered with small bumps called papillae (pah-PIH-lee). The papillae are made up of small scales that give them a velvety appearance. Larger papillae have a single sensory bristle that helps velvet worms to feel their surroundings.

Along the sides of the bodies are breathing holes, or spiracles (SPIH-reh-kulz). The spiracles lead to a network of respiratory tubes inside the body, similar to insects and spiders. The head has a pair of soft antennae, clawlike jaws, and soft, fleshy papillae on either side of the mouth. Inside the mouth is a rough, tonguelike structure that helps to grind food. The cone-shaped legs are stumpy and unsegmented, but there are 13 to 43 pairs of legs, depending on the age, sex, and species of velvet worm. Each leg is tipped with 3 to 5 pads and a pair of claws.

GEOGRAPHIC RANGE

Velvet worms are found in Mexico, Central America, Chile, tropical West Africa, South Africa, southeast Asia, New Guinea, Australia, and New Zealand.

HABITAT

All velvet worms live in leaf litter, under stones or logs, or in soil in moist and humid habitats, such as tropical and subtropical forests.

DIET

Velvet worms are carnivores (KAR-nih-vorz), or meat eaters, and eat mainly insects, spiders, other arthropods, and snails.

BEHAVIOR AND REPRODUCTION

As with arthropods, which include insects, spiders, and their relatives, velvet worms must molt, or shed their exoskeleton, in order to grow. These secretive animals capture prey with threads of clear, sticky slime shot from the oral papillae. The slime is also used to discourage predators and can be squirted up to 1.6 feet (0.5 meters) in distance. During the dry season, or periods of low temperature, velvet worms crawl down into crevices in the soil and remain there until conditions on the surface improve.

A MISSING LINK?

Velvet worms have changed very little since their marine ancestors first came on land about 400 million years ago. Discovered in 1826, velvet worms were first thought to be a kind of slug. Later scientists realized that they shared features of both segmented worms (Annelida) and arthropods, and they were placed in their own phylum. They have been called the "missing link" that connects these two groups, but recent studies show that they are more closely related to arthropods than annelids.

Mating has been observed in very few species. Males produce special chemicals, or pheromones (FEH-re-moans), from glands located at the bases of their legs to attract females. In some species, males deposit sperm packets directly into the female's reproductive opening. In other species, the packets are placed on the female's body and are absorbed directly through the exoskeleton. The sperm is sometimes stored for several months before the eggs are fertilized.

Some velvet worms deposit their eggs in the soil, and the young develop and are nourished inside the egg until they hatch later. Others also produce eggs, but they hatch inside the female's body and young are born live. A few species give live birth to young that are nourished by the mother's body until they are born, headfirst. Whether born or hatched, all young velvet worms resemble small adults.

VELVET WORMS AND PEOPLE

Velvet worms are particularly valuable research animals. Their distributions are studied to help track the movements of continents over millions of years. Their sticky slime is also being studied as a possible glue for special kinds of surgery.

CONSERVATION STATUS

Eleven species of velvet worms are listed by the World Conservation Union (IUCN). Three species are listed as Critically Endangered, which means they face an extremely high risk of extinction in the wild. Two species are listed as Endangered or facing a very high risk of extinction in the wild. Four species are listed as Vulnerable or facing a high risk of extinction in the wild. One species is listed as Lower Risk, or at risk of becoming threatened with extinction in the future. Another is Data Deficient and lacks sufficient information to determine its vulnerability to extinction. The greatest threat to their existence is habitat loss.

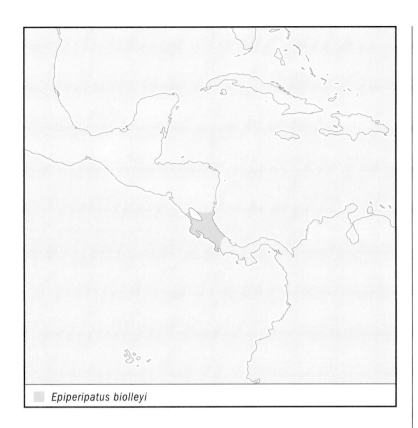

Epiperipatus biolleyi

NO COMMON NAME
Epiperipatus biolleyi

Physical characteristics: *Epiperipatus biolleyi* adults measure up to 1.5 to 2 inches (38 to 52 millimeters) in length and are rusty brown or pinkish with dark papillae and a stripe along the back. Antennae and legs are gray. Females have 30 pairs of legs, while males have 26 to 28.

Geographic range: They are found in Costa Rica.

Habitat: *Epiperipatus biolleyi* (abbreviated as *E. biolleyi*) live in low mountain forests inside rotting logs or in natural cavities in the soil.

Diet: Nothing is known about their diet in the wild.

Behavior and reproduction: *E. biolleyi* avoid light and walk at speeds up to 0.4 inches (10 millimeters) per second. Individuals found in the wild often carry scars and missing legs.

Velvet worms eat mainly insects, spiders, other arthropods, and snails (Illustration by Dan Erickson. Reproduced by permission.)

Sperm packets are deposited directly into the reproductive opening. They are viviparous.

***Epiperipatus biolleyi* and people:**   *E. biolleyi* are not known to impact people or their activities.

Conservation status: This species is not considered endangered or threatened.   ■

FOR MORE INFORMATION

Books:

Tavolacci, J., ed. *Insects and Spiders of the World.* Volume 9, *Stonefly-Velvet Worm. Velvet Worm.* New York: Marshal Cavendish, 2003.

Periodicals:

Ghiselin, M. T. "A Moveable Feaster." *Natural History* 94, no. 9 (September 1985): 54-60.

Mendez, R. "Keeping a Missing Link—The Velvet Worm." *1997 Invertebrates in Captivity Proceedings,* 72-74.

Monge-Nágera, J., and J. P. Alfaro. "Geographic Variation of Habitats in Costa Rican Velvet Worms (Onychophora: Peripatidae)." *Biogeographica* 71, no. 3 (1995): 97-108.

New, T. R. "Onychophora in Invertebrate Conservation: Priorities, Practice and Prospects." *Zoological Journal of the Linnean Society* 114, no. 1 (1995): 77-89.

New, T. R. "Velvet Worms: Charismatic Invertebrates for Conservation." *Wings* 27, no. 2 (Fall 2004): 12-15.

Sunnucks, P., and N. Tait. "Tales of the Unexpected." *Nature Australia* 27, no. 1 (2001): 60-69.

Web sites:

Introduction to the Onychophora. http://www.ucmp.berkeley.edu/onychoph/onychophora.html (accessed on January 18, 2005).

The Onychophora. http://www.mnhn.fr/assoc/myriapoda/ONYCHO.HTM (accessed on January 18, 2005).

Onychophora Homepage. http://www.sciref.org/onychophora/ (accessed on January 18, 2005).

phylum
C H A P T E R

PHYSICAL CHARACTERISTICS

Water bears are mostly microscopic, measuring 0.00787 to 0.0472 inches (0.2 to 1.2 millimeters) in length. They have bilateral symmetry (bye-LAT-er-uhl SIH-muh-tree) and can only be divided into similar halves along one plane. The outside of the body, or cuticle (KYU-tih-kuhl), may have platelike scales, spines, and other appendages. Most species are whitish or clear, but some land-dwelling, or terrestrial (te-REH-stree-uhl), species are yellow, orange, green, red, or greenish black.

Their bodies are made up of five indistinct segments, including the head and four trunk segments. Each trunk segment bears a pair of stumpy, segmented legs. The first three pairs are used for walking, while the last pair is used for clinging. Terrestrial and freshwater species have legs with fewer segments that end in two or four claws. Most marine water bears have telescoping legs that can be withdrawn inside their bodies. Depending on the species, these legs have up to 13 claws or four toelike structures with varying numbers of claws. In some species, the toes are tipped with suction cups or sticky, rod-shaped discs, like the feet of a gecko.

Water bears feed through a mouth with bristlelike jaws called stylets (STAI-lehts). The stylets are used to puncture cell walls so fluids are sucked into the mouth. Because they are small and live in moist or wet environments, water bears do not have a circulatory or respiratory system. They breathe directly through the body wall. Some species have kidneylike organs that

phylum

class

subclass

order

monotypic order

suborder

family

remove waste and regulate body salts, while others rely on special glands located at the bases of the legs.

Both young and adult water bears shed the cuticle, or molt, just like insects, spiders, and other arthropods. The mouthparts and surrounding structures, as well as the toes and claws, are produced by special glands after the new cuticle has formed.

GEOGRAPHIC RANGE

Water bears are found on all continents and in all oceans.

HABITAT

Water bears require water and are found in a wide variety of marine, freshwater, and terrestrial habitats. Some species live in hot, radioactive springs, while other live in ice caves formed by glaciers and other sheets of ice. Many marine species are found along beaches. Those living on land are found in primitive plants and plantlike organisms growing on rocks, logs, and soil, such as mosses, liverworts, and lichens.

DIET

Water bears eat plants, microscopic animals, and bacteria. Terrestrial species either suck juices from mosses and lichens or eat bacteria growing on these organisms. Some marine species are parasites (PAIR-uh-sites) and live and feed on other animals, such as sea cucumbers and barnacles. A few species rely on bacteria living inside special organs in their heads to provide nutrition in the form of proteins and sugars.

BEHAVIOR AND REPRODUCTION

Although many species of water bears are slow and lumbering like bears, species that prey on other microscopic animals are fairly quick and can move faster than the human eye can follow.

Water bears can survive extreme conditions for months, even years, by shutting down all life processes, a phenomenon known as cryptobiosis (KRIP-toe-bye-OH-sihs). Cryptobiosis is triggered mainly by lack of water, or dehydration (dih-high-DRAY-shun), and very low temperatures. Water bears in cryptobiosis as a result of dehydration are said to be in the tun (tuhn) stage.

Most water bears require males and females to reproduce. Some males place sperm directly into special sperm-storing organs on the female's body. Some females have special structures that are inserted into the male, allowing them to grab sperm inside the male's body. A few species are parthenogenic (PAR-thih-no-JEH-nik) and capable of producing young without mating. In some species, individuals have reproductive organs of both males and females. Most water bears are thought to lay eggs. Young water bears resemble the adults, but may have fewer claws and other structures.

WATER BEARS AND PEOPLE

The cryptobiotic abilities of water bears have long been of interest to scientists. Several species in the tun stage have been exposed to cosmic radiation, vacuum, and temperatures close to absolute zero and have survived, clearing the way to use them as experimental animals in space. Scientists are also analyzing the proteins and sugars produced by water bears during the tun stage to protect their delicate tissues under extreme conditions. These and other studies may help to explain how life began and developed on Earth.

CONSERVATION STATUS

No water bears are considered endangered or threatened.

TUNS OF FUN

Water bears are the only animals capable of stopping all life functions and still be alive. They survive harsh conditions in the barrel-like tun stage. Tun is another name for a wine barrel or cask. Water bear tuns can be picked up by winds and carried hundred of miles. Tuns have been revived from moss specimens collected more than 100 years ago. They can survive 20 days at temperatures of -328°F (-200°C).

GIANT YELLOW WATER BEAR
Richtersius coronifer

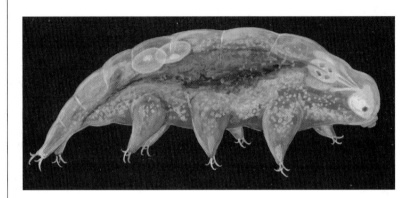

Giant yellow water bears live on mosses in high mountain habitats up to 18,300 feet (5,600 meters) and in Arctic habitats. (Illustration by Amanda Humphrey. Reproduced by permission.)

Physical characteristics: This species is a relatively large (up to 0.039 inches or 1 millimeter) water bear. They are usually yellow to orange with large black eyes. Each leg has two equally sized claws.

Geographic range: This species is found in the Arctic, Sweden, Turkey, Nepal, and Colombia.

(Specific distribution map not available.)

Habitat: Giant yellow water bears live on mosses in high mountain habitats up to 18,300 feet (5,600 meters) and in Arctic habitats.

Diet: This species is believed to suck fluids from the cells of mosses.

Behavior and reproduction: Giant yellow water bears can survive severe dehydration for up to 9 years. They are also capable of tolerating temperatures down to -320°F (-196°C) whether they are in the tun stage or not.

This species requires males and females to reproduce, but can also switch to parthenogenesis.

Giant yellow water bears and people: This species has possible uses as an experimental animal in outer space. They are capable of surviving high temperatures, vacuum, and cosmic radiation.

Conservation status: Giant yellow water bears are not considered endangered or threatened. ■

FOR MORE INFORMATION

Books:

Kinchin, Ian M. *The Biology of Tardigrades.* London: Portland, 1994.

Periodicals:

Romano, F.A. "On Water Bears." *Florida Entomologist* 86 (2003): 134-137.

Wright, J. C., P. Westh, and H. Ramløv. "Cryptobiosis in Tardigrada." *Biological Reviews of the Cambridge Philosophical Society* 67 (1992): 1-29.

Web sites:

Hunting for Water Bears in the Backyard. http://www.microscopy-uk.org.uk/mag/indexmag.html?http://www.microscopy-uk.org.uk/mag/artjun00/mmbearp.html (accessed on January 19, 2005).

The Incredible Water Bear. http://www.microscopy-uk.org.uk/mag/index-mag.html?http://www.microscopy-uk.org.uk/mag/artjun00/mmbearp.html (accessed on January 19, 2005).

Water Bears-Tardigrades. http://www.tardigrades.com (accessed on January 19, 2005).

REMIPEDES

Remipedia

Class: Remipedia

Number of families: 2 families

phylum

● **class**

subclass

order

monotypic order

suborder

family

PHYSICAL CHARACTERISTICS

Remipedes (REM-mih-peeds) are wormlike crustaceans that lack both color and eyes and measure 0.35 to 1.8 inches (9 to 45 millimeters) long. They have a short, distinct head and, depending on species, a long body trunk with 10 to 32 segments. Most of the trunk segments have a pair of flattened, paddlelike limbs directed out from the sides. The head has a pair of threadlike sensory processors and two pairs of antennae. The second pair of antennae is long and feathery.

The mouthparts are found inside the head. They include three pairs of jawlike appendages: a pair of mandibles (MAN-dih-bulz), or biting mouthparts, and two pairs of maxillae (mack-SIH-lee). The first pair of maxillae is tipped with fanglike projections. The fangs inject an unknown chemical that paralyzes and kills prey. The second pair of maxillae is followed by a nearly identical pair of mouthparts called maxillipeds (mack-SIH-leh-pehds). The fingerlike maxillipeds are actually attached to the first trunk segment, which is tightly joined to the head.

GEOGRAPHIC RANGE

Remipedes are found in underwater sea caves along the shores of the Bahamas, Canary Islands, Cuba, eastern Mexico, northwestern Australia, and the Indian Ocean.

HABITAT

Remipedes live only in completely submerged sea caves near the shores of islands and some continents. They live with other cave-dwelling, or troglodytic (TRAH-gloh-DIH-tik), crustaceans and fish.

DIET

They are predators and eat troglodytic shrimp and fish. Remipedes are closely associated with the sand or mud at the bottom of caves. In captivity they gather these materials into a small ball, hold it over their mouth, then eat it. Some scientists think that they are using bacteria in the sediment as either a food source or for some physiological purpose.

BEHAVIOR AND REPRODUCTION

Remipedes usually swim upside down in open water inside caves. They are sometimes found swimming, resting, or grooming on the bottom. The antennae are cleaned by drawing them through the trunk limbs, while the trunk limbs are cleaned with the mouthparts.

Remipedes are hermaphrodites (her-MAE-fro-daits), with individuals having the reproductive organs of both males and females. The egg-producing organs, or ovaries (OH-veh-reez), are located in the head. The tubes or ducts leading from the ovaries to the outside of the body open in the trunk segment that has the seventh pair of trunk limbs. The male reproductive organs open at the fourteenth pair of trunk limbs. The males produce sperm packets. Very little is known about how remipedes develop, other than the juveniles resemble the adults and have fewer trunk segments.

REMIPEDES AND PEOPLE

Remipedes do not have any immediate impact on humans or their activities.

CONSERVATION STATUS

No remipedes are considered endangered or threatened. However, one species, *Speleonectes lucayensis,* is protected by Lucayan National Park on Grand Bahama Island. The cave habitats of all remipedes are threatened by logging, development, pesticides, and sewage disposal.

SWIMMING TO THEIR OWN BEAT

Remipedes have puzzled scientists since their discovery in a cave in the Bahama Islands in 1980. Their wormlike bodies and other features are considered primitive and similar to those of the ancestors of all crustaceans. Yet their internal and venom-injecting mouthparts and trunk limbs directed sideways from the body are recognized as unique features among crustaceans. They swim about on their backs in caves by rhythmically beating these paddlelike limbs.

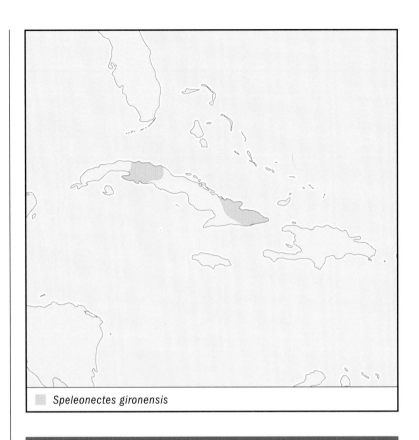

Speleonectes gironensis

NO COMMON NAME
Speleonectes gironensis

Physical characteristics: *Speleonectes gironensis* measure up to 0.55 inches (14 millimeters) in length. The maximum number of trunk segments is 25. The last pair of appendages on the end of the body trunk is twice as long as the last body trunk segments.

Geographic range: *Speleonectes gironensis* (abbreviated to *S. gironensis*) are found only in the undersea caves along the coast of Matanzas and Holguin Provinces, Cuba.

Habitat: *S. gironensis* are found in caves from 39 feet (12 meters) and deeper.

Diet: They eat mostly small cave crustaceans.

Speleonectes gironensis *are found only in the undersea caves along the coast of Matanzas and Holguin Provinces, Cuba. (Illustration by Jonathan Higgins. Reproduced by permission.)*

Behavior and reproduction: They swim in open water. Nothing is known about their reproductive behavior.

***Speleonectes gironensis* and people:** This species does not impact humans or their activities.

Conservation status: This species is not considered endangered or threatened. ■

FOR MORE INFORMATION

Books:

Yager, Jill. "The Reproductive Biology of Two Species of Remipedes." In *Crustacean Sexual Biology,* edited by R. T. Bauer and J. W. Martin. New York: Columbia University Press, 1991.

Periodicals:

Yager, J. "Remipedia, a New Class of Crustacea from a Marine Cave in the Bahamas." *Journal of Crustacean Biology* 1 (1981): 328-333.

Yager, J. "*Speleonectes gironensis,* New Species (Remipedia: Speleonectidae), from Anchialine Caves in Cuba, with Remarks on Biogeography and Ecology." *Journal of Crustacean Biology* 14 (1994): 752-762.

Yager, J., and W. F. Humphreys. " *Lasionectes exleyi,* sp. nov., the First Remipede Crustacean Recorded from Australia and the Indian Ocean, with a Key to the World Species." *Invertebrate Taxonomy* 10 (1996): 171-187.

Web sites:

Introduction Remipedia. http://www.ucmp.berkeley.edu/arthropoda/crustacea/remipedia.html (accessed on January 20, 2005).

Remipedia: Species. http://www.crustacea.net/crustace/remipedia/index.htm (accessed on January 20, 2005).

class

CHAPTER

PHYSICAL CHARACTERISTICS

Cephalocarids (sef-fal-oh-KAR-ids) are small crustaceans, measuring 0.078 to 0.146 inches (2 to 3.7 millimeters) in length. The eyeless head is short, broad, and covered by a horseshoe-shaped shield. There are two pairs of antennae and two pairs of jaws. The first pair of antennae is not branched; it is uniramous (YU-neh-RAY-mus). The second pair is branched or biramous (BY-ray-mus). The second pair of jaws is also biramous. It is the maxillae (mack-SIH-lee), which follows the uniramous first pair of jaws and resembles the appendages on the rest of the body. Maxillipeds (mack-SIH-leh-pehds), fingerlike limbs associated with the mouth, are absent. The thorax, or midbody, has eight segments, each with a pair of paddlelike, biramous limbs. The abdomen or tail section has 11 segments with no limbs at all. The tip of the tail, or telson, has a pair of long, threadlike, uniramous appendages.

GEOGRAPHIC RANGE

Cephalocarids live on the east and west coasts of North and South America, the Caribbean Islands, New Caledonia, New Zealand, and Japan.

HABITAT

Cephalocarids are usually found on or just below the surface of the muck that settles on the sea bottom, from shallow waters to depths of 5,250 feet (1,600 meters). This muck is rich in plant and animal materials. A few species are found in

Cephalocarids | 71

sand or the rubble that accumulates around coral reefs.

DIET

Using the rhythmic beat of their paddle-like limbs, cephalocarids draw water with bits of food into their mouth. As they spread their limbs, food-carrying water is pulled into a groove on the underside of their bodies that leads to the mouth.

BEHAVIOR AND REPRODUCTION

Cephalocarids swim and burrow through the muck by using their limbs. They sometimes fold their bodies in half to clean themselves.

Cephalocarids are hermaphrodites (her-MAE-fro-daits), with individuals having both male and female reproductive organs. Eggs are carried by small appendages on the midbody. The hatching cephalocarid is eyeless and has only three pairs of functional limbs, all located on the head. This is one of its three stages as a larva (LAR-vuh), or young animal that must go through changes in form before becoming an adult. As the larvae (LAR-vee; plural of larva) grow and molt, or shed their exoskeletons, additional body segments and limbs are added.

CEPHALOCARIDS AND PEOPLE

Cephalocarids are of scientific interest because they are thought to have features similar to the most ancient of crustaceans.

CONSERVATION STATUS

No cephalocarids are considered threatened or endangered.

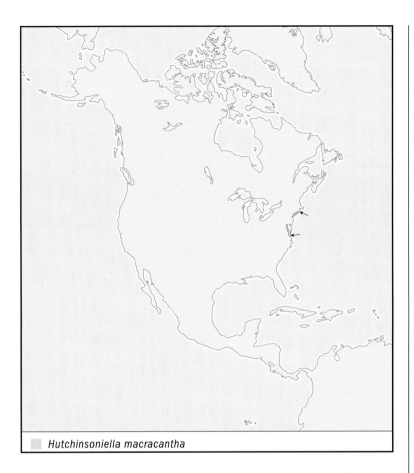

Hutchinsoniella macracantha

NO COMMON NAME
Hutchinsoniella macracantha

Physical characteristics: The head and midbody segments are wider than the abdomen or tail section. Some pairs of limbs are reduced in size and resemble small rounded projections.

Geographic range: This species is found along the coast of the United States from Long Island to Virginia and eastward on the continental slope.

Habitat: *Hutchinsoniella macracantha* live in the muck that settles on the sea bottom.

Diet: They eat bits of plant and animal materials.

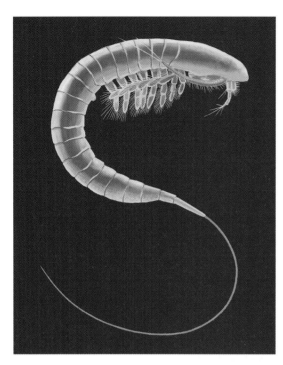

Hutchinsoniella macracantha *live in the muck that settles on the sea bottom. (Illustration by John Megahan. Reproduced by permission.)*

Behavior and reproduction: *Hutchinsoniella macracantha* are usually found on or just below the surface of the sea bottom. The larva molts 19 times before reaching adulthood.

***Hutchinsoniella macracantha* and people:** This species is not known to impact humans or their activities.

Conservation status: This species is not considered threatened or endangered. ■

FOR MORE INFORMATION

Books:

Hessler, R. R. *Cephalocarida: Living Fossil Without a Fossil Record.* In *Living Fossils.* N. Eldredge and S. M. Stanley, eds. New York: Springer Verlag, 1984.

Schram, F. *Crustacea.* Oxford, U.K.: Oxford University Press, 1986.

Periodicals:

Sanders, H. L. "The Cephalocarida, a New Subclass of Crustacea from Long Island Sound." *Proceedings of the National Academy of Sciences* 41 (1955): 61-66.

Web sites:

Brachypods (Cephalocarida). http://www.crustacea.net/crustace/ www/ brachyp.htm (accessed on January 21, 2005).

Introduction to the Cephalocarida. http://www.ucmp.berkeley.edu/ arthropoda/crustacea/cephalocarida.html (accessed on January 21, 2005).

FAIRY SHRIMPS, TADPOLE SHRIMPS, AND CLAM SHRIMPS AND WATER FLEAS

Branchiopoda

Class: Branchiopoda
Number of families: 29 families

phylum
class
subclass
order
monotypic order
suborder
family

PHYSICAL CHARACTERISTICS

Branchiopods (BRAN-kee-oh-pods) come in a variety of forms and are difficult to define as a group. They have two pairs of antennae, both of which are uniramous (YU-neh-RAY-mus), or unbranched at their bases. They all have mouthparts that are either lacking or greatly reduced in size. The maxillipeds (mack-SIH-leh-pehds), or leglike structures that are associated with the mouth, are absent. A shieldlike carapace (CARE-eh-pes) covers the head and segments of the thorax or midbody. The number of segments and limbs varies. The thoracic (thuh-RAE-sik) or midbody limbs are leaflike and are used for swimming, filtering water, breathing, or gathering food. The abdomen or tail usually does not have any appendages underneath, but does have threadlike appendages on the tip. The Branchiopoda is divided here into different groups: fairy shrimps, tadpole shrimps, and clam shrimps and water fleas.

Fairy shrimps are medium-sized branchiopod crustaceans and usually measure from 0.39 to 1.18 inches (10 to 30 millimeters) in length. Some predatory species may reach 3.9 inches (100 millimeters). Their limbs are flat and leaflike, and they differ from other branchiopods because they have no carapace. Most fairy shrimps have 11 thoracic segments, but some species have few as 10 or as many as 17 or 19. Nearly all species are translucent and lack any kind of coloration. However, the egg sacs carried by females are usually brilliant orange, red, or blue. The threadlike appendages at the tail in some species are red or orange. The males of some species have specialized antennae that are used to grasp the females during mating.

Tadpole shrimps range in length from 0.4 to 1.6 inches (10 to 40 millimeters), with some species measuring 4 inches (110 millimeters). Like fairy shrimps, they also have 11 thoracic segments. A large, flat carapace covers the head and midbody of tadpole shrimps. The carapace is attached only to the head and partially covers the abdomen. They have a pair of compound eyes located on the front margin of the carapace, each with multiple lenses. The broad carapace and narrow abdomen give these animals a tadpolelike appearance. The carapace ranges from silvery gray, yellowish, olive, to dark brown and is sometimes spotted. Their bodies are usually translucent, but may be pinkish or reddish due to the presence of hemoglobin (HE-meh-GLO-bihn) in their blood. Hemoglobin is a protein in blood that captures oxygen.

Clam shrimps and water fleas usually range in size from 0.008 to 0.7 inches (0.2 to 17 millimeters). They resemble clams and other bivalve mollusks that have hinged shells. These branchiopods are flattened from side to side and are protected by a large, hinged or folded carapace that mostly or completely covers their bodies and limbs. Their bodies are divided into two regions, the head and body trunk. In clam shrimps the halves of the carapace are hinged like a clam and nearly cover the entire body. The carapace even has growth rings, just like a clam. The bodies of water fleas are never completely covered by the carapace. Their carapaces fold over their backs like an upside down taco, leaving their heads exposed. The body trunk of clam shrimps are made up of 10 to 32 segments, each with a pair of flattened, leaflike limbs. The trunks of water fleas have only 4 to 6 limbs located toward the head. They use their larger pair of antennae for swimming, while the smaller pair is used to sense their environment.

GEOGRAPHIC RANGE

Branchiopods are found on all continents.

HABITAT

Most fairy shrimps live in temporary rain pools, but some species prefer high mountain lakes, Arctic or Antarctic ponds, or saline lakes. They usually swim in open water and prefer habitats that are free of fish and other predators. Tadpole shrimps live only on the bottom of temporary rain pools, avoiding predation by fish entirely. Clam shrimps also prefer temporary pools and ponds, although some species live in permanent bodies of water covered with thick mats of algae (AL-jee), or plantlike growths that live in water. They are usually found burrowing in mud. Water fleas are sometimes common in lakes, ponds, slow-moving streams, and rivers. A few species are found in the sea. Depending on the species, they are found swimming in open water, on vegetation, or on the bottom. One species lives in water collected on mosses living up in the tree canopy of tropical cloud forests in Puerto Rico.

DIET

Most fairy shrimps use their specialized leg bases to filter bacteria and algae from the water and direct it to a groove under their bodies. The groove leads directly to the mouth. Some species eat microscopic animals, such as rotifers, crustacean larvae (LAR-vee) or young, and even other fairy shrimps. Some species are predatory and attack other crustaceans. Tadpole shrimps eat anything, living or dead, including bacteria, algae, microscopic animals, insect larvae, tadpoles, other crustaceans, plant roots and shoots. Clam shrimps are mostly filter feeders, eating whatever flows through their mouths in water, but they can also scrape and tear at their food and will scavenge almost any organism in their environment. Some species also scrape algae from rocks and eat bacteria or prey on microscopic animals.

BEHAVIOR AND REPRODUCTION

Both fairy shrimps and water fleas move up and down through the water on a daily cycle. They remain protected in deeper waters during the day and swim to the surface at night to feed. Fairy shrimps swim upside down in a rhythmic motion. Water fleas use their legs to produce a constant current of water that allows them to filter food particles. The food items are collected in a groove at the base of their legs and mixed with mucus to form a bolus or mass that is moved forward toward the mouth. Clam shrimps use their second antennae in addition to their legs for swimming, sometimes in an upside down position, performing spiral or staggered movement. They use their forefeet to collect food, while the hind appendages are modified as mandibles (MAN-dih-bulz) for biting and grinding large food particles.

INSTANT SHRIMP: JUST ADD WATER

Some fairy shrimp eggs are called cysts (cists). Cysts are resistant to drought and extreme temperatures and remain dormant or inactive until conditions are more favorable for development. In 1960 the cysts of *Artemia* were first sold through comic books as Sea Monkeys. The cysts hatch just hours after adding water. Today, people around the world still buy kits promising animals that develop quickly, swim upside down, breathe through their feet, and reproduce with or without sex.

Tadpole shrimps usually require males and females to reproduce. Some species can produce young without mating, a process called parthenogenesis (PAR-thih-no-JEH-nih-sus). Some species are hermaphroditic (her-MAE-fro-DIH-tik), with individuals having both male and female reproductive organs. Different populations of the same species may use different types of reproductive methods depending on circumstances, allowing them to survive and reproduce under all kinds of environmental conditions. Fertilized eggs are carried in a brood pouch for several hours before they are released into the water. The eggs of some species are incredibly tough and can survive without water and in freezing temperatures for up to one hundred years. The eggs hatch as larvae and develop rapidly. The bodies of larvae have only mouthparts and antennae as appendages. Under the right conditions, tadpole shrimps will molt, or shed their external skeletons, numerous times in just 24 hours. They gain new pairs of limbs with each molt. Adulthood is usually reached in about two weeks after hatching.

Most species of fairy shrimps reproduce by mating or by parthenogenesis and lay eggs. The antennae of the males are specially equipped to hold the female during mating. The eggs are fertilized inside the female's body. Depending on the species, up to 4,000 eggs are laid in a special pouch that is carried outside the body. Eventually, the eggs are released into the water, where they sink to the bottom or float on the surface and later wash up on shore.

Clam shrimps reproduce by mating or by parthenogenesis, or both. The female carries up to several hundred eggs attached to a specialized structure that are laid when she molts. In other species, the eggs are stored in a special pouch attached to the carapace. A few species lay eggs that are resistant to drying out and are distributed by wind or water.

Water fleas reproduce mostly by parthenogenesis but, depending on conditions, will also mate. Reproduction usually begins as temperatures warm in spring. Reproductive activity drops off in summer due to overcrowding and lack of food. In some species a second peak in the population may occur in fall. Eggs are carried in a special chamber between the body and carapace. Some eggs hatch right away, while others enter a resting state called diapause (DYE-uh-pawz). Eggs in diapause are capable of surviving without water and in extreme temperatures. Most eggs develop into females. The development of males is triggered by environmental conditions such as crowding, availability of food, or the shortening day length as fall approaches.

FAIRY SHRIMPS, TADPOLE SHRIMPS, CLAM SHRIMPS, WATER FLEAS, AND PEOPLE

Eggs of fairy shrimp are collected, cleaned, dried, packed, and sold to pet stores and fish farms as food for fish. They also provide people living in parts of Libya with their major source of animal protein. Two species from the hills of northeastern Thailand are fished by local people and used in a variety of dishes. The tadpole shrimps are sometimes considered pests of rice fields. In large numbers, these animals expose and eat the roots of rice seedlings as they roam the bottom in search of food. However, in Japan, *Triops longicaudatus* is used to help control weeds in rice fields. Some species of *Triops* are sold in kits for rearing as pets. Water fleas are a critical link in the food webs of many aquatic habitats and ensure the survival of fish populations.

CONSERVATION STATUS

Twenty-eight species of fairy shrimps are listed by the World Conservation Union (IUCN). Six are considered Critically Endangered or facing an extremely high risk of extinction in the wild; nine are Endangered or facing a very high risk of extinction in the wild. Ten are Vulnerable or facing a high risk of extinction in the wild; one is Lower Risk/Conservation Dependent, meaning if the conservation program were to end, the animal would be placed in one of the threatened categories. One is Lower Risk/Near Threatened or at risk of becoming threatened with extinction in the future, and one is listed as Data Deficient, which means there is not enough information to make a judgment about the threat of extinction. Five of the Endangered species live in the United States, three of which live in California. They are threatened by the development of land for farming, home, and business interests. Efforts are underway in California to protect the habitats of these species.

The IUCN also lists a tadpole shrimp in California, *Lepidurus packardi*, as Endangered. It is threatened by habitat destruction. No species of clam shrimps or water fleas are considered endangered or threatened.

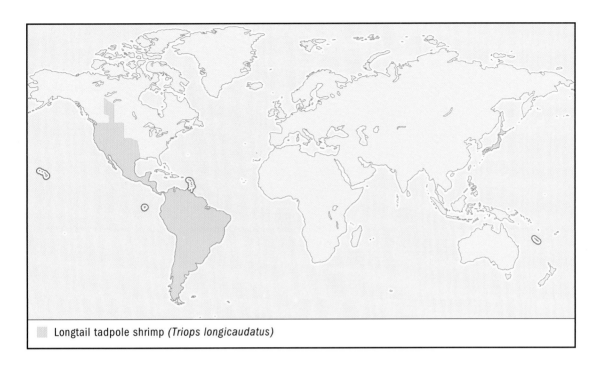

Longtail tadpole shrimp (*Triops longicaudatus*)

LONGTAIL TADPOLE SHRIMP
Triops longicaudatus

Physical characteristics: The longtail tadpole shrimp is a large species that reaches up to 1.5 inches (40 millimeters) in length. The second maxilla is absent.

Geographic range: The species is found in North America (including Hawaii but not Alaska), Central America, South America, Japan, the West Indies, the Galápagos Islands, and New Caledonia.

Habitat: The longtail is the most widely distributed of all tadpole shrimps. It is found in a wide variety of temporary waters, including rice fields.

Diet: Longtail tadpole shrimps scavenge both living and dead plant and animal materials. They also prey on microscopic animals, insect larvae, other small crustaceans, and even each other.

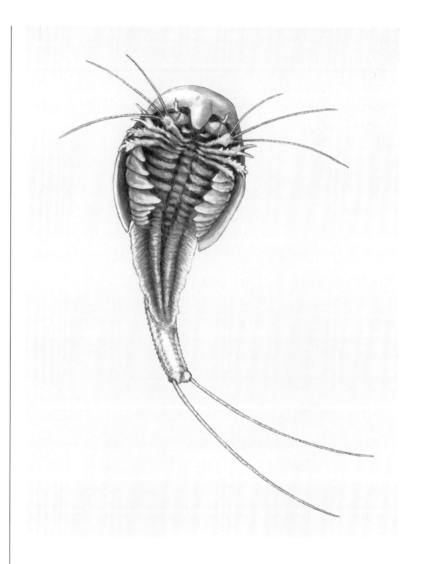

Longtail tadpole shrimps scavenge both living and dead plant and animal materials. They also prey on microscopic animals, insect larvae, other small crustaceans, and even each other. (Illustration by Bruce Worden. Reproduced by permission.)

Behavior and reproduction: They root about on the bottom of temporary pools in search of food. When oxygen levels are low, they swim upside down near the water surface.

They reproduce by mating or parthenogenesis.

Longtail tadpole shrimps and people: The longtail tadpole shrimp is sometimes considered a pest in rice fields mainly in the United States and Spain, where it damages the roots and leaves of rice plant seedlings. In large numbers this species stirs up the muddy bottom, blocking out sunlight needed by developing plants. In Japan, rice plants are too big to be eaten. Instead, the tadpole shrimps attack unwanted weeds. As a result, they are considered to be beneficial. Their dried eggs are sold in breeding kits to schools and to people interested in raising unusual pets.

Conservation status: This species is not considered endangered or threatened. ■

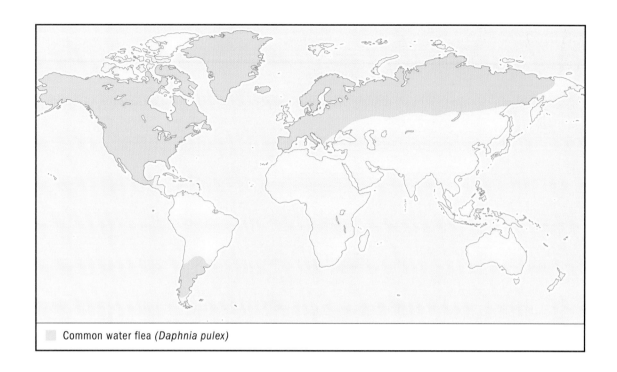

Common water flea (Daphnia pulex)

COMMON WATER FLEA
Daphnia pulex

Physical characteristics: Common water fleas are small, measuring 0.008 to 0.1 inches (0.2 to 3 mm) in length. They are flattened from side to side. A large, folded carapace covers all but the head. They have two pairs of antennae and five pairs of leaflike limbs.

Geographic range: Common water fleas are found in North America, Europe, and the cooler regions of South America.

Habitat: Common water fleas live in freshwater lakes, ponds, rivers, and streams.

Diet: They eat algae and microscopic animals such as rotifers.

Behavior and reproduction: Water fleas migrate up and down through the water on a daily cycle. They reproduce by parthenogenesis in spring and early summer. Late in the season, some of these eggs develop into males, marking the beginning of a period of reproduction by mating. Eggs produced by mating, or sexual reproduction, have

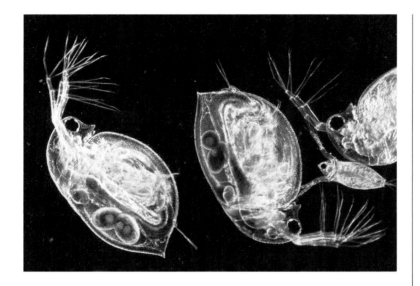

thick shells. Females produce three to nine eggs at a time. The young take six to eight days after hatching to reach adulthood.

Common water fleas and people: Common water fleas are kept in laboratories as living test subjects for the detection of water pollutants.

Conservation status: Common water fleas are not considered endangered or threatened. ■

FOR MORE INFORMATION

Books:

Bliss, D. E. *Biology of the Crustacea.* New York: Academic Press, 1982–1985.

Erikson, C., and D. Belk. *Fairy Shrimp of California's Puddles, Pools and Playas.* Eureka, CA: Mad River Press, 1999.

Pennak, Robert W. *Freshwater Invertebrates of the United States,* 3rd ed., *Protozoa to Mollusca.* New York: John Wiley and Sons, 1989.

Schram, Frederick R. *Crustacea.* New York: Oxford University Press, 1986.

Thorp, J. H., and A. P. Covich, eds. *Ecology and Classification of North American Freshwater Invertebrates,* second edition. New York: Academic Press, 2001.

Web sites:

Cladocera. http://www.cladocera.uoguelph.ca/ (accessed on February 8, 2005).

Fairy Shrimp. http://www.vernalpool.org/inf_fs.htm (accessed on February 8, 2005).

Introduction to the Branchiopoda. http://www.ucmp.berkeley.edu/arthropoda/crustacea/branchiopoda.html (accessed on February 8, 2005).

subclass

C H A P T E R

PHYSICAL CHARACTERISTICS

Most leptostracans are 0.19 to 0.59 inches (5 to 15 millimeters) in length, but the largest species measure up to 1.96 inches (50 millimeters). Their transparent bodies are covered by a loose whitish shield, or carapace, that is folded over their backs. The carapace (CARE-eh-pes) is flattened from side to side and covers the thorax or midbody, leaving the head and long abdomen exposed. At the front of the carapace is a beaklike projection, or rostrum (RAH-strem), that extends out over the head.

The head has red compound eyes set on stalks. The first pair of antennae is usually branched, or biramous (BY-ray-mus). The second pair of antennae is uniramous (YU-neh-RAY-mus) and not branched. The mandibles (MAN-dih-bulz), or biting mouthparts, are uniramous. Maxillipeds (mack-SIH-leh-pe-hds), the leglike appendages associated with the mouth, are absent. The thorax and abdomen are distinct. The thorax has eight pairs of leaflike limbs that are all similar to one another in appearance. The seven-segmented abdomen or tail section has six pairs of limbs called pleopods (ple-o-pawds). The first four pairs are biramous. Each pair is hooked together so that they work together when swimming. The last two pairs of pleopods are small and uniramous. The tail segment at the tip of the abdomen is tipped with a long, forked projection.

GEOGRAPHIC RANGE

Leptostracans are found in all the world's oceans.

HABITAT

Most leptostracans are found from seashores to depths of 1312.32 feet (400 meters), but one species lives in deep-sea waters at depths of more than 6,561 feet (2,000 meters). Although some species prefer open waters, most live on mud bottoms that have very little oxygen.

DIET

Leptostracans stir up materials from the bottom and filter out bits of food suspended in the water. Some species are scavengers and feed on accumulations of dead organisms that have settled on the ocean floor.

BEHAVIOR AND REPRODUCTION

Adult males sometimes swim long distances in search of mates using the first four pairs of pleopods. Young individuals and adult females rest on the bottom for hours. Their leaflike limbs beat rhythmically to move oxygen-carrying water through the carapace. In captivity leptostracans burrow in mud and often remain motionless. Inactivity and slow heartbeat allow them to live in environments with very little oxygen.

The eggs of most leptostracans are thought to be carried in a special chamber located beneath the carapace. The young develop within the eggs. They hatch resembling adults, but are distinguished by having a small fourth pair of pleopods. Water temperature has a tremendous influence on growth rates of immature leptostracans. Males develop gradually as they molt, or shed their external skeletons. Females continue to resemble immature leptostracans until they are ready to reproduce.

LEPTOSTRACANS AND PEOPLE

Nebalia bipes is an important food for live fish raised in captivity.

CONSERVATION STATUS

No leptostracans are considered endangered or threatened.

Dahlella caldariensis

NO COMMON NAME
Dahlella caldariensis

Physical characteristics: The largest individuals of *Dahlella caldariensis* (abbreviated to *D. caldariensis*) measure approximately 0.31 inches (8.1 millimeters) long from the base of the rostrum to the tip of the tail. The rostrum is three times longer than wide and almost half as long as the carapace. The eyes lack color; eyestalks are banana-shaped with tiny, toothlike bumps along the front margin.

Geographic range: This species lives near deep-sea geysers, known as hydrothermal vents, near the Galápagos Islands and the East Pacific Rise.

Habitat: *D. caldariensis* is found in vent openings and clumps of mussels and vestimentiferans at depths of 8,040 to 8,595 feet (2,450 to 2,620 meters).

Diet: Not much is known about their feeding habits. However, it has been suggested that the rough eyestalks might be used to scrape surfaces to loosen bits of food, such as encrustations of bacteria and other organisms.

Behavior and reproduction: Nothing is known about their behavior or reproduction.

***Dahlella caldariensis* and people:**   Nothing is known.

Conservation status: This species is not considered endangered or threatened.   ■

FOR MORE INFORMATION

Books:

Brusca, R. C., and G. J. Brusca. *Invertebrates.* Second edition. Sunderland, MA: Sinauer Associates, 2003.

Hessler, R. R., and F. R. Schram. *Leptostraca as Living Fossils.* In *Living Fossils,* edited by N. Eldredge and M. Stanley. Berlin: Springer-Verlag, 1984.

Periodicals:

Briggs, D. E. G., M. D. Sutton, and D. J. Siveter. "A new phyllocarid (Crustacea: Malacostraca) from the Silurian Fossil-Lagerstätte of Herefordshire, UK." *Proceedings of the Royal Society: Biological Sciences* 271, no. 1535 (2004): 131-138.

Web sites:

The Biology of Sea Fleas. http://www.museum.vic.gov.au/crust/nebbiol .html (accessed on February 14, 2005).

Invertebrate Anatomy Online: Nebalia pugettensis. http://www.lander .edu/rsfox/310nebaliaLab.html (accessed on February 14, 2005).

Leptostraca. http://crustacea.nhm.org/peet/leptostraca/ (accessed on February 14, 2005).

order

PHYSICAL CHARACTERISTICS

Typical mantis shrimps have long bodies that are cylinder-shaped or slightly flattened from top to bottom. They vary considerably in color, depending on the species or the individual. Some are brightly colored, while others are marked so that they blend in with their surroundings. At the front of the head are moveable segments that bear the eyestalks and two pairs of antennae. The antennae are sensitive to odors and disturbances in the water.

Mantis shrimps have the most highly developed eyes of all crustaceans, and their vision is excellent. Each compound eye is made up of multiple lenses. The eyes are often iridescent, appearing like jewels, and are mounted on the end of a periscope-like stalk to give them a clear view in all directions. A specialized band of lenses across each eye is unique and divides the eyes into three distinct visual regions. Mantis shrimps have the ability to see shapes accurately under all light conditions and to gauge distances, allowing them to use their lightning-quick raptorial limbs with deadly accuracy. The middle band of lenses is used to see infrared, visible, and ultraviolet light. The other two regions can see polarized light. Polarized light travels in parallel planes. Parts of the antennae and tails of mantis shrimps reflect polarized light and may provide them with the ability to locate and communicate with one another.

A shieldlike carapace (CARE-eh-pes) covers the thorax or midbody, and the abdomen is distinctly segmented. The thorax has eight pairs of limbs. The first five pairs, the maxillipeds (mack-SIH-leh-pehds), are associated with the mouth and are used for prey capture and eating. The second pair of maxillipeds is very conspicuous and resembles the front legs of a praying mantis. They are called grabbing, or raptorial (rap-TORE-ee-all), limbs and are used to stab or club prey. When not in use, they are kept folded like jack knives under the head and body. Mantis shrimps can replace lost or damaged raptorial limbs. Damaged limbs are forcibly removed with the other maxillipeds. The lost limb is replaced with the next molt and grows to full size after three more molts. Three more pairs of maxillipeds follow the raptorial limbs. The remaining three pairs of thoracic midbody limbs are used for walking.

The abdomen has five pairs of leaflike limbs called pleopods (PLEE-oh-pawds). They are used for swimming and also have gills for breathing. The abdomen ends in a large, fanlike tail made up of the flat tail segment, and a pair of appendages, or uropods (YUR-oh-pawds).

Male and female mantis shrimps are easily distinguished. Males have a pair of long, slender sperm-transferral organs located at the bases of the last pair of walking legs. The female's reproductive organs appear as a narrow slit that opens underneath the body between the first pair of walking legs. In some species the males have larger bodies than the females, with larger raptorial limbs and tails.

GEOGRAPHIC RANGE

Mantis shrimps live in the ocean off nearly all landmasses in tropical and subtropical waters.

HABITAT

Most mantis shrimps prefer to live in shallow tropical or subtropical seas, but a few species live in cooler waters of the sub-Antarctic. They are usually found along the shore in habitats affected by the tides or just beyond. Some species dig or occupy abandoned burrows with several entrances in muddy or sandy sea bottoms down to 33 feet (10 meters) below the surface. Other species live in hollows among rocks and corals.

DIET

Mantis shrimps are predators that hunt and kill animals for food. They attack fish, mollusks, and other crustaceans.

BEHAVIOR AND REPRODUCTION

The behavior of mantis shrimps is defined by their raptorial limbs. Species with toothed or spiny limbs grab and stab their prey and are called spearers. Spearers lie in wait at the entrance to their burrows in mud or sand and wait for a soft-bodied fish or shrimp to come within range. Mantis shrimps that use their raptorial limbs like clubs are called smashers. Smashers actively search for prey, usually animals with hard bodies or shells, crippling them with powerful blows. They drag their smashed victims into hollows among rocks and coral before they begin eating. Depending on the species, resting animals plug the entrance to their burrow with rocks or with their raptorial limbs or tail.

Some species of mantis shrimps are nocturnal (nahk-TER-nuhl), or active only at night, especially on moonlit nights. Others are diurnal (die-UR-nuhl), or active during the day. Still others species are crepuscular (kreh-PUS-kyuh-lur), coming out only just after sunset or before sunrise.

Most mantis shrimps live alone, but males and females will come together briefly only to mate. Males and sometimes females will actively seek a mate. Males perform elaborate mating behaviors to attract the attention of the female. Females will accept one or more males as mates during this time. In a few species, males and females mate for life, a period that may last 15 to 20 years. These life-long mates share one burrow. The females tend to the eggs, while the male hunts for himself and his mate.

Males and females mate belly to belly. Males deposit sperm directly into the female where it is stored in a special pouch just inside the opening to her reproductive organs. The eggs are fertilized inside her body just as they are being laid. The eggs may not be laid right away. The female may choose to wait until ocean currents are available for dispersing the eggs. Eggs are glued together in a mass and take anywhere from 10 days to two months to hatch. During this time the female carefully tends the eggs and is guarded by the male. The hatchlings may leave the burrow immediately, or remain in the burrow for a week to two months.

Newly hatched mantis shrimps have long slender bodies and bulging eyes. They pass through several distinct developmental stages in about three months before reaching adulthood. Some species are benthic (ben-thik) and start out on the sea bottom. Others are pelagic (peh-LAJ-ihk) and immediately set off in the open sea. All species eventually develop into pelagic larvae (LAR-vee) or young and settle to the bottom as post-larvae. Postlarvae are very similar to the adults in both shape and behavior.

MANTIS SHRIMPS AND PEOPLE

Mantis shrimps are especially sensitive to pollution. Their presence or absence in coral reefs allows scientists to gauge the environmental health of the habitat. Some mantis shrimp species are popular pets in saltwater aquariums. *Squilla mantis* is a very tasty species. Efforts are underway to culture them as human food in the Mediterranean and Adriatic seas.

CONSERVATION STATUS

No mantis shrimps are considered endangered or threatened.

LIGHTNING FAST AND PACKS A PUNCH

The strike of the raptorial limbs of mantis shrimps is one of the fastest movements in nature. They can strike at prey in just 2 milliseconds. The blink of a human eye takes 100 milliseconds. Two of the larger smasher species, *Hemisquilla ensigera* and *Odontodactylus scyllarus*, can strike with a force nearly equal to that of a .22 caliber bullet and are known to have smashed the double-layered safety glass of public aquariums.

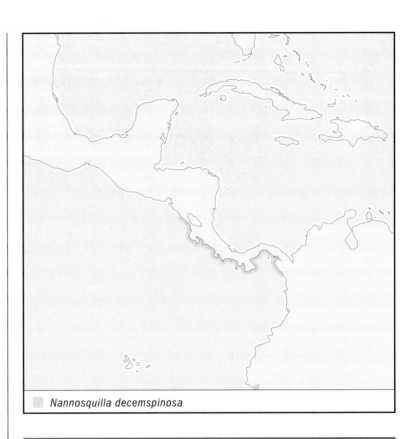

Nannosquilla decemspinosa

NO COMMON NAME
Nannosquilla decemspinosa

Physical characteristics: This small species measures up to 0.98 inches (25 millimeters) in length and is marked to match its background.

Geographic range: This species can be found off the Pacific coast of Panama.

Habitat: They live in shallow waters on muddy bottoms close to shore.

Diet: This species is a spearer that waits inside the entrance of its burrow to ambush soft-bodied fish and crustaceans.

Behavior and reproduction: When washed up on shore by high tides or storms, *Nannosquilla decemspinosa* turns itself into a wheel

and rolls back to the water at 72 revolutions per minute, or 1.5 body lengths per second. If it slows down before reaching the shore, it uses its entire body as a spring to move upward and forward into the next roll.

Males actively search for females and engage in mating displays in front of their burrows. After mating, the male will guard the female until the larvae swim out to sea and then he leaves.

Nannosquilla decemspinosa and people: Its ability to roll like a wheel makes this species a scientific curiosity.

Conservation status: *Nannosquilla decemspinosa* is not considered endangered or threatened. ■

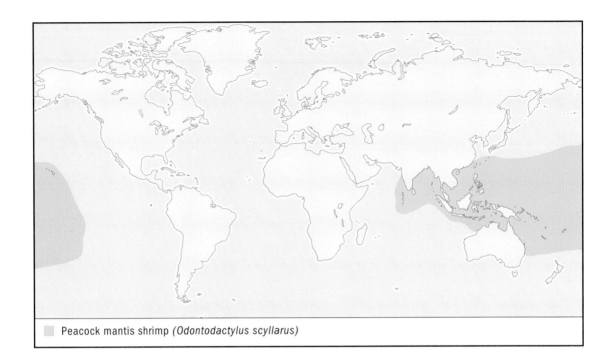

Peacock mantis shrimp (*Odontodactylus scyllarus*)

PEACOCK MANTIS SHRIMP
Odontodactylus scyllarus

Physical characteristics: The body of a peacock mantis shrimp reaches a length of 6.7 inches (170 millimeters). Males and females are distinctively colored. Mature males are bright green with crimson and blue appendages; females are more olive or brown. Young individuals are bright yellow.

Geographic range: This species is found in the Indo-Pacific Ocean, including Hawaii.

Habitat: They live on coral reefs.

Diet: The peacock mantis shrimp is a smasher that hunts hard-shelled animals like clams, snails, and crabs.

Behavior and reproduction: This species is usually diurnal, but may hunt at night during a full moon. They line their burrows with pieces of coral, rock, and shell.

The peacock mantis shrimp is a smasher that hunts hard-shelled animals like clams, snails, and crabs. (© Tony Wu/ www.silent-symphony.com. Reproduced by permission.)

Males actively search for females and engage in mating displays in front of their burrows. After mating, the male will guard the female until the larvae swim out to sea, and then he leaves.

Peacock mantis shrimps and people: This brightly colored species is popular with hobbyists who keep saltwater aquariums.

Conservation status: The peacock mantis shrimp is not considered endangered or threatened. ■

FOR MORE INFORMATION

Periodicals:

Caldwell, R. L., and H. Dingle. "Stomatopods." *Scientific American* 234 (1975): 80-89.

"Earth Almanac: Eyes and Claws of a Killer Shrimp." *National Geographic* 190, no. 3 (September 1996).

Patek, S. N., W. L. Korff, and R. L. Caldwell. "Biomechanics: Deadly Strike Mechanism of a Mantis Shrimp." *Nature* 428 (2004): 819-820.

Web sites:

Lurker's Guide to Stomatopods. http://www.blueboard.com/mantis/ (accessed on February 14, 2005).

Secrets of the Stomatopod. http://www.ucmp.berkeley.edu/aquarius/ (accessed on February 14, 2005).

Stomatopoda: Families. http://www.crustacea.net/crustace/stomatopoda/index.htm (accessed on February 14, 2005).

BATHYNELLACEANS
Bathynellacea

Class: Malacostraca

Order: Bathynellacea

Number of families: 2 families

PHYSICAL CHARACTERISTICS

Bathynellaceans (bath-ee-nel-AYS-see-ans) range in length from 0.02 to 0.14 inches (0.5 to 3.5 millimeters). They do not have eyes and lack any body coloration. The body is divided into a head, thorax, and abdomen. The head may or may not have a beaklike projection, or rostrum. The first pair of antennae, called antennules, is uniramous, or unbranched. The segmented thorax has seven or eight pairs of simple biramous, or branched, legs. There are no leglike thoracic limbs associated with the mouthparts. The six-segmented abdomen may or may not have one or two pairs of small limbs. Bathynellaceans do have a pair of limbs on the end of the body called uropods. The uropods are found on either side of a central projection, or telson.

GEOGRAPHIC RANGE

Bathynellaceans are found on all continents except Antarctica. They are not known to be from Central America, from islands that are volcanic in origin, and from some other islands, such as New Caledonia, Fiji, and the Caribbean islands.

HABITAT

Bathynellaceans are found mostly underground near freshwater habitats or in caves. They are sometimes collected on the surface in waters that are fed by underground water sources, such as wells, in sands along the shores of rivers and lakes, or in springs. At least one African species lives in hot springs and can tolerate temperatures up to 130°F (55°C). A few species can tolerate slightly salty water and are found near the seashore or in other brackish waters.

DIET

Bathynellaceans eat plant materials, worms, microscopic animals, and bacteria. Some species may be specialists and feed on just one or two of these groups of organisms.

BEHAVIOR AND REPRODUCTION

Bathynellaceans crawl through the sand with a combination of swimming and walking movements. Although they are very awkward swimmers in open water, they are extremely agile animals and move easily through the narrow spaces between grains of sand.

Although both male and female bathynellaceans are known, their mating behavior has never been observed. Unlike most crustaceans that carry their eggs or young, female bathynellaceans lay their eggs one at a time in the surrounding sand. The young animal hatches from the egg as a larva with only working antennae and mouthparts. Adulthood is reached through a series of molts, or shedding of the exoskeleton. Additional appendages are added with each molt. The number of molts varies among species.

BATHYNELLACEANS AND PEOPLE

Bathynellaceans help to improve water quality and flow by breaking down bits of plants and animals that wash into underground water systems.

CONSERVATION STATUS

No species of bathynellaceans are considered endangered or threatened.

TAPPING IN TO BATHYNELLACEANS

Bathynellaceans eat bits of plants and animals washed into the ground from the Earth's surface. Bacteria, fungi, and other microscopic organisms break down in their waste products. These activities help to clean the water and keep it flowing through the filtering sands that surround underground springs. Without these organisms these natural filters would soon become clogged and prevent the flow of fresh, clean water from underground sources into wells, springs, lakes, and rivers.

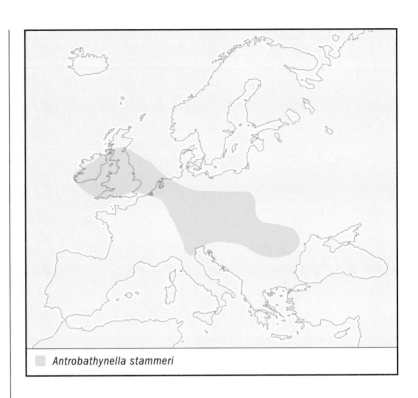

Antrobathynella stammeri

NO COMMON NAME
Antrobathynella stammeri

Physical characteristics: Males and females have a row of four spines at the base of the uropods. The spine closest to the front of the body is larger and distinctly separated from the others. The base of the seventh leg of the male has a clear, cone-shaped bump on the inside.

Geographic range: *Antrobathynella stammeri* are widely distributed in Europe, from Ireland to Romania.

Habitat: *Antrobathynella stammeri* are found in underground springs and all surface habitats fed by them.

Diet: They eat bits of plant materials and worms.

Behavior and reproduction: *Antrobathynella stammeri* are agile crawlers soon after they hatch from the eggs.

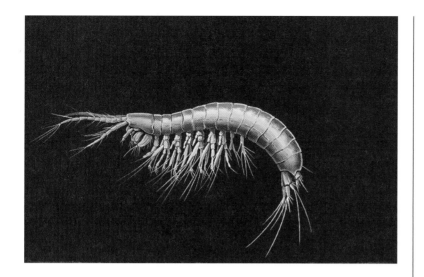

This species reproduces throughout the year. The young take about nine months to reach adulthood. Adults must continue to molt before they can reproduce. Adult males molt four times and females five. Animals in captivity live up to two years, probably longer in the wild.

***Antrobathynella stammeri* and people:** This species probably contributes to keeping underground springs fresh and flowing.

Conservation status: *Antrobathynella stammeri* is not considered endangered or threatened. ▪

FOR MORE INFORMATION

Books:

Coineau, N. *Syncarida.* In *Encyclopaedia Biospeologica* 2, edited by C. Juberthie and V. Decou. Bucarest, Romania: Société de Biospéologie, 1998.

Web sites:

Lowry, J.K. *Crustacea, the Higher Taxa: Description, Identification, and Information Retrieval.* Version 2 October 1999. http://crustacea.net/ (accessed on February 15, 2005).

Syncarida. http://www.lucidcentral.com/keys/lwrrdc/public/Aquatics/adcrust/html/SYNCARID.htm (accessed on February 15, 2005).

order

phylum

class

subclass

● order

monotypic order

suborder

family

PHYSICAL CHARACTERISTICS

Anaspidaceans (an-ah-spih-DAY-see-ans) are usually dull brown. They measure up to 1.9 inches (50 millimeters), but some species are less than 0.39 inches (10 millimeters). They have a head, thorax, and abdomen. They may or may not have a beaklike rostrum. The eyes are found either on the tips of stalks or on the head. Some species do not have eyes at all. The first pair of antennae, or antennules (an-TEN-yuls), is either branched or not. The second pair of antennae is biramous (BY-ray-mus) or branched. The mandibles are uniramous (YU-neh-RAY-mus) or unbranched. They do not have a shieldlike carapace covering the head and thorax. The first thoracic (thuh-RAE-sik) segment is tightly joined with the head. It has a pair of maxillipeds, thoracic limbs associated with the mouth.

The pairs of thoracic legs are either unbranched or branched. In biramous legs, the inner branch is called the endopod (IHN-doh-pawd), while the outer branch is called the exopod (EHK-soh-pawd). The flaplike gills, organs used for breathing underwater, are located on the bases of the legs. The movements of the exopods keep oxygen-carrying water flowing over the gills. The abdomen also has segments. There are one, two, or five pairs of pleopods (PLEE-oh-pawds), or limblike structures attached to the underside of the abdomen. The tip of the abdomen has a pair of long appendages called uropods (YUR-oh-pawds). The uropods are found on either side of a central tail segment, or telson . The uropods and telson sometimes form a fanlike tail.

GEOGRAPHIC RANGE

Anaspidaceans are found only in southeastern Australia (including Tasmania), New Zealand, Chile, and Argentina.

HABITAT

The larger species of anaspidaceans usually prefer to live in cool mountain streams, lakes, and swamps. Stream-dwelling species forage on boulders and smaller rocks on the stream bottom. Species living in swamps are found in the burrows of crayfish. Lake species live in mats of algae growing on the bottom. Smaller species live in the sands surrounding underground springs.

DIET

Anaspidaceans eat plant and animal materials. Larger species scavenge these materials by scraping them off rocks submerged in water.

BEHAVIOR AND REPRODUCTION

Anaspidaceans are poor swimmers and usually crawl about their habitat. The exopods of their thoracic legs move constantly to circulate oxygen-carrying water over the flaplike gills. When they walk, their thoracic and abdominal limbs move together in a smooth, rhythmic motion.

Both males and females are known, but mating has not been observed. Unlike most crustaceans that carry their eggs or young, female anaspidaceans lay their eggs individually on plants or stones. They do not guard or provide any care for them. The eggs hatch in 30 to 60 days as larvae (LAR-vee) that have working antennae and mouthparts only. Adulthood is reached through a series of molts, or sheddings of the exoskeleton. Additional appendages are added with each molt. Sometimes young anaspidaceans hatch with fewer than the adult number of appendages, adding additional appendages as they molt.

ANASPIDACEANS AND PEOPLE

Anaspidaceans and bathynellaceans are considered to be very primitive relatives of krill, crabs, shrimps, lobsters, and crayfish. Studying them may reveal how these animals have evolved, or gradually changed to survive in their environment, over millions of years.

SOMETHING FISHY DOWN UNDER

Water pollution is not the only threat to aquatic animals in Australia. Like all native freshwater crustaceans, anaspidaceans evolved in the absence of trout. Australian colonists introduced these fish from Europe. Without natural defenses against trout, anaspidaceans can only survive in isolated branches of streams and rivers that are out of reach from these hungry predators. Four species of anaspidaceans are listed as Vulnerable, but more species may be considered as scientists learn more about them.

CONSERVATION STATUS

Four species of Australian anaspidaceans are listed by the World Conservation Union (IUCN) as Vulnerable, or facing a high rate of extinction in the wild. These include the Tasmanian anaspid crustacean (*Allanaspides helonomus*), Hickman's Pygmy Mountain shrimp (*Allanaspides hickmani*), Great Lake Shrimp (*Paranaspides lacustris*), and *Eucrenonaspides oinotheke*.

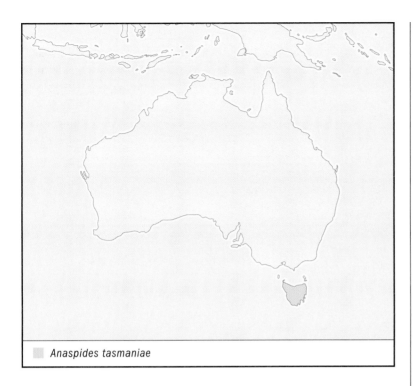
Anaspides tasmaniae

NO COMMON NAME
Anaspides tasmaniae

Physical characteristics: The body of this species is long, and the eyes are on stalks. The thoracic and abdominal segments are similar in length. The pleopods are long and leglike. The telson and uropods form a fanlike tail.

Geographic range: This species is found only in Tasmania, Australia.

Habitat: *Anaspides tasmaniae* live in freshwater streams and shallow pools.

Diet: They feed on both plant and animal tissues.

Behavior and reproduction: This species searches constantly for food, chewing on large pieces of plants or scraping the surfaces of pebbles with its mouth. They will also scavenge the bodies of small,

Anaspides tasmaniae searches constantly for food, chewing on large pieces of plants or scraping the surfaces of pebbles with its mouth. (Illustration by Michelle Meneghini. Reproduced by permission.)

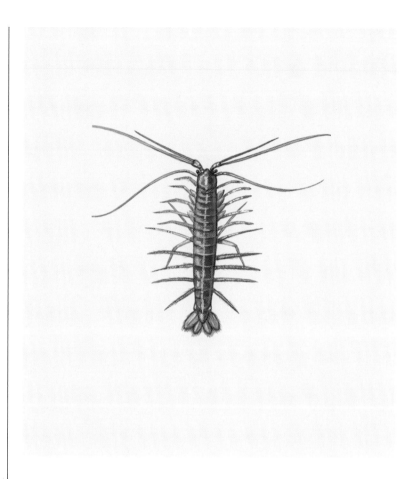

dead animals. They walk by using both thoracic and abdominal appendages. To avoid danger, they will snap their body trunk and jump straight up.

Mating has not been observed. Eggs are laid on plants or bark under water. The young hatch as juveniles with fewer appendages than adults.

***Anaspides tasmaniae* and people:** *Anaspides tasmaniae* are of interest to scientists studying crustacean evolution.

Conservation status: This species is not considered endangered or threatened. ■

FOR MORE INFORMATION

Books:

Schram, F. *Crustacea.* Oxford, U.K.: Oxford University Press, 1986.

Periodicals:

Swain, R., and C. I. Reid. "Observations on the Life History and Ecology of *Anaspides tasmaniae.*" *Journal of Crustacean Biology* 3 (1983): 163-172.

Web sites:

Lowry, J. K. *Crustacea, the Higher Taxa: Description, Identification, and Information Retrieval.* Version: 2 October 1999. http://www .crustacea.net/crustace/www/anaspida.htm (accessed on February 15, 2005).

KRILL

Euphausiacea

Class: Malacostraca

Order: Euphausiacea

Number of families: 2 families

phylum

class

subclass

● **order**

monotypic order

suborder

family

PHYSICAL CHARACTERISTICS

Krill are shrimplike in appearance and measure 1.57 to 5.9 inches (40 to 150 millimeters) in length. Their red-spotted bodies are transparent, with their internal organs visible from the outside. They have two pairs of antennae, both of them branched, or biramous (BY-ray-mus). Their large compound eyes are set on stalks. Each compound eye has many individual lenses. The head and segmented thorax are closely joined together, forming a region known as the cephalothorax (SEH-feh-lo-THOR-acks). The cephalothorax is covered by a shield-like carapace that does not cover the feathery gills located on the bases of some legs.

The thorax has eight pairs of biramous limbs. Thoracic (thuh-RAE-sik) limb pairs six through eight form a netlike structure that is used to strain food out of the water. Krill do not have any thoracic limbs associated with the mouth. The abdomen has six segments, plus a flaplike tail segment, or telson. The first five segments each have a pair of paddlelike limbs, or pleopods (PLEE-oh-pawds). These special pleopods are used for swimming and are also called swimmerets (SWI-meh-rehts).

Many species are called "light-shrimp" because they have light-producing tissues in their eyestalks, legs, and abdomen. These displays of yellowish green or blue light are probably used to locate mates or confuse predators.

GEOGRAPHIC RANGE

Krill are found in all oceans.

HABITAT

Krill swim in water off the coast, out in the open ocean, and around polar ice. Most krill feed and mate close to the surface, but a few species live at depths of up to 16,404 feet (5,000 meters).

DIET

Krill eat free-floating organisms known as plankton, which are microscopic plants and animals.

BEHAVIOR AND REPRODUCTION

Krill filter their food from the water using their bristly thoracic legs like a basket. Water is squeezed through the basket, leaving the plankton behind. The food is moved toward the mouth with the other legs. Krill grow by molting, or shedding their external skeletons. They molt and grow throughout their lives. When food is scarce, their bodies actually shrink with each molt. Smaller bodies require less food (energy) to maintain. When threatened, krill sometimes molt instantly, leaving a empty external skeleton behind as a decoy.

Eighteen species of krill form massive, shapeless swarms that sometimes stretch the length of several city blocks. These swarms usually spend the day at lower depths to avoid being eaten by other animals. Many fish, sea birds, and marine mammals regularly prey on krill. Krill rise to the surface of the ocean to feed. Although krill can use their swimmerets to move around for short distances, they are mostly dependent on ocean currents to cover large distances. They also have the ability to adjust the buoyancy (BOI-en-see) of their bodies so they can rise or sink to different levels in the water.

Krill require both males and females to reproduce. Reproduction only takes place when there is plenty of food. The male produces sperm packets and uses his legs to transfer them to the opening of the female's reproductive organs. The female stores the sperm in a special pouch until she is ready to lay her eggs. The eggs are fertilized as they leave her body.

After hatching, krill pass through several juvenile stages in a few months. They hatch as larvae (LAR-vee) that have only antennae and mouthparts as appendages. The first pair of antennae, or antennules, is used for swimming. This stage is followed by larval stages that have thoracic limbs used for swimming. These are followed by a larval stage in which the

Blue whales measure up to 100 feet (meters) in length and weigh in at 300,000 pounds (136,080 kilograms). Hungry whales swim through swarms of krill, which are only one one-thousandth of their size, with mouths and throats wide open, swallowing as much as 50 tons (45.36 metric tons) of water in one gulp. The krill are screened out by comblike plates and swallowed. Blue whales may eat 3 to 4 tons (2.72 to 3.63 metric tons), or 40,000,000 krill every day.

antennae are no longer used for swimming. With each molt the larvae increase in size and add more body segments and appendages until they reach adulthood.

Adult krill lose their male and female characteristics after the summer mating season and return to a more juvenilelike form. They regain their adult characteristics in spring in preparation for the new mating season. Krill live between two and 10 years, depending on the species.

KRILL AND PEOPLE

Krill are fished commercially and are used as feed for fish, especially on farms that raise salmon and yellowtail tuna. In Japan and other parts of the world, the protein-rich bodies of krill are processed and added to foods for human consumption.

CONSERVATION STATUS

No species of krill are listed by the World Conservation Union (IUCN) as endangered or threatened. Still, over-fishing and climate change could threaten krill populations and the animals that depend on them.

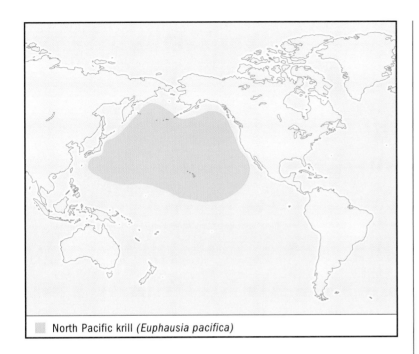

North Pacific krill (*Euphausia pacifica*)

NORTH PACIFIC KRILL
Euphausia pacifica

Physical characteristics: North Pacific krill measure about 0.75 inches (19 millimeters) and weigh about 0.003 ounces (0.1 grams).

Geographic range: They are found in the North Pacific Ocean, from North America to Japan.

Habitat: North Pacific krill live in open water at the edge of the continental shelf or just beyond. They are found at the surface to depths of about 984.24 feet (300 meters).

Diet: They eat plankton.

Behavior and reproduction: North Pacific krill rise to the surface to feed at night. They sink to lower levels during the day and seldom feed there, even if food is abundant.

Males take part in one breeding season and live about two years. Females live longer and take part in two breeding seasons.

North Pacific krill rise to the surface to feed at night. They sink to lower levels during the day and seldom feed there, even if food is abundant. (Illustration by Bruce Worden. Reproduced by permission.)

North Pacific krill and people: This species is fished commercially in the United States, Canada, and Japan.

Conservation status: North Pacific krill are not considered endangered or threatened.   ■

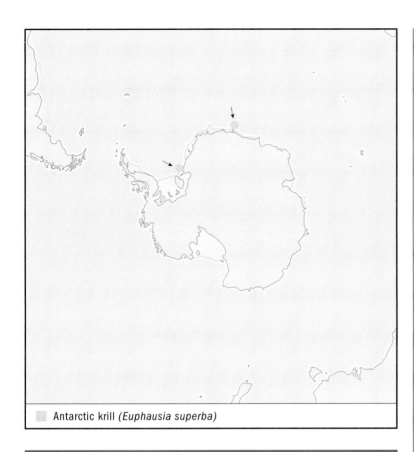

Antarctic krill (*Euphausia superba*)

ANTARCTIC KRILL
Euphausia superba

Physical characteristics: Adult Antarctic krill measure up to 2.5 inches (65 millimeters) in length and weigh up to 0.07 ounces (2 g). Their gut is green due to their diet of free-floating, microscopic plant organisms or phytoplankton.

Geographic range: They live in the oceans surrounding Antarctica.

Habitat: Antarctic krill are found from the surface to depths of 1,640 feet (500 meters). Their massive swarms are found under and around the edges of sea ice.

Diet: They eat mostly phytoplankton, but will also feed on small crustaceans.

Behavior and reproduction: Antarctic krill swarms may reach densities of 30,000 krill per 35 cubic feet (0.99 cubic meters). Some swarms are made up almost entirely of a single sex or age group. They rise to the surface at night to feed and sink to lower depths during the day.

Females lay several batches of eggs during the 5-month breeding season. Each batch may have up to 10,000 eggs. The eggs sink to the bottom. The larvae spend 10 days rising back to the surface to feed and develop. They reach maximum size in three to five years and may live for a total of seven years.

Antarctic krill and people: This krill species is fished commercially by several countries. Nearly 100,000 tons (90,000 metric tons) are caught each year. They are processed as food for humans, domestic animals, farm-raised fish, and sport fishing bait.

Conservation status: Antarctic krill are not considered endangered or threatened. However, krill fishing limits were set in 1982 by the Convention on the Conservation of Antarctic Marine Living Resources. Part of the Antarctic Treaty System, the Convention is intended to encourage the recovery of whale populations. ■

FOR MORE INFORMATION

Books:

Brusca, Richard C., and Gary J. Brusca. *Invertebrates.* Sunderland, MA: Sinauer Associates, 2003.

Periodicals:

Brierly, A. S., et al. "Antarctic Krill Under Sea Ice: Elevated Abundance in a Narrow Band Just South of Ice Edge." *Science* 295 (March 8, 2002): 1890-1892.

Hamner, W. M. "Krill-Untapped Bounty From the Sea?" *National Geographic* 165, no. 5 (May 1984): 626-643.

Nakagawa, Y., Y. Endo, and H. Sugisaki. "Feeding Rhythm and Vertical Migration of the Euphausiid *Euphausia pacifica* in Coastal Waters of North-eastern Japan During Fall." *Journal of Plankton Research* 25, no. 6 (2003): 633-644.

Web sites:

Krill. http://www.enchantedlearning.com/subjects/invertebrates/crustacean/Krillprintout.shtml (accessed on February 17, 2005).

AMPHIONIDS

Amphionidacea

Class: Malacostraca

Order: Amphionidacea

Number of families: 1 family

PHYSICAL CHARACTERISTICS

There is only one species of amphionid, *Amphionides reynaudii*. Adult males are unknown; females are about 1 inch (2.6 centimeters) long. Their bodies are divided into a head, thorax, and abdomen. The head and thorax are completely covered by a thin, membranelike carapace. There is a considerable amount of space between the carapace and the underside of the body. The head has a pair of compound eyes on stalks that are believed to produce light. Compound eyes have multiple lenses. Both pairs of antennae are branched, or biramous (BY-ray-mus). The second pair of antennae also has a single, large, leaflike flap on their bases.

The thorax has seven segments. Segments 3 and 7 have feathery gills. Juvenile males have seven pairs of thoracic limbs, but the last pair is absent in females. Pairs 1 through 6 are biramous. Only the first pair of limbs, the maxillipeds, is used for swimming. The remaining limbs are sticklike and useless for swimming. In females, the fifth pair of thoracic limbs is very long, and the sixth pair has the openings to the reproductive system. The last pair of thoracic limbs (juvenile males only) is unbranched, or uniramous (YU-neh-RAY-mus).

The abdomen is divided into six segments. The first five segments each has a pair of appendages underneath called pleopods (PLEE-oh-pawds). In females, the first pair of pleopods is long, ribbonlike, and uniramous. They reach toward the head and are about half the length of the carapace. They are used to close off the underside of the carapace to form a brood chamber when protecting eggs. The remaining four pairs of pleopods are much shorter and biramous. The tip of the abdomen has a pair of long appendages called uropods (YUR-oh-pawds). The uropods are found on either side of a flaplike tail, or telson. The uropods and telson together form a fanlike tail.

GEOGRAPHIC RANGE

Amphionids live in all oceans. Because they are found throughout the world, no distribution map is provided.

HABITAT

Amphionids are marine and are most common near the equator. Young animals live with other plankton at depths of 90 to 300 feet (30 to 100 meters). Plankton is made up of free-floating, often microscopic, plant and animal life. Adult females have been found at depths of 5,577 feet (1,700 meters).

DIET

Immature amphionids probably eat algae (AL-jee) and other microscopic organisms. Adult females have reduced mouthparts and digestive tracts. This suggests to scientists that the amphionids must rely on energy from food they ate before reaching adulthood.

BEHAVIOR AND REPRODUCTION

There is very little information on behavior and reproduction. Younger animals live with other plankton in the upper layers of the ocean, while adults live and breed in deeper waters. The light-producing eyestalks may be used to attract or locate mates.

The larvae (LAR-vee) molt, or shed their exoskeletons, up to 13 times before reaching the postlarval stage. Postlarvae resemble the adult in shape and behavior, but are not able to reproduce. The number of larval stages varies from region to region and among individuals living in the same place.

Nothing is known about their mating habits. The eggs pass from openings at the bases of the sixth pair of thoracic limbs

AN ORDER IS BORN

Amphionids were formerly grouped with coral and snapping shrimps on the basis of their similar larval forms. In 1973, they were reclassified in the new order Amphionidacea. This placement was based on the adult female's unique brood chamber and the ribbonlike structure of the pleopods. Before anything was known about their development, scientists thought the various larval stages of the only known species were distinct species and described them as new.

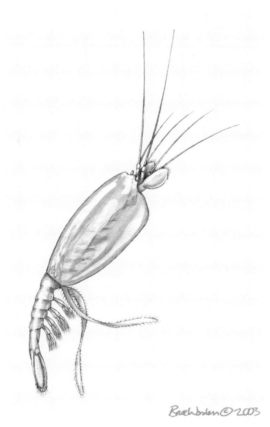

into the brood chamber underneath the thorax. It is likely that they are fertilized in the chamber. The developing eggs probably remain in the chamber until they hatch. Hatchlings probably escape through the gap created when the female loosens or removes her ribbonlike pleopods.

AMPHIONIDS AND PEOPLE

These unique crustaceans are of interest to scientists who study crustaceans and how they survive in their environment.

CONSERVATION STATUS

This species is not considered endangered or threatened.

FOR MORE INFORMATION

Books:

Holthuis, L. B. *The Recent Genera of the Caridean and Stenopodidean Shrimps (Decapoda); with an Appendix on the Order Amphionidacea.* Leiden, The Netherlands: Nationaal Natuurhistorisch Museum, 1993.

These unique crustaceans are of interest to scientists who study crustaceans and how they survive in their environment. (Illustration by Bruce Worden. Reproduced by permission.)

Periodicals:

Heegaard, P. "Larvae of Decapod Crustacea: The Amphionidae. Dana Expedition," *Report* 77 (1969): 1-67.

Lindley, J. A., and F. Hernández. "The Occurrence in Waters Around the Canary and Cape Verde Islands of *Amphionides reynaudii*, the Sole Species of the Order Amphionidacea (Crustacea: Eucarida)." *Revista de la Academia Canaria de las Ciencias* 11, nos. 3-4 (1999): 11-119.

Williamson, D. I. "*Amphionides reynaudii* (H. Milne Edwards), Representative of a Proposed New Order of Eucaridan Malacostraca." *Crustaceana* 25, no. 1 (1973): 35-50.

**CRABS, SHRIMPS,
AND LOBSTERS**

Decapoda

Class: Malacostraca

Order: Decapoda

Number of families: 151 families

order

CHAPTER

PHYSICAL CHARACTERISTICS

Decapods, including crabs, shrimps, lobsters, and crayfishes, are among the most familiar of all crustaceans. They come in a wide variety of sizes, ranging from tiny pea crabs to the giant Japanese spider crab *Macrocheira kaempferi* with spidery legs spanning up to 12 feet (3.7 meters) across. Many species have distinctive color patterns, and some are able to change their colors. Despite their incredible variety, all decapods have the same basic body plan with three body regions: head, thorax, and abdomen. The head and thorax are closely joined together, or fused, to form the cephalothorax (SEH-feh-lo-THOR-acks). A shieldlike carapace (CARE-eh-pes) covers the cephalothorax. The carapace also covers the sides of the body and protects the breathing organs, or gills.

The head sometimes has a beaklike projection called a rostrum and two distinct pairs of long antennae. The first pair of antennae, or antennules (an-TEN-yuls), is branched, or biramous (BY-ray-mus). They are used mostly to detect odors. The second pair of antennae is uniramous (YU-neh-RAY-mus), or not branched. This pair is used mainly as organs of touch. The compound eyes are set on the tips of stalks. Each compound eye has multiple lenses. Depending on the species, the uniramous jaws, or mandibles, are used for slicing flesh, grinding plant materials, or crushing shells.

The first three segments of the thorax are closely joined, or fused, with the head. The appendages of these first three segments are called maxillipeds (mack-SIH-leh-pehds). Maxillipeds are thoracic (thuh-RAE-sik) limbs that work together with the mouthparts. The leglike limbs, or pereopods (PAIR-ee-oh-pawds), of the remaining five thoracic segments are either uniramous or weakly biramous and are used mainly for walking. The first few pairs of legs, especially the first pair, often have claws that are used for feeding, mating, and defense. Fast, slender claws are used to grab alert prey. Large strong claws with toothlike surfaces are used to crush the shells of clams, snails, and other hard-shelled prey.

The six-segmented abdomen has pairs of appendages underneath called pleopods (PLEE-oh-pawds). In lobsters, crayfishes, and shrimps, the abdomen is long, thick, and powerful and is used for swimming. At the end of the abdomen is a pair of slender biramous appendages, the uropods (YUR-oh-pawds). In between the uropods is a taillike segment called the telson. The telson is not tightly joined with, or fused, to the last abdominal segment. The telson and uropods work together to form a fanlike tail. Hard-bodied decapods, such as lobsters, snap their abdomens with fanlike tails forward underneath their bodies to propel themselves backward through the water. Shrimps and other softer-bodied species use their abdomens and tails to swim forward in the water. However, the bodies of crabs are relatively short and compact. They have lost most of their abdominal appendages. The crab's abdomen is short, flat, and folded forward under the body. It plays no role in swimming and has just a few pairs of pleopods that are used only for carrying eggs (females) or mating (males).

GEOGRAPHIC RANGE

Decapods are found worldwide.

HABITAT

Approximately ninety percent of all species live in the ocean. They are found in all kinds of habitats, including mud flats, mangrove forests, rocky shores, muddy or sandy beaches, sea grass beds, coral reefs, open water, and sea bottoms, including deep sea geysers known as hydrothermal vents. Many species dig burrows in these habitats and come out only under the protection of dark to look for food. Freshwater species live in a variety of habitats, including mountain streams, rivers, ponds, and along lakeshores. Only one percent of all decapods are terrestrial. These species are sometimes found at elevations of up to 3,280 feet (1,000 meters) or as far as 9 miles (15 kilometers) away from the ocean. They still depend on the sea and must return there to reproduce.

DIET

As a group, decapods are omnivorous, which means they eat both plant and animal materials. Lobsters, shrimps, and many crabs mostly prey on other animals, including fish, worms, mollusks, and other crustaceans. Occasionally, when the opportunity arises, they will scavenge the dead bodies of these and other marine animals. Some crabs and shrimps are filter feeders. They use their bristly antennae, maxillipeds, or legs to strain out bits of food floating in the water. Other filter feeders stir up sand and mud to strain out food that has settled on the bottom. Many marine and freshwater decapods eat plants, but will sometimes feed on animal flesh when it is available.

BEHAVIOR AND REPRODUCTION

Decapods show many complicated and even amazing behaviors. For example, Caribbean spiny lobsters form a long row of up to 65 individuals that march single-file toward deeper water. It is not well understood why they do this, although it may have something to do with avoiding storms during the winter. Juvenile red king crabs often gather together into mounds that may contain thousands of individuals. This behavior is believed to prevent them from being eaten by predators.

Some species form special relationships with other organisms. Certain shrimps establish cleaning stations where fishes line up to have their parasites removed. Fish parasites are worms, crustaceans, and other animals that live on their bodies and eat their blood and other body fluids. Other shrimps share a burrow with a fish. The fish watches for danger as the shrimp builds and maintains the burrow.

Some species make signals that are seen or heard by other members of the same species. Decapods that spend some or most of their lives on land produce sounds by rubbing one part of their body against another. Marine and freshwater species release special chemicals, or pheromones (FEH-re-moans), into the water along with their waste through special glands on the antennae. The pheromones are used to attract mates.

Except for one kind of crayfish, all decapods require males and females to reproduce. In some shrimps, the adults mature

first as males and later develop into females. A few species keep both male and female reproductive structures and are called hermaphrodites (her-MAE-fro-daits).

Decapods have many kinds of courtship. In fiddler crabs the male has claws that are much larger than those of the females. Useless for feeding, the oversized male claws are used only for fighting with other males and attracting females. Depending on the species, mating is very brief or may occur only after males and females have spent long periods of time together. In these cases the female can only mate just after she molts, or sheds her external skeleton (exoskeleton). As they prepare to molt, adult females release pheromones to attract males. A male will sometimes grasp the female with its legs for several days or weeks until she finally molts. Sperm is transferred to the female as a fluid or inside packets. The sperm is deposited directly into the reproductive organs of the female or into a special storage sac in her body. In some species the male stands guard over the female to prevent other males from mating with her.

Most female decapods hold their egg masses with their pleopods. They keep the eggs clean and make sure that plenty of oxygen-carrying water is circulated around them. Just before hatching, the eggs release a chemical that tells the female to shake the mass to help release the larvae (LAR-vee), or young animals, into the water as they hatch. After hatching, parental care is rare. Young crayfishes will stay with their female parents for protection. In some tropical crabs that breed in freshwater trapped at the bases of plants growing on tree limbs, the females provide food for their larvae and protect them from predators.

DECAPODS AND PEOPLE

Most of the crustaceans harvested as food for humans are in the order Decapoda. Shrimps and crayfishes are raised on aquatic farms and sold as food throughout the world. Depending on where and what decapods eat, some species can become poisonous to the people that eat them. Others, if they are not cooked properly, may carry parasites that infest the bodies of people and make them sick.

In some areas, land crabs are considered pests in rice fields. They eat the rice plants and dig burrows that drain water away from the plants. The accidental introduction of the European green crab to the eastern coast of the United States has caused serious harm to clam beds harvested for food. Foreign species of crayfishes have damaged crops and threatened to reduce populations of native crayfish species.

CONSERVATION STATUS

There are 197 species of decapods listed by the World Conservation Union (IUCN), most of which are species of freshwater crayfish that live in very small or limited habitats. They are especially vulnerable to habitat destruction and loss and may become threatened in the future.

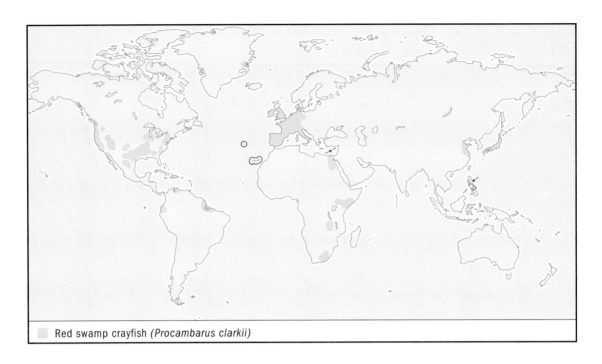

Red swamp crayfish *(Procambarus clarkii)*

SPECIES ACCOUNTS

RED SWAMP CRAYFISH
Procambarus clarkii

Physical characteristics: The dark red, nearly black body of the red swamp crayfish measures up to 4.7 inches (120 millimeters). Its pincherlike claws are long and slender, with bright bumps and red tips.

Geographic range: Originally from the southern United States and northern Mexico only, this species is now widely established in Europe, Africa, Central and South America, and Southeast Asia.

Habitat: This species is tolerant of a wide range of habitats, even slightly salty water. They prefer to live in slow moving streams, swamps, and ponds, where there are plenty of plants growing along the shores and leaves on the bottom. Their populations are the largest in habitats that flood each year.

Diet: Red swamp crayfishes are omnivorous and eat many different kinds of plants and small animals, such as snails, insects, fishes, and tadpoles.

The red swamp crayfish is tolerant of a wide range of habitats, even slightly salty water. (Gerard Lacz/Peter Arnold, Inc.)

Behavior and reproduction: During the dry season they will sometimes dig burrows down 2 feet (0.6 meters) or more to reach water.

Adult males have two body forms. The first form has large claws, hooks at the bases of some legs, and spends its time looking for a mate. After mating, males molt into the second form, which has smaller claws. Females can store sperm for long periods of time. They brood their eggs for two to three weeks and produce two generations each year. The hatchlings resemble small crayfishes and stay with the female for several weeks. They live for a total of twelve to eighteen months in the wild.

Red swamp crayfishes and people: This species is sold as a pet and as fish bait. It has been introduced around the world because it grows fast and can live in a wide variety of habitats. Red swamp crayfishes were introduced to eastern Africa to eat snails that carry parasites harmful to humans.

Conservation status: The World Conservation Union (IUCN) does not consider this species to be threatened or endangered. ■

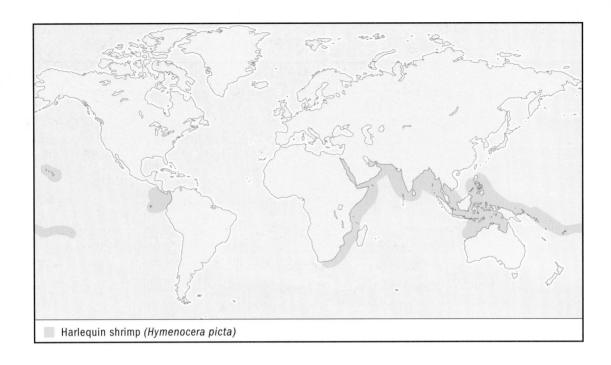
Harlequin shrimp *(Hymenocera picta)*

HARLEQUIN SHRIMP
Hymenocera picta

Physical characteristics: Adult Harlequin shrimp measure about 2 inches (50 millimeters) in length. The claws on the second pair of legs are very large, distinctly flat, and platelike in shape. Both the body and claws have bright purple markings or red blotches on a white or cream-colored background.

Geographic range: This species is found along the shores of East Africa, the Red Sea to Indonesia, and across northern Australia to Hawaii, Panama, and the Galápagos Islands.

Habitat: This species lives in and hides among coral reefs.

Diet: Harlequin shrimp pry sea stars off coral reefs with their large, flat claws and eat them.

Behavior and reproduction: Pairs are territorial. Single individuals are much more active than those in pairs.

Adult males and females live and defend their territory together. Females molt every eighteen to twenty days and mate soon after. They produce about one thousand eggs at a time. Eggs hatch within eighteen days. The larvae are well developed and spend a short time floating in the water with other plankton. Plankton is made up of plants and animals that live in open water and are at the mercy of ocean currents.

Harlequin shrimps and people: Harlequin shrimp are popular pets because they are easy to breed and raise in captivity. They might also play a role in conserving coral reefs because they eat small, coral-eating crown-of-thorns sea stars.

Conservation status: The World Conservation Union (IUCN) does not consider this species to be threatened or endangered. ■

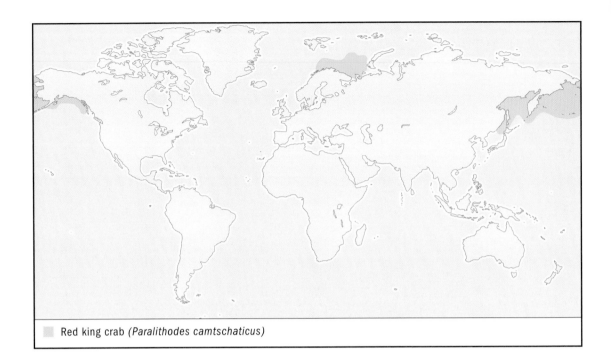

Red king crab (*Paralithodes camtschaticus*)

RED KING CRAB
Paralithodes camtschaticus

Physical characteristics: Red king crabs are a very large, reddish brown species with a carapace measuring up to 11 inches (280 millimeters) wide. Their legs stretch more than 6 feet (1.8 meters) across. Both the carapace and legs are covered with lots of sharp spines. The right claw is larger than the left. Only three pairs of walking legs are visible.

Geographic range: This species lives in the Sea of Japan to northern British Columbia. It was introduced into the Barents Sea and has spread westward to Norway.

Habitat: Red king crabs live at depths of 10 to 1,190 feet (3 to 366 meters) and prefer open habitats with sandy or muddy bottoms.

Diet: They prey on a variety of bottom-dwelling invertebrates, including brittle stars, sea stars, sand dollars, and sea urchins, barnacles, worms, mollusks, and sponges.

Behavior and reproduction: Two-year-old juveniles often gather by the hundreds or thousands to form spectacular mounds known as pods in shallow water. The pods are thought to discourage predators; they disperse shortly after dusk, as the crabs forage for prey, and form again before dawn.

Mating occurs just after the female molts, and her exoskeleton is still soft. The male uses his small fifth pair of walking legs to spread sperm over the female's pleopods. Anywhere from 150,000 to 400,000 eggs come out of the female's body right away, but they take almost a year to hatch. The larvae do not resemble the adults and molt four times before settling on the ocean bottom.

Red king crabs and people: Red king crabs were once the target of one of the most valuable fisheries off Alaska in United States waters. Commercial harvesting is carried out with large baited pots.

Two-year-old juveniles often gather by the hundreds or thousands to form spectacular mounds known as pods. (Eiichi Kurasawa/Photo Researchers, Inc.)

Conservation status: The World Conservation Union (IUCN) does not consider this species to be threatened or endangered. However, populations off the coast of Alaska and in the western Bering Sea have suffered as a result of over-fishing. A population introduced to the Barents Sea appears to be growing. ■

Sand fiddler crab (*Uca pugilator*)

SAND FIDDLER CRAB
Uca pugilator

Physical characteristics: The carapace of adult sand fiddler crabs are about 1 inch (26 millimeters) wide. The eyestalks are very long and slender. The claws of males are distinctly unequal in size, while those of females are smaller and equal in size.

Geographic range: This species is found along the eastern coast of the United States, from Cape Cod, Massachusetts, south to Pensacola, Florida.

Habitat: Sand fiddler crabs live on sandy beaches that open to the sea or on sand-mud beaches in protected areas along salt marsh edges and tidal creek banks.

Sand fiddler crabs live on sandy beaches that open to the sea or on sand-mud beaches in protected areas along salt marsh edges and tidal creek banks. (David & Hayes Norris/Photo Researchers, Inc.)

Diet: They eat bits of plants, bacteria, and other organisms.

Behavior and reproduction: Sand fiddler crabs feed at low tide, scraping up mud with their claws and pulling out bits of food with their mouth parts. Males only use their small claw to feed, while females use both claws. They dig and live in simple burrows in the sand and come out only at low tide to feed. When the tide starts to come in, they will plug the burrow entrance overhead with sand.

Males sit near the entrances of their burrows, where mating occurs, waving their large claw and beating it against the sand to attract females. The female remains in the burrow for about two weeks, until the eggs are about ready to hatch. The larvae do not resemble the adults, and are released into the water at night during high tide and carried away by the current. After six to eight weeks and five molts, the larvae return and settle on the bottom.

Sand fiddler crabs and people: They are occasionally sold as pets.

Conservation status: The World Conservation Union (IUCN) does not consider this species to be threatened or endangered. ■

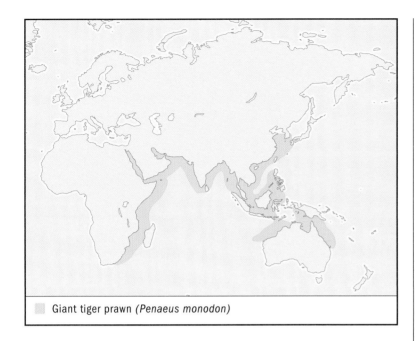

Giant tiger prawn (*Penaeus monodon*)

GIANT TIGER PRAWN
Penaeus monodon

Physical characteristics: The dark bodies of adult giant tiger prawn have several distinct black and white bands and reach 13.2 inches (336 millimeters) in length.

Geographic range: They are found off the eastern coast of Africa and the Red Sea, east to India, Australia, and Japan.

Habitat: Juveniles live near the shore and in mangrove estuaries (EHS-chew-AIR-eez). The adults prefer waters with silty or sandy bottoms and live down to depths of 525 feet (162 meters).

Diet: Giant tiger prawn eat mostly smaller shrimps, crabs, mollusks, and other animals, as well as algae (AL-jee). They will also swallow sand and silt mixed with bacteria and bits of plants and animals. Bacteria are single-celled organisms that break down the tissues of dead organisms.

Behavior and reproduction: During the day, giant tiger prawn remain buried on the sea bottom. Groups of two hundred to three

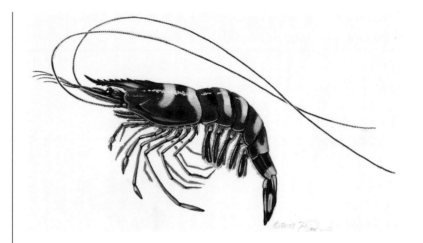

Groups of two hundred to three hundred individuals have been observed swimming in shallow water at dawn and dusk. (Illustration by Jonathan Higgins. Reproduced by permission.)

hundred individuals have been observed swimming in shallow water at dawn and dusk.

Giant tiger prawn mate at night, just above the sea bottom, right after the female molts. The male deposits sperm in a special structure underneath the female's thorax. Females release 250,000 to 800,000 eggs into the water, where they hatch in less than eighteen hours. They do not resemble the adults and have only mandibles and two pairs of antennae for appendages. The non-feeding larvae use these appendages to swim in the water. The larvae reach adulthood in about twelve days and live less than a total of two years.

Giant tiger prawns and people: Giant tiger prawn are harvested by boats dragging nets in the water. They are an important species for aquatic farms because they grow large very quickly and bring a high price at the market.

Conservation status: The World Conservation Union (IUCN) does not consider this species to be threatened or endangered. ■

FOR MORE INFORMATION

Books:

Bliss, D. E. *Shrimps, Lobsters and Crabs.* New York: Columbia University Press, 1989.

Debelius, H. *Crustacea Guide of the World.* Frankfurt, Germany: IKAN, 1999.

Factor, J. R. *Biology of the Lobster.* New York: Academic Press, 1995.

Periodicals:

Herrnkind, W. F. "Strange March of the Spiny Lobster." *National Geographic* (June 1975) 147, no. 6: 819-831.

Web sites:

Crayfish Homepage. http://crayfish.byu.edu/ (accessed on March 15, 2005).

Crustacean Gallery. http://www.mov.vic.gov.au/crust/page1.html (accessed on March 15, 2005).

Crustacean Printouts. http://www.enchantedlearning.com/subjects/invertebrates/crustacean/index.shtml (accessed on March 15, 2005).

Fiddler Crabs (Genus *Uca*). http://www.fiddlercrab.info/ (accessed on March 15, 2005).

Lobster FAQs. http://www.nefsc.noaa.gov/faq/fishfaq7.html (accessed on March 15, 2005).

Class: Malacostraca

Order: Mysida

Number of families: 4 families

order

PHYSICAL CHARACTERISTICS

The bodies of mysids are usually glassy and transparent, although deep-sea species are often red. Many species have dark, star-shaped patterns made up of clusters of special cells. These clusters of cells give some mysids the ability to change colors to match their background. They can turn dark against a black background or a dark olive green if they are living among green algae (AL-jee).

Most mysids resemble wormlike shrimp and measure between 0.39 to 1.18 inches (10 to 30 millimeters) long. Both pairs of antennae are branched, or biramous (BY-ray-mus). Males have bristles on the bases of the second pair of antennae. The compound eyes are black and mounted on flexible stalks. Each compound eye has multiple lenses. The head and segmented thorax are tightly joined together in a single body region called the cephalothorax (SEH-feh-lo-THOR-acks). A shieldlike carapace covers the head and most of the cephalothorax and is tightly attached with, or fused to, the first 3 or 4 thoracic (thuh-RAE-sik) segments.

The thorax has eight pairs of biramous thoracic limbs, or pereopods (PAIR-ee-oh-pawds). The first and sometimes second pairs of pereopods have pincherlike claws and are used for feeding. The bases of some pereopods in females have plates that form a brooding chamber called the marsupium (mar-SUE-pee-uhm).

The abdomen has six segments. All segments are similar in appearance except for the last, which is twice as long as the others. Each of the first five abdominal segments has a pair of biramous appendages, or pleopods (PLEE-oh-pawds), underneath. The pleopods are usually smaller in the female and sometimes in the male. Males have specialized pleopods that are used for mating. At the tip of the abdomen is a flaplike tail, or telson. On either side of the telson is a biramous uropod (YUR-oh-pawd). Together the telson and uropods form a fanlike tail.

GEOGRAPHIC RANGE

Mysids live on all continents and in all oceans.

HABITAT

Mysids live in a wide variety of aquatic environments. Most species are found in the open sea or along the coast, usually on or near the bottom. Some species burrow in the sand or mud, while others are found in open waters. Species living in open waters are called pelagic (peh-LAJ-ihk) species. Deep-sea mysids are found at depths of 18,700 to 23, 622 feet (5,700 to 7, 200 meters). Other species live in estuaries and other brackish aquatic habitats. A few species live in underground springs or in coastal sea caves.

DIET

Most mysids are filter feeders. They strain tiny bits of plant and animal materials from the water as they swim over the bottom. These species also use their pincherlike claws to capture small animals when they are available. Prey items include small crustaceans and mollusks.

BEHAVIOR AND REPRODUCTION

Mysids spend much of their time swimming. They can swim up, down, forward, and backward with equal agility. When threatened they quickly jerk backward by flexing the abdomen and fanlike tail forward against the thorax. Females have very small pleopods and use their pereopods for swimming. Burrowing species rise up into the water at night to feed and sink down to the safety of the bottom during the day to avoid predators. Some species form swarms that may reach several miles in length and three or more feet in diameter.

Both males and females are required for reproduction. Females produce chemicals, or pheromones (FEH-re-moans), to attract males. Males and females sometimes align their bodies,

belly-to-belly and head-to-tail, to mate. The male's sperm is either injected or washed into the female's marsupium. Within 30 minutes eggs are released into the marsupium and fertilized.

After hatching the young remain and develop in the marsupium for several weeks or months, depending on species and water temperature. The young eventually leave the marsupium with a full set of appendages and reach adulthood in about a month at water temperatures of 68°F (20°C).

MYSIDS AND PEOPLE

Some mysids are harvested and processed for use as fish food or bait. In Asia, mysids are commonly sold as food for humans. They are also used as research animals because they are easy to collect, handle, and keep in the laboratory.

CONSERVATION STATUS

The World Conservation Union (IUCN) considers two species of mysids, both of which live in sea caves, to be Critically Endangered: *Bermudamysis speluncola* and *Platyops sterreri*. This means these mysids are facing an extremely high risk of extinction in the wild. Mysids are threatened by pollution of coastal waters, dredging of canals, groundwater drainage, and continual use of pesticides. Underground waters are threatened by tourism, agriculture, and urban development.

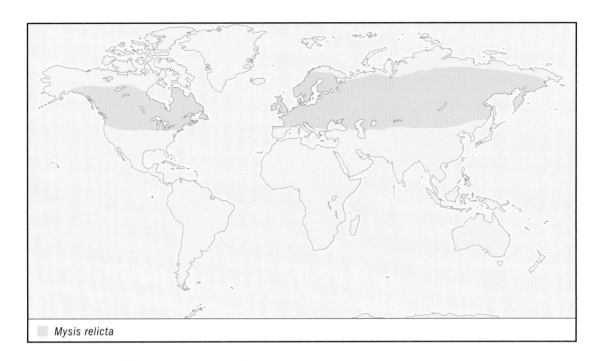

Mysis relicta

NO COMMON NAME
Mysis relicta

Physical characteristics: Adults measure 0.59 to 0.98 inches (15 to 25 millimeters) long. The telson is wide and split at the tip.

Geographic range: In North America *Mysis relicta* is found in the Great Lakes of North America; Green Lake, Trout Lake, and Lake Geneva in Wisconsin; the Finger Lakes of New York; and a few Canadian shield lakes. It has been introduced into other lakes in the western United States, Alabama, and Maine. This species is also found in Europe, Scandinavia, and Russia.

Habitat: This species prefers to live in cold, freshwater lakes at temperatures of 39° to 57°F (4° to 14°C).

Diet: *Mysis relicta* is a filter feeder, a scavenger, and a predator.

Behavior and reproduction: This species moves up into open water at night and remains near the bottom during the day. They usually live in the dark; their eyes are easily damaged by strong light.

Brood size is determined by the size of the female. Females measuring 0.51 to 0.59 inches (13 to 15 millimeters) carry 10 to 20 eggs, while females 0.66 to 0.82 inches (17 to 21 millimeters) carry as many as 25 to 40 eggs. The hatchlings remain in the marsupium for one to three months. They live a total of one or two years. Females reproduce once to twice in their lifetime.

Mysis relicta and people: *Mysis relicta* are prey for many species of fish valued as food for humans. These include lake trout, brown trout, rainbow trout, kokanee salmon, burbot, smelts, alewives, and others.

Conservation status: *Mysis relicta* is not considered endangered or threatened. ◼

Stygiomysis cokei

NO COMMON NAME
Stygiomysis cokei

Physical characteristics: Adults measure 0.35 to 0.86 inches (9.0 to 22.0 millimeters). The carapace is about one-fifth of the entire length of the body. The first pair of antennae (antennules) are about one-half the body length. The marsupium is made up of four plates. The telson has fifteen spines arranged in five groups of three and is about one-sixth the length of the body.

Geographic range: *Stygiomysis cokei* is found in coastal inland caves near Quintana Roo, Yucatan Peninsula, Mexico; in Mayan Blue Cave; Carwash Cave; and Naharon Cave.

Habitat: These cave dwellers live in the freshwater layer at depths of 32.8 to 65.6 feet (10 to 20 meters). They are also found in the upper layers with slightly brackish waters. They prefer habitats with

These cave dwellers live in the freshwater layer at depths of 32.8 to 65.6 feet (10 to 20 meters). (Photograph by Jerry Carpenter. Reproduced by permission.)

relatively constant temperatures ranging between 76.1° to 77.9°F (24.5° to 25.5°C).

Diet: *Stygiomysis cokei* is primarily a filter feeder.

Behavior and reproduction: Little is known about how this species behaves under natural conditions. When disturbed, they will swim with awkward movements. Nothing is known about their reproductive behavior.

***Stygiomysis cokei* and people:** This species is not known to impact humans or their activities directly.

Conservation status: This species is not considered endangered or threatened. ■

FOR MORE INFORMATION

Books:

Brusca, Richard C., and Gary J. Brusca. *Invertebrates.* Sunderland, MA: Sinauer Associates, 2003.

Mauchline, J. *The Biology of Mysids and Euphausiids.* Part I. *The Biology of Mysids.* London: Academic Press, 1980.

Periodicals:

Grossnickle, N. E. "Feeding Habits of *Mysis relicta*—An Overview." *Hydrobiology* 93 (1982): 101-107.

Web sites:

"Biology of Opposum [sic] Shrimps." *Mysidacea Gallery.* http://www
.museum.vic.gov.au/crust/mysibiol.html (accessed on February 21,
2005).

Mysis relicta. http://nas.er.usgs.gov/queries/FactSheet.asp?SpeciesID=
1142 (accessed on February 22, 2005).

LOPHOGASTRIDS
Lophogastrida

Class: Malacostraca

Order: Lophogastrida

Number of families: 2 families

PHYSICAL CHARACTERISTICS

Lophogastrids (loh-foh-GAS-trids) are long, shrimplike, and usually measure 0.39 to 3.15 inches (10 to 80 millimeters) in length, but one species reaches 13.78 inches (350 millimeters). Both pairs of antennae are branched, or biramous (BY-ray-mus). The outer branches of the second pair of antennae, or exopods, are short and flaplike. The compound eyes are set on stalks. Each eye has multiple individual lenses. The first pair of jaws, or mandibles, is biramous. The larger branch is used to crush food. The smaller branch is used for handling food and for cleaning. The second pair of branched jaws is called the maxillae (mack-SIH-lee). They are bristly and used to filter particles of food from the water.

A shieldlike carapace covers the head and segmented thorax. The carapace is loosely attached to the body and extends forward out over the head in a beaklike projection. It also covers the sides of the body down to the bases of the thoracic limbs. The thoracic limbs, or pereopods (PAIR-ee-oh-pawds), are biramous. Special plates form the marsupium (mar-SOUP-ee-uhm), a special brood pouch for carrying eggs.

Both males and females have well-developed biramous limbs, or pleopods (PLEE-oh-pawds), on the underside of the abdomen. The tip of the abdomen has a pair of long appendages called uropods (YUR-oh-pawds). The uropods are found on either side of a long, pointed tail-segment, or telson. The uropods and telson of this species are distinct and do not form a fanlike tail.

GEOGRAPHIC RANGE

Lophogastrids live in all oceans except the Arctic. Most species are found in the Pacific and Indian oceans.

HABITAT

Lophogastrids usually swim in deep, open waters down to depths of 3,280 feet (1,000 meters). Some species are found in waters as shallow as 164 feet (50 meters).

DIET

Most lophogastrids are thought to be predators. They prey on free-floating animals called zooplankton. Only one species, *Gnathophausia*, seems to use its bristly mouthparts as filters to strain large particles of food from the water.

DEEP-SEA DEFENSES

The brilliant red color of giant red mysids appears black in the dim light that penetrates the waters of their deep-sea home. This makes them virtually invisible to many predators. But if they are discovered, they can spit out a glowing fluid. The sudden splash of light startles and distracts predators, giving the mysid a chance to escape. If all else fails, their hard, spiny carapace will discourage even the hungriest of predators.

BEHAVIOR AND REPRODUCTION

Little is known about the behavior of lophogastrids. They are very difficult to observe in the wild. Recently they have been raised in captivity at the Monterey Bay Aquarium in California. Lophogastrids spend all their time swimming and use their pleopods to propel through the water. They use their pereopods to keep oxygen-carrying water flowing through their gills.

It is likely that both males and females are required for reproduction, but mating has never been observed. The eggs are kept in the brood pouch until they hatch. The hatchlings have a complete set of thoracic limbs.

LOPHOGASTRIDS AND PEOPLE

Lophogastrids are probably an important food source for many fish that are eaten by people.

CONSERVATION STATUS

No lophogastrids are considered endangered or threatened.

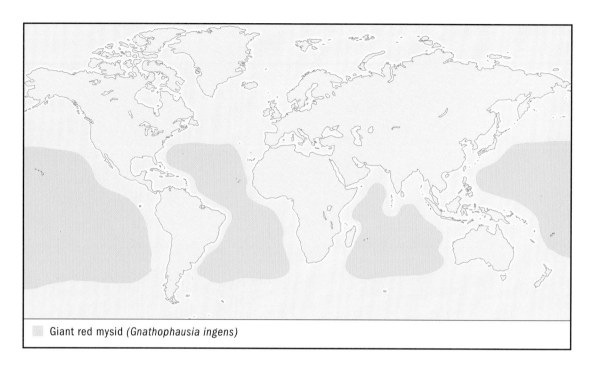

Giant red mysid (*Gnathophausia ingens*)

SPECIES ACCOUNT

GIANT RED MYSID
Gnathophausia ingens

Physical characteristics: The giant red mysid is the largest crustacean that lives in open water. It measures up to 13.78 inches (350 millimeters) in length. The carapace has a very long, beaklike projection that extends almost to the end of the first pair of antennae, or antennules. The flaplike exopods of the second pair of antennae are long with sharply pointed tips. The back of the carapace is extended as a spine that reaches back to the second abdominal segment. The carapace is folded inward underneath the body to form a partially enclosed gill chamber.

Geographic range: Giant red mysids live in deep waters below the tropical and subtropical waters of the Atlantic, Pacific, and Indian oceans.

Habitat: They live in deep, open waters, usually at depths of 1,300 to 4,920 feet (396 to 1,500 meters).

Diet: Giant red mysids eat large particles filtered from the seawater, as well as small dead organisms found in the water.

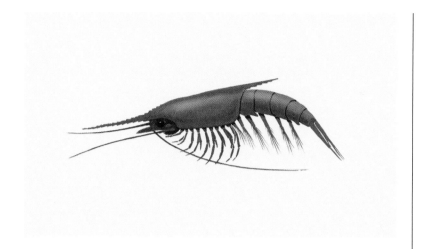

The giant red mysid is the largest crustacean that lives in open water. It measures up to 13.78 inches (350 millimeters) in length. (Illustration by John Megahan. Reproduced by permission.)

Behavior and reproduction: Little is known about the behavior of this species. *Gnathophausia ingens* has a very long period of larval development that is estimated to be about 530 days. Adult females probably have more than one brood and live for almost 3000 days. From hatching to adult, an individual giant red mysid molts 13 times.

Giant red mysids and people: This species is probably eaten by larger fishes that are fished commercially and sold as human food.

Conservation status: Giant red mysids are not considered endangered or threatened. ■

FOR MORE INFORMATION

Books:

Schram, F. R. *Crustacea.* Oxford, U.K.: Oxford University Press, 1986.

Periodicals:

Childress, J. J., and M. H. Price. "Growth Rate of the Bathypelagic Crustacean *Gnathophausia ingens* (Mysidacea: Lophogastridae). I. Dimensional Growth and Population Structure." *Marine Biology* 50 (1978): 47-62.

Web sites:

Giant Red Mysid (Gnathophausia ingens). http://www.mbayaq.org/efc/living_species/default.asp?hOri=0&hab=9&inhab=179 (accessed on February 22, 2005).

Class: Malacostraca

Order: Cumacea

Number of families: 8 families

phylum

class

subclass

● **order**

monotypic order

suborder

family

PHYSICAL CHARACTERISTICS

Cumaceans (koo-MAY-see-ans) are strange-looking crustaceans with a large shieldlike carapace and slender abdomen. Their bodies resemble a comma lying on its side. Most cumaceans measure 0.039 to 0.39 inches (1 to 10 millimeters) long, but one species reaches 1.57 inches (40 millimeters). The head may or may not have a beaklike projection, or rostrum. In some species there is one compound eye on the middle of the head. Others have two compound eyes or no eyes at all. Each compound eye has multiple lenses and is not set on a stalk. The first pair of antennae, or antennules, is either branched (biramous), or not (uniramous). The second pair of antennae is uniramous. The mandibles, or jawlike structures, are uniramous and are usually used for grinding food.

The carapace covers the head and extends back over the first three of the eight thoracic segments. A sharp, beaklike extension of the carapace projects forward over the head. The first three segments are tightly joined, or fused, to the head. The first two pairs of thoracic limbs or maxillipeds (mack-SIH-leh-pehds) work with the mouth to handle food, while the third pair is leglike and used for walking. In females, the second pair of maxillipeds has special plates on their bases to hold eggs. The remaining pairs of thoracic limbs are called pereopods (PAIR-ee-oh-pawds). Depending on species, they are either uniramous (YU-neh-RAY-mus) or biramous (BY-ray-mus) and are used for walking.

The segmented abdomen is distinct and slender. The number of pairs of abdominal appendages, or pleopods (PLEE-oh-pawds), ranges from 0 to 5. In males the pleopods are fully developed, reduced in size, or absent. With the exception of one species, pleopods are not found on females. The tip of the abdomen has a pair of slender, well-developed appendages called uropods (YUR-oh-pawds). The uropods are biramous. In between the uropods is a single, long, tail segment, or telson.

GEOGRAPHIC RANGE

Cumaceans live around the world in oceans, seas, bays, and estuaries to the deepest trenches.

HABITAT

Most species live in the ocean and brackish waters, but some are found in habitats where water is fresh for at least short periods of time. Many live on the bottom, just below the surface in soft mud or sand. They prefer habitats where there is some water current, but little wave action. One group lives on algae growing on rocks and broken bits of coral.

DIET

Most cumaceans eat tiny particles of plants. These materials are broken down into bits by grinding them down with grains of sand in their mouth or by using their mandibles to scrape particles off larger pieces. One group has sharp mandibles, suggesting that they might prey on microscopic animals.

BEHAVIOR AND REPRODUCTION

Cumaceans spend most of their time in mud or sand. They need to stay close to the surface so they can move oxygen-carrying water over their gills. The first pair of maxillipeds is used to move water forward from the walking legs through the carapace toward the head. Some species leave the bottom and swim up into the water after dark.

Males and females are required for reproduction. In most species the males spend at least some of their time swimming in open water in search of a mate. In some species the males

WHO KNOWS?

So little is known about cumaceans that it is unlikely that anyone would know if any species were threatened or endangered. They are sometimes found in large numbers, but their distributions are patchy in both small areas and over large distances. Under these circumstances it is difficult to determine if a drop in population numbers or their absence is a result of some environmental disturbance, or simply part of a little-understood natural cycle.

do not swim, but have special antennae that are used to grab the female's abdomen. They hang on to their mates with their antennae until they have mated. Females carry their eggs in a special brood pouch under the thorax until they hatch. The larvae (LAR-vee) do not live in open water like most other crustaceans. Instead, they live in the same places as the adults and molt, or shed their exoskeletons, until they reach adulthood. Once they reach adulthood, they stop molting.

CUMACEANS AND PEOPLE

Some species are an important food source for young fish, such as salmon and cod. These fishes are caught and sold as food for people.

CONSERVATION STATUS

No species of cumaceans are considered endangered or threatened.

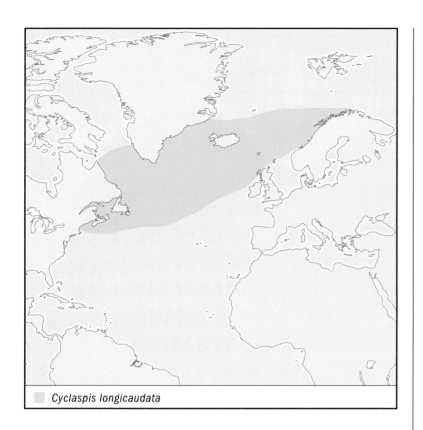

Cyclaspis longicaudata

NO COMMON NAME
Cyclaspis longicaudata

Physical characteristics: The smooth carapace of *Cyclaspis longicaudata* is almost ball-shaped. The abdomen is very long and slender; males have five pairs of pleopods.

Geographic range: They live in the cold waters of the North Atlantic, from northern Norway to the northeastern United States.

Habitat: They live on the bottom in sandy mud at depths from 395 to 16,400 feet (120 to 5,000 meters).

Diet: Nothing is known about what they eat.

Behavior and reproduction: Nothing is known about their behavior or how they reproduce. The shape of their bodies suggests that

The shape of their bodies suggests that Cyclaspis longicaudata *spend little time swimming, except possibly when the males are looking for a mate. (Illustration by John Megahan. Reproduced by permission.)*

they spend little time swimming, except possibly when the males are looking for a mate. Some populations reproduce year-round.

***Cyclaspis longicaudata* and people:**   This species does not directly impact people or their activities.

Conservation status: This species is not considered endangered or threatened. ■

FOR MORE INFORMATION

Books:

Brusca, R. C., and G. J. Brusca. *Invertebrates.* Second edition. Sunderland, MA: Sinauer Associates, 2003.

Ruppert, E. E., and R. S. Fox. *Seashore Animals of the Southeast.* Columbia: University of South Carolina Press, 1988.

Periodicals:

Watling, L. "Revision of the Cumacean Family Leuconidae." *Journal of Crustacean Biology* 11 (1991): 56-82.

Web sites:

Lowry, J. K. *Crustacea, the Higher Taxa: Description, Identification, and Information Retrieval.* Version: 2 October 1999. http://www.crustacea.net/crustace/www/cumac.htm (accessed on February 18, 2005).

Welcome to the Cumacean Page. http://nature.umesci.maine.edu/cumacea.html (accessed on February 18, 2005).

order

PHYSICAL CHARACTERISTICS

Most tanaids are small, shrimplike crustaceans measuring 0.039 to 0.078 inches (1 to 20 millimeters), but the largest species may reach 3.15 inches (80 millimeters). Some species have color patterns of mostly yellowish and blue or gray. Both pairs of antennae are branched, or biramous (BY-ray-mus). The compound eyes, each having multiple lenses, are on the tips of stalks. The head and first two segments of the thorax are closely joined together into one region, the cephalothorax (SEH-feh-lo-THOR-acks). A shieldlike carapace covers the cephalothorax. All of the thoracic and abdominal limbs are biramous. The first two pairs are called maxillipeds, but they are not part of the mouth. The second pair of maxillipeds has pincherlike claws. The remaining five segments of the thorax each have a pair of limbs called pereopods (PAIR-ee-oh-pawds). The pereopods are usually similar in shape and used for swimming. In some species the first pair is flat and probably used for digging.

In females, the bases of some of the legs form flattened plates and are used to form a brood pouch, or marsupium (mar-SOUP-ee-uhm). The appendages underneath the abdomen, called pleopods (PLEE-oh-pawds), are either present or absent. If present, they are usually used for swimming. But in species that live in tubes, the pleopods are used to create a flow of oxygen-carrying water through the tube. The last two abdominal segments are tightly joined with the tail segment, or telson. On either side of the telson is an appendage called the uropod

(YUR-oh-pawd). The telson and uropods together form a fanlike tail.

GEOGRAPHIC RANGE

Most tanaids live in the ocean, but a few species prefer the brackish waters of estuaries where rivers meet the ocean.

HABITAT

Most tanaids live at a wide variety of depths on the bottom of oceans and estuaries. Many species live at depths of more than 656 feet (200 meters); some are found below 29, 527 feet (9,000 meters). A few species live in the open ocean as free-floating plankton. Still others live in the cracks of sea turtle shells, while others live inside snail shells occupied by hermit crabs. Other species glue bits of sand and other particles into open-ended tubes and live inside.

DIET

Most tanaids eat bits of plants, animals, and other microorganisms. Larger pieces of food are handled by the maxillipeds and passed on to the mouth. In some species, the smaller branches of the pereopods and the first pair of pleopods have special structures that are used to stir up mud and sand and strain out bits of food. A few predatory species use their maxillipeds and mouthparts to attack small animal prey.

BEHAVIOR AND REPRODUCTION

Nothing is known of the behavior of tanaids.

Both males and females are usually required for reproduction. Some species are hermaphrodites (her-MAE-fro-daits), with individuals having the reproductive organs of both males and females. The eggs are held in the marsupium until they hatch. The hatchlings, or larvae (LAR-vee), go through several distinct larval stages inside the marsupium. They do not leave the pouch until they have developed most of their appendages. Unlike many crustacean larvae, tanaids do not live in the open water with other plankton.

TANAIDS AND PEOPLE

Tanaids do not affect people or their activities.

CONSERVATION STATUS

No species of tanaids is considered endangered or threatened.

Apseudes intermedius

NO COMMON NAME
Apseudes intermedius

Physical characteristics: The last five thoracic segments have rounded bristly expansions on their sides. The marsupium is not well developed in this species. The telson is twice as long as it is wide. The outer branch of the biramous uropods has seven segments.

Geographic range: This species is found around the Cape Verde Islands, the Mediterranean Sea, and off the coast of Brazil (Rio de Janeiro).

Habitat: They live in shallow waters, in sandy or muddy bottoms.

Diet: This species eats bits of plant and animal materials, as well as microorganisms. They probably stir up bits of food from the bottom with their pereopods and pleopods.

Behavior and reproduction: Nothing is known about the behavior of this species. In some habitats tanaids are the most abundant of all animals. Males and females are known; hermaphrodites are not.

***Apseudes intermedius* and people:** This species does not directly impact people or their activities.

Conservation status: *Apseudes intermedius* is not considered endangered or threatened. ■

FOR MORE INFORMATION

Books:

Brusca, Richard C., and Gary J. Brusca. *Invertebrates.* Sunderland, MA: Sinauer Associates, 2003.

Martin, Joel W., and George E. Davis. *An Updated Classification of the Recent Crustacea.* Los Angeles: Natural History Museum of Los Angeles County, Science Series 39, 2001.

Web sites:

Tanaidacea Homepage. http://tidepool.st.usm.edu/tanaids/ (accessed on February 21, 2005).

Apseudes intermedius *eat bits of plant and animal materials, as well as microorganisms. (Illustration by Dan Erickson. Reproduced by permission.)*

order

phylum

class

subclass

● **order**

monotypic order

suborder

family

PHYSICAL CHARACTERISTICS

Mictaceans (mik-tah-SEE-ans) resemble long, slender shrimps. They range in length from 0.078 to 0.14 inches (2 to 3.5 millimeters). This species does not have a shieldlike carapace covering the head and segmented thorax. However, a plate does cover the head and the first segment of the thorax, which is tightly joined with the head. The head plate covers the sides of head and the bases of the mouthparts. Mictaceans may or may not have stalked eyes. The first pair of thoracic limbs is associated with the mouth. The remaining seven pairs are used for swimming. Pairs 1 through 5, or 2 through 6, are branched, or biramous (BY-ray-mus). Gills are absent. The abdomen is six-segmented. The first five abdominal segments have pairs of uniramous (YU-neh-RAY-mus) or unbranched appendages called pleopods (PLEE-oh-pawds). At the end of the abdomen is a pair of slender biramous appendages called uropods (YUR-oh-pawds). In between the uropods is a slender, taillike segment called the telson. The telson and uropods do not join together to form a fanlike tail.

GEOGRAPHIC RANGE

Mictaceans are found off the coasts of northeastern South America, southeastern Australia, Bermuda, the Bahamas, and the Cayman Islands.

HABITAT

Mictaceans are found in underground sea caves or deep-sea habitats.

DIET

No one is sure what mictaceans eat. The small body size and the shape of their mouthparts suggests that they scavenge dead plants and animals.

BEHAVIOR AND REPRODUCTION

The animals move both by walking and swimming. It is believed that males and females must mate to reproduce, but mating has never been observed.

MICTACEANS AND PEOPLE

Mictaceans are of special interest to scientists studying the lives and evolution of crustaceans. Evolution is how organisms slowly change and adjust to their environments over millions of years.

CONSERVATION STATUS

Only one species of mictacean, *Mictocaris halope* from Bermuda, is listed as Critically Endangered by the World Conservation Union (IUCN). This means that it faces extremely high risk of extinction in the wild.

EXTINCTION IS FOREVER

Three-fifths of the world's mictaceans live in anchialine (aeng-KEY-eh-lihn) caves. Anchialine comes from Greek meaning "near the sea." Anchialine caves are formed when sea water floods underground spaces in limestone or volcanic rock. There is no surface connection with the ocean. These sometimes incredibly old habitats are home to many unusual animal species found nowhere else. Pollution, collapse, or other disturbances in caves might cause these animals to die out forever, or become extinct.

Mictocaris halope

NO COMMON NAME
Mictocaris halope

Physical characteristics: The body is long, slender, and colorless. Adults measure 0.12 to 0.14 inches (3 to 3.5 millimeters) in length. The head has a beaklike projection, or rostrum. Working eyes are absent, but eyestalks are present. The inner branches of the uropod have two segments. The telson is spiny along its back margin.

Geographic range: *Mictocaris halope* is found in Bermuda.

Habitat: *Mictocaris halope* lives on or near rocks at the bottom of underground sea caves.

Diet: They may strain bits of plant food from the water.

Behavior and reproduction: This species spends most of its time swimming, but is occasionally found crawling over or resting on

Mictocaris halope *lives on or near rocks at the bottom of underground sea caves. (Illustration by John Megahan. Reproduced by permission.)*

rocks. Mating has never been observed. Eggs are carried in a pouch, or marsupium (mar-SOUP-ee-uhm), formed by special plates on the leg bases. The young larvae (LAR-vee) hatch without their last pair of appendages.

***Mictocaris halope* and people:** This species is not known to impact people or their activities.

Conservation status: This species is listed as Critically Endangered by the World Conservation Union (IUCN), which means it faces extremely high risk of extinction in the wild. *Mictocaris halope* is very sensitive to the water quality of the caves in which it lives. ∎

FOR MORE INFORMATION

Books:

Brusca, Richard C., and Gary J. Brusca. *Invertebrates.* Sunderland, MA: Sinauer Associates, 2003.

Periodicals:

Bowman, T. E., and T. M. Iliffe. "*Mictocaris halope*, a New Unusual Peracaridan Crustacean from Marine Caves on Bermuda." *Journal of Crustacean Biology* 5 (1985): 58-73.

Web sites:

Anchialine Caves and Cave Fauna of the World. http://www.tamug.edu/cavebiology/index2.html (accessed on February 22, 2005).

Mictacea (Pericarida, Malacostraca) http://www.crustacea.net/crustace/www/mictacea.htm (accessed on February 22, 2005).

PHYSICAL CHARACTERISTICS

Spelaeogriphaceans (speh-lee-oh-grih-FAY-see-ans) are blind with long, cylinder-shaped bodies. Adults measure from 0.12 to 0.28 inches (3.1 to 7.2 millimeters) and have three distinct body regions: head, thorax, and abdomen. The head has a distinct, beaklike projection called the rostrum. Both pairs of antennae are long and branched, or biramous (BY-ray-mus). The eyestalks are present, but the eyes are not. The jaws, or mandibles, are uniramous (YU-neh-RAY-mus) or unbranched. A short, shieldlike carapace covers the back of the head and the first two segments of the segmented thorax. The first thoracic segment is firmly attached, or fused, to both the head and the carapace. There is one pair of maxillipeds, thoracic limbs that work together with the mouthparts.

The remaining pairs of thoracic limbs are called pereopods (PAIR-ee-oh-pawds). The pereopods are used for walking and are also used to move oxygen-carrying water past the body. The abdomen has six segments. Each of the first five segments of the abdomen has a pair of biramous limbs called pleopods (PLEE-oh-pawds). The first four pairs of pleopods are well developed and paddlelike; the fifth pair is very small. At the end of the abdomen is a pair of slender biramous appendages called the uropods (YUR-oh-pawds). In between the uropods is a slender, taillike segment called the telson. The telson is not tightly joined with, or fused to, the last abdominal segment. The telson and uropods do not join together to form a fanlike tail.

phylum
class
subclass
● **order**
monotypic order
suborder
family

GEOGRAPHIC RANGE

Spelaeographaceans are known only from small regions of South Africa, Brazil, and Western Australia.

HABITAT

They are found in freshwater streams or pools in caves or in underground springs.

DIET

Spelaeographaceans are thought to feed on bits of plants that are washed into the caves and underground springs. They use their mouthparts to sweep up small particles off rocks.

BEHAVIOR AND REPRODUCTION

Very little is known about these animals. They do not burrow or swim. Instead, they walk around on the bottom of freshwater habitats in caves or underground springs. Males and females are known, but mating has never been observed. The females carry ten to twelve eggs in the brood pouch located under the thorax and surrounded by the carapace.

SPELAEOGRIPHACEANS AND PEOPLE

Spelaeographaceans are of special interest to scientists studying the lives and evolution of crustaceans. Evolution is how organisms slowly change and adjust to their environments over millions of years.

CONSERVATION STATUS

No species of spelaeographaceans are considered endangered or threatened. The South African *Spelaeogriphus lepidops*, known from a single cave, is protected locally.

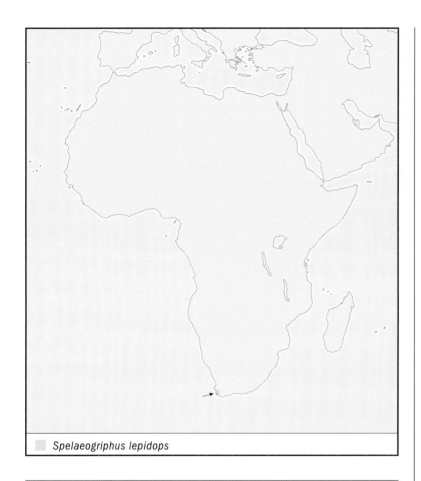

Spelaeogriphus lepidops

NO COMMON NAME
Spelaeogriphus lepidops

Physical characteristics: This species is white, or transparent, with food clearly visible in the gut. Adults range in length from 0.22 to 0.28 inches (5.6 to 7.2 millimeters).

Geographic range: *Spelaeogriphus lepidops* lives only in one stream and pool in the Bat Cave system in Table Mountain, near Cape Town, South Africa.

Habitat: *Spelaeogriphus lepidops* lives in a freshwater stream and pool in a cave.

Spelaeogriphaceans are of special interest to scientists studying the lives and evolution of crustaceans. Evolution is how organisms slowly change and adjust to their environments over millions of years. (Illustration by Dan Erickson. Reproduced by permission.)

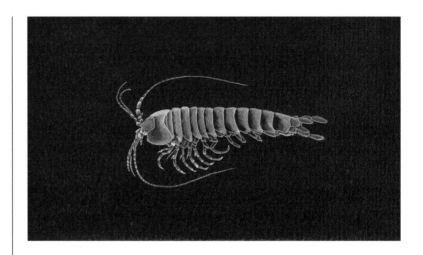

Diet: This species probably eats bits of plants that wash down into the cave from bogs on top of Table Mountain.

Behavior and reproduction: *Spelaeogriphus lepidops* use their mouthparts like brushes to sweep up bits of plant materials into their mouths. Males and females are known, but mating has never been observed. Observations of animals in captivity suggest that they hatch with the full number of thoracic segments.

Spelaeogriphus lepidops and people: This is one of many unique kinds of animals that are found only on Table Mountain.

Conservation status: The Bat Cave system and its unique animals are all protected. Special collecting permits are required even for scientists. ■

FOR MORE INFORMATION

Books:

Schram, F. R. *Crustacea.* Oxford, U.K.: Oxford University Press, 1986.

Periodicals:

Gordon, I. "On *Spelaeogriphus*, a New Cavernicolous Crustacean from South Africa." *Zoology* 5 (1957): 31-47.

Poore, G. B., and W. F. Humphreys. "First Record of Spelaeogriphacea (Crustacea) from Australia; A New Genus and Species from an Aquifer in the Arid Pilbara of Western Australia." *Crustaceana* 71 (1998): 721-742.

Web sites:

Profile/General Info [Table Mountain National Park] http://www .cpnp.co.za/main.html (accessed on March 14, 2005).

Spelaeogriphacea (Pericarida, Malacostraca). http://www.crustacea .net/crustace/www/spelaeog.htm (accesssed on March 14, 2005).

THERMOSBAENACEANS
Thermosbaenacea

Class: Malacostraca

Order: Thermosbaenacea

Number of families: 4 families

PHYSICAL CHARACTERISTICS

Adult thermosbaenaceans (ther-mohs-bee-NAY-cee-ans) are small, blind, and have slender bodies measuring up to 0.20 inches (5.2 millimeters). Their short head does not have a beaklike projection, or rostrum. They may or may not have eyestalks, but they never have eyes. The first pair of antennae (antennules) is branched, or biramous (BY-ray-mus). The second pair of antennae are uniramous (YU-neh-RAY-mus) or not branched. A short, shieldlike carapace covers the head and segmented thorax. The carapace of adult females has a large, bulging area that forms a brood chamber inside for storing eggs until they hatch. The first thoracic segment of both males and females is tightly joined, or fused, to the head.

The thorax has five to seven pairs of leglike biramous limbs called pereopods (PAIR-ee-oh-pawds). The pereopods are usually used for walking and sometimes swimming. The abdomen has six segments, but only the first two have appendages. The abdominal appendages, called pleopods (PLEE-oh-pawds), are well developed, narrow and rounded, or very small. At the end of the abdomen is a pair of slender biramous appendages, the uropods (YUR-oh-pawds). In between the uropods is a taillike segment called the telson. The telson in this species is not tightly joined with, or fused to, the last abdominal segment. The telson and uropods do not join together to form a fanlike tail.

GEOGRAPHIC RANGE

Thermosbaenaceans are found in the North Atlantic Ocean, the Mediterranean Sea, and the southeastern Indian Ocean.

HABITAT

Most thermosbaenaceans live in underground springs or in caves with brackish waters. Brackish water is less salty than seawater. Others live along the seashore or in underground caves filled with seawater. A few species live in hot springs at temperatures of 111 to 118°F (44 to 48°C).

DIET

Thermosbaenaceans living in hot springs eat blue-green algae and other organisms growing underwater on rocks. Other species are thought to use their brushlike mouthparts to sweep up small plant particles off the bottom and into their mouths.

BEHAVIOR AND REPRODUCTION

Thermosbaenaceans usually walk, but sometimes use their legs for swimming. Males and females are known, but mating has never been recorded. Thermosbaenaceans are unique among their crustacean relatives in that the eggs are kept in a brood pouch on their back formed by the swollen carapace. The young resemble the adults when they hatch. In one species, they hatch before the sixth and seventh pairs of legs are fully developed.

THERMOSBAENACEANS AND PEOPLE

Thermosbaenaceans do not impact people or their activities.

CONSERVATION STATUS

No species of thermosbaenaceans is considered endangered or threatened.

SOME LIKE IT HOT!

Thermosbaena mirabilis only lives in two baths fed by hot springs at the oasis of El Hamma in southern Tunisia. They thrive in warm, slightly salty water at temperatures between 98.6 to 116.6°F (37 to 47°C). These heat-loving animals stop moving when the temperature dips down to a relatively "chilly" 95°F (35°C) and die at around 86°F (30°C).

Thermosbaena mirabilis

NO COMMON NAME
Thermosbaena mirabilis

Physical characteristics: The adult body is sort of cylinder-shaped and measures up to 0.14 inches (3.5 millimeters). The thorax has five pairs of biramous pereopods. The telson is large and is about as long as the last three abdominal segments combined.

Geographic range: This species is known to live in just a few hot springs in Tunisia.

Habitat: This species lives in hot springs with lots of dissolved minerals, at temperatures usually higher than 111°F (44°C).

Diet: *Thermosbaena mirabilis* eats several species of bacteria known as blue-green algae. Bacteria are one-celled organisms that break down wastes and tissues of other organisms.

Behavior and reproduction: They walk over the surfaces of rock in search of food. Hatching young resemble the adults and have five pairs of pereopods.

***Thermosbaena mirabilis* and people:**   This species is not known to impact people or their activities.

Conservation status: *Thermosbaena mirabilis* is not considered endangered or threatened.   ■

FOR MORE INFORMATION

Books:

Schram, F. R. *Crustacea.* Oxford, U.K.: Oxford University Press, 1986.

Periodicals:

Wagner, H. P. "A Monographic Review of the Thermosbaenacea (Crustacea: Peracarida)." *Zoologische Verhandelingen* 291 (1994): 1-338.

Web sites:

Thermosbaenaceans.   http://www.geocities.com/mediaq/thermo.html (accessed on March 14, 2005).

PILLBUGS, SLATERS, AND WOODLICE

Isopoda

Class: Malacostraca

Order: Isopoda

Number of families: Approximately 120 families

order

phylum

class

subclass

 order

monotypic order

suborder

family

PHYSICAL CHARACTERISTICS

Isopods come in a variety of shapes and sizes. Most species have long bodies and are somewhat flat from top to bottom. They are mostly small, ranging from 0.02 to 0.6 inches (0.5 to 15 millimeters) in length. However, the largest species, *Bathynomus giganteus*, is an ocean bottom-dwelling creature that measures up to 19.7 inches (500 millimeters).

All isopods have three major body regions: head, thorax, and abdomen. Both pairs of antennae are unbranched, or uniramous (YU-neh-RAY-mus). The first pair is usually small, while the second is long and well developed. Unlike most crustaceans, the compound eyes, if present, are not set on stalks. Each compound eye has multiple lenses. The jaws, or mandibles, are uniramous and quite variable. Depending on the species, they are used to grind plant tissues, slice flesh, or pierce the tissues of living animals.

The first thoracic segment is tightly joined, or fused, to the head. Its uniramous limbs are called maxillipeds (mack-SIH-leh-pehds). Maxillipeds are thoracic limbs that work together with the mouthparts. Isopods do not have a shieldlike carapace that covers the head and thorax. Most species have seven pairs of walking legs called pereopods (PAIR-ee-oh-pawds). The pereopods are usually short, but in some species they are long and spiderlike. Plates on the underside of the thorax form a brood pouch, or marsupium (mar-SOUP-ee-uhm). The marsupium is where the eggs are kept and young hatch.

The six-segmented abdomen of terrestrial (te-REH-stree-uhl) species, or isopods that live on land, have two or more pairs of appendages called pleopods (PLEE-oh-pawds). The pleopods are white, egg-shaped, and are used for breathing. These species also take oxygen into their bodies directly through their external skeleton, or exoskeleton. The abdomen of all species ends with a pair of biramous (BY-ray-mus), or branched, uropods (YUR-oh-pawds), or tail appendages. Between the uropods is a taillike segment called the telson. The telson is tightly joined, or fused, to one or more abdominal segments.

Parasitic isopods, species that spend most or all of their lives feeding and living on fish and other crustaceans in the ocean, look different from other species. The females have wide thoracic segments, while segments that make up the abdomen tend to be much narrower. Males have body segments of similar width and are more egg-shaped in outline, similar to pillbugs. Both pairs of antennae of parasitic isopods are usually very small.

GEOGRAPHIC RANGE

Isopods are found worldwide.

HABITAT

Terrestrial isopods called pillbugs and woodlice are found in moist situations in a variety of habitats, including deserts. A few blind species live in ant nests. They are usually found under rocks, logs, tree barks, or other objects. Slaters are found along rocky seashores splashed by ocean waves. They also spend time in the water. Others prefer shallow waters associated with oceans, such as bays and estuaries (EHS-chew-AIR-eez). However, most species live in the ocean. There, parasitic species feed on the blood of fish and other crustaceans, such as barnacles, crabs, and shrimps.

DIET

Isopods eat plant and animal tissues. Terrestrial species search the forest floor for living and dead plants and fungi, as well as dead bodies and animal waste. At least 10% of their diet is their own waste, which they need to replenish vital nutrients to maintain normal growth rates.

Species that live in the ocean eat algae (AL-jee) and other bits of vegetation, including wood. Some isopods scavenge dead fish and other animals on the ocean bottom. Others are parasites, either all their lives, or only during their early developmental stages.

BEHAVIOR AND REPRODUCTION

Terrestrial isopods usually come out at night to feed. During the heat of the day, they instinctively hide in dark places beneath rocks, logs, and leaf litter where there is life-sustaining moisture. Under hot, dry conditions they release odors that are attractive to other isopods of the same species. They pile on one another as a defense of against losing precious body moisture. Some desert species actually live in family groups, with adults caring for their young in burrows throughout most of the summer. Thirsty pillbugs can take up water through their uropods and channel it through grooves along the sides of their bodies to the mouth.

The brownish and gray colors help terrestrial isopods to hide from predators. They also have special glands in their thorax that produce an unpleasant odor. The European pillbug has a marking similar to that of the European black widow spider. Predators usually avoid this venomous spider. The similarly marked isopod fools potential predators into thinking that it is also a dangerous spider. Pillbugs can also protect themselves from predators and from drying out by rolling up into a ball to protect their delicate undersides.

Like all crustaceans, isopods must molt, or shed their exoskeletons, to grow. Isopods are unusual in that they molt one half at a time. The rear half of the body molts first and is followed two or three days later by the front half. It is only during this time that the eggs of the mature female can be fertilized. Both males and females are usually required for reproduction. But in some parasitic species, young adults start out as males and later become females.

Males climb on the backs of females to mate. The males curl the abdomen around so that the underside comes into contact with hers. Males use their pleopods to transfer the sperm to the genital openings of the females. After mating the female releases a dozen to several hundred eggs into the marsupium. They will remain there from eight to twelve weeks. Depending on the species, one or two broods are produced each year. The pale juveniles leave the marsupium and resemble the adults. However, they lack the last pair of thoracic legs, or pereopods. The juveniles become larger and darker with each molt, eventually gaining the full number of limbs.

Most isopods live one or two years, but some may live as long as five. The longest-lived species, *Armadillo officinalis*, is known to live up to nine years.

PILLBUGS, SLATERS, WOODLICE, AND PEOPLE

Wood burrowing and feeding species living in oceans and estuaries can severely damage pilings, docks, and other underwater wooden structures. Pillbugs seldom cause any damage, but large numbers may eat seedlings and other garden and greenhouse plants.

CONSERVATION STATUS

Forty-one species of isopods are listed by the World Conservation Union (IUCN). Two are listed as Data Deficient, which means there is not enough information to make a judgment about the threat of extinction. Twenty-two are considered Vulnerable, or facing a high risk of extinction in the wild. Seven are listed as Endangered, or facing very high risk of extinction in the wild. Nine are listed as Critically Endangered, or facing an extremely high risk of extinction in the wild. The last species, the Socorro isopod, *Thermosphaeroma thermophilum*, is Extinct in the Wild, which means it is no longer alive except in captivity or through the aid of humans.

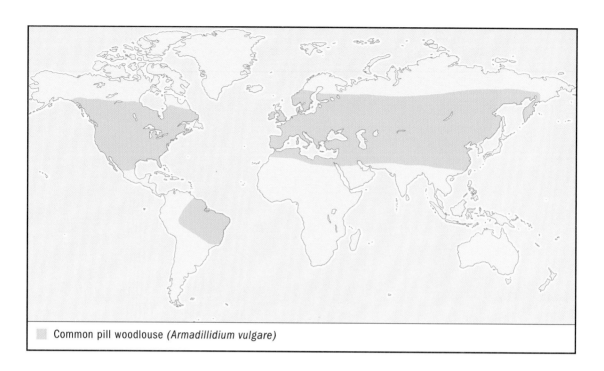

Common pill woodlouse (*Armadillidium vulgare*)

SPECIES ACCOUNTS

COMMON PILL WOODLOUSE
Armadillidium vulgare

Physical characteristics: The bodies of common pill woodlouses are egg-shaped, with adults measuring up to 0.7 inches (18 millimeters). They are dark gray, brown to red and usually have distinct rows of spots. The antennae are visible from above, but the legs are not.

Geographic range: Originally from southern Europe and North Africa, this species is now found throughout the world in temperate climates.

Habitat: Common pill woodlouses are found in many different kinds of habitats, including forests, grasslands, and even coastal and desert sand dunes. They are very common in cultivated fields, gardens, and greenhouses. Most individuals are found under rocks, logs, and other objects where there is plenty of moisture.

Diet: They eat young plant shoots, as well as dead and decaying plant matter.

Behavior and reproduction: Common pill woodlouses roll up into a ball to protect themselves. They move slowly on the ground in search of food and mates, traveling up to 43 feet (13 meters) a day under ideal summer conditions. During the winter they move only about half as far. During this time they may burrow as much as 10 inches (250 millimeters) beneath the surface of the soil.

Their reproductive cycles are triggered by rising temperatures and longer daylight hours. Mating usually occurs from late spring to early summer, sometimes even later in the year, just before the female goes through her molt. Females can store sperm in a special sac for up to one year. They produce one brood per year in the northern parts of their range, while those to the south produce two or three. Each brood has up to 100 eggs, but only half survive to become juveniles.

Common pill woodlouses and people: Large numbers of common pill woodlouses are sometimes considered pests in gardens and greenhouses because they will nibble on young plants.

Conservation status: Common pill woodlouses are not considered endangered or threatened. ■

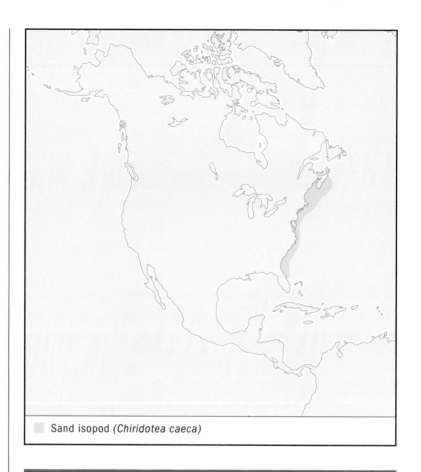

Sand isopod (*Chiridotea caeca*)

SAND ISOPOD
Chiridotea caeca

Physical characteristics: Adult sand isopods are flat from top to bottom and measure up to 0.6 inches (15 millimeters) in length and 0.3 inches (7 millimeters) across. Their bodies are almost paddlelike when viewed from above. The thorax is almost round and is followed by a long and pointed abdomen. The legs are thick and feathery in appearance.

Geographic range: They live in the western Atlantic Ocean, from Nova Scotia south to Florida.

Habitat: Sand isopods live along the shore and just beyond in the water, where they burrow in coarse, sandy bottoms.

Diet: Very little is known about the diet and feeding ecology of this burrowing species, but they are thought to be predators.

Behavior and reproduction: The rear pereopods are used to burrow in the sand. Mating occurs while adult sand isopods are buried in the substrate and may take up to several days. The females molt while they are in the grasp of the males. Two to six dozen eggs are produced in one brood each year. Juveniles measuring 0.1 (2.5 millimeters) long and 0.05 inches (1.25 millimeters) wide appear in spring and molt at least six times before reaching adulthood.

Sand isopods and people: This species does not impact people or their activities.

Conservation status: Sand isopods are not considered endangered or threatened. ■

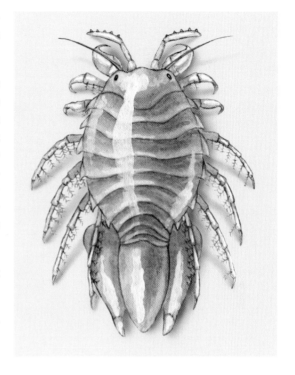

Sand isopods live along the shore and just beyond in the water, where they burrow in coarse, sandy bottoms. (Illustration by Bruce Worden. Reproduced by permission.)

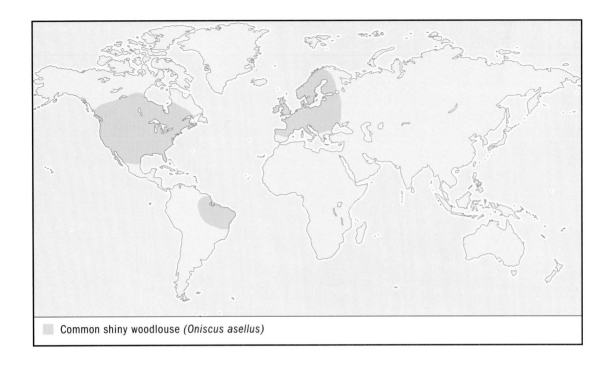

Common shiny woodlouse *(Oniscus asellus)*

COMMON SHINY WOODLOUSE
Oniscus asellus

Physical characteristics: The body of the common shiny wood-louse is egg-shaped, has a shiny grayish brown back, and reaches a length of approximately 0.6 inches (16 millimeters). It has a pair of long antennae.

Geographic range: Originally from only western and northern Europe, this species is now also established in both eastern Europe and North America.

Habitat: The common shiny woodlouse lives in almost any damp habitat, particularly in forests. It is usually found under rocks and logs.

Diet: It eats plant materials, especially the leaves of lime, ash, and alder trees.

Behavior and reproduction: This species cannot roll up into a ball for protection. They avoid light and seek out areas with high levels of moisture. They tend to latch on firmly to rocks and other surfaces.

The common shiny woodlouse lives in almost any damp habitat, particularly in forests. It is usually found under rocks and logs. (Stephen P. Parker/Photo Researchers, Inc.)

Common shiny woodlice and people: This common garden and greenhouse species does little damage to plants.

Conservation status: The common shiny woodlouse is not considered endangered or threatened. ■

FOR MORE INFORMATION

Books:

Raham, R. G. "Pill Bug Strategies." In *Dinosaurs in the Garden: An Evolutionary Guide to Backyard Biology*. Medford, NJ: Plexus Publishing, 1988.

Sutton, S. *Woodlice*. Oxford, U.K.: Pergamon Press, 1980.

Tavolacci, J., editor. *Insects and Spiders of the World*. Volume 7. *Owlet Moth-Scorpion. Pill Bug*. New York: Marshal Cavendish, 2003.

Periodicals:

McDermott, J. J. "Biology of *Chiridotea caeca* (Say, 1818) (Isopoda: Idoteidae) in the Surf Zone of Exposed Sandy Beaches along the Coast of Southern New Jersey, U.S.A." *Ophelia* 55 (2001): 123-135.

Web sites:

Minibeast Profiles: Sowbugs and Pillbugs. http://members.aol.com/YESedu/MBP05.html (accessed on March 14, 2005).

"Pillbugs. Oniscidea." *Critter Catalog.* http://www.biokids.umich.edu/critters/information/Oniscidea.html (accessed on March 14, 2005).

Sowbugs and Pillbugs. http://www.zoo.org/educate/fact_sheets/sowbug/sowbug.htm (accessed on March 14, 2005).

World List of Marine, Freshwater and Terrestrial Isopod Crustaceans. http://www.nmnh.si.edu/iz/isopod/ (accessed on March 14, 2005).

AMPHIPODS

Amphipoda

Class: Malacostraca

Order: Amphipoda

Number of families: 155 families

PHYSICAL CHARACTERISTICS

Amphipods come in a wide variety of shapes and sizes, but most have long, c-shaped bodies that are flat from side to side. Amphipods usually measure 0.2 to 0.6 inches (5 to 15 millimeters) in length, but some deep-sea species reach up to 9.8 inches (250 millimeters).

All amphipods have bodies that are made up of three regions: head, thorax, and abdomen. Both pairs of antennae are well developed and unbranched, or uniramous (YU-neh-RAY-mus). The compound eyes, if present at all, are not set on stalks. Each compound eye has multiple lenses. The eight-segmented thorax has eight pairs of uniramous appendages. The first thoracic (thuh-RAE-sik) segment is tightly joined, or fused, to the head. Its appendages are called maxillipeds (mack-SIH-leh-pehds). Maxillipeds are thoracic limbs that work together with the mouthparts. The remaining seven pairs of thoracic limbs are called pereopods (PAIR-ee-oh-pawds). The first two pairs of pereopods end in pincherlike claws that are used for grasping. The last five pairs of pereopods are used for burrowing, crawling, and jumping. Respiratory organs, or gills, are also found on the thorax.

The six-segmented abdomen has three pairs of appendages called pleopods (PLEE-oh-pawds). The pleopods are used for swimming and for moving oxygen-carrying water through the burrow. Another three pairs of abdominal appendages are called uropods (YUR-oh-pawds). The uropods are used for burrowing, jumping, and swimming. At the end of the abdomen is a

phylum

class

subclass

● **order**

monotypic order

suborder

family

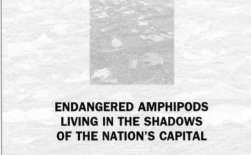

small, taillike segment called the telson. Depending on the species, the telson is sometimes fused to the last abdominal segment.

GEOGRAPHIC RANGE

Amphipods are found worldwide.

HABITAT

Most amphipods live on the ocean bottom and burrow in mud or debris. Many live in the open sea and are usually found on floating, jellylike animals, such as jellies and ctenophores. Others burrow into sandy beaches. About 1,200 species are found in fresh water, where they live among decaying leaves. About one hundred species live in moist habitats on land.

DIET

Amphipods eat plants, small animals, or scavenge dead bodies. One group lives on the bodies of marine mammals and eats their skin. Others attach themselves to the bodies of jellies or feed inside the bodies of tunicates.

BEHAVIOR AND REPRODUCTION

Some marine amphipods spend their entire lives attached to floating mats of algae or to jellies and their relatives. One group lives as external parasites on the bodies of dolphins, porpoises, and whales. Beach hoppers and their relatives live under decaying vegetation or dig burrows in mud or sand.

Both males and females are required for reproduction. Males attach themselves to the females and transfer their sperm directly to the opening of her reproductive organs. Females brood their eggs in a pouch under the thorax made up of special thoracic plates. Newly hatched amphipods look very similar to the adults.

AMPHIPODS AND PEOPLE

In many freshwater and marine habitats, amphipods help break down and recycle decaying plant and animal matter. They are also eaten by other animals that are harvested as food for people.

CONSERVATION STATUS

Seventy-one species of amphipods are listed by the World Conservation Union (IUCN). Two species are listed as Extinct, or no longer in existence; seven as Critically Endangered, facing extremely high risk of extinction in the wild; six as Endangered or facing a very high risk of extinction in the wild; and fifty-six as Vulnerable or facing high risk of extinction in the wild. Nearly all of these are freshwater species found in caves or underground springs. The parasitic species of dolphins, porpoises, and whales are not listed, even though many of their hosts may be considered threatened or endangered.

Skeleton shrimp (*Caprella californica*)

SKELETON SHRIMP
Caprella californica

Physical characteristics: Skeleton shrimp measure up to 1.38 inches (35 millimeters) in length. They have long, slender bodies with very small abdomens. The pincherlike claws of the pereopods are used for grasping and climbing.

Geographic range: This species is found only along the coast of central and southern California.

Habitat: Skeleton shrimp live just below the tide line, where they cling to algae and the slender, plantlike structures of some groups of marine animals.

Diet: They eat both plant and animal tissues found on the bottom or floating in the water.

Behavior and reproduction: Skeleton shrimp scrape the sea bottom to gather food.

Fertilized eggs are brooded in a chamber made by broad, leaflike thoracic appendages. The newly hatched juveniles look very much like the adults.

Skeleton shrimp and people: Skeleton shrimp do not impact people or their activities.

Conservation status: Skeleton shrimp are not considered to be threatened or endangered. ■

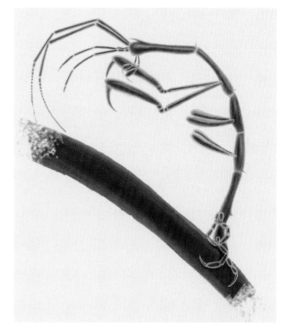

Skeleton shrimp live just below the tide line, where they cling to algae and some groups of marine animals. (Illustration by John Megahan. Reproduced by permission.)

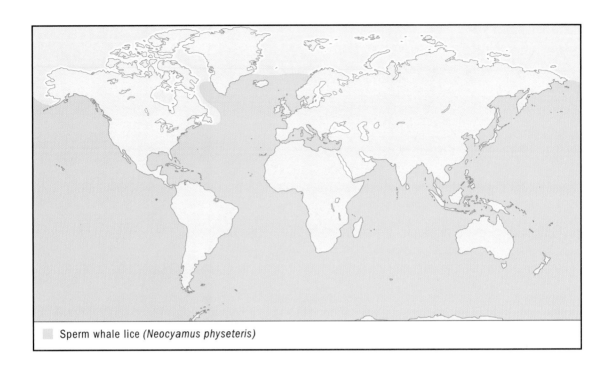

Sperm whale lice *(Neocyamus physeteris)*

SPERM WHALE LICE
Neocyamus physeteris

Physical characteristics: Unlike many amphipods, the yellow to orange bodies of this species are flattened top-to-bottom, not side-to-side. They measure up to 0.4 inches (10 millimeters). They use their hooklike claws to latch on to the skin of sperm whales. Their thoracic gills are clearly visible and resemble clumps of tiny fingers.

Geographic range: Sperm whale lice are found on sperm whales, which occur in all of the world's oceans.

Habitat: They live only on the bodies of sperm whales.

Diet: They scavenge organisms attached to the whale's skin and eat the skin itself.

Behavior and reproduction: Sperm whale lice spread to other whales by jumping onto them when infested whales rub up against other whales. Whale calves are infested by amphipods that come off their mothers when they touch.

Eggs are brooded in a pouch made by broad, leaflike appendages underneath the thorax. Newly hatched sperm whale lice strongly resemble the adults.

Sperm whale lice and people: This species does not impact people or their activities.

Conservation status: Sperm whale lice are not considered by the World Conservation Union (IUCN) to be threatened or endangered, although their only habitat, the sperm whale, is listed as Endangered, or facing very high risk of extinction in the wild. ■

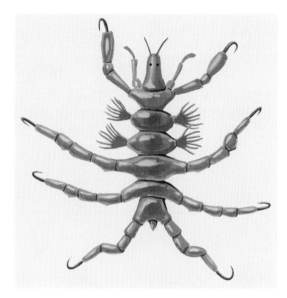

Sperm whale lice are found on sperm whales, which occur in all of the world's oceans.
(Illustration by John Megahan. Reproduced by permission.)

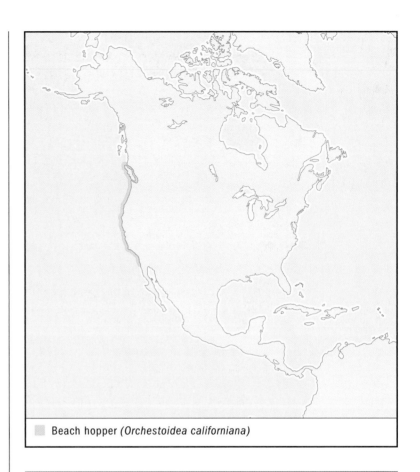

Beach hopper (*Orchestoidea californiana*)

BEACH HOPPER
Orchestoidea californiana

Physical characteristics: Beach hoppers measure up to 1.1 inches (28 millimeters) in length. They have curved bodies that are flat from side-to-side. Their compound eyes are very small. The long second pair of antennae is bright orange to rosy red.

Geographic range: Beach hoppers are found along the west coast of North America, from Vancouver Island, British Columbia, south to Laguna Beach, California.

Habitat: They live on beaches with fine sand and backed by dunes.

Diet: They eat seaweed washed up on the beach.

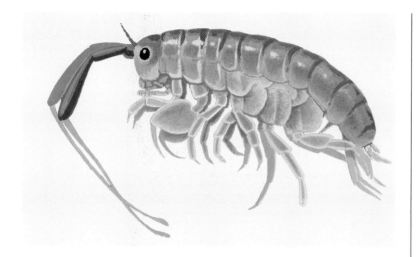

Beach hoppers feed at night to avoid both the daytime heat and being eaten by shorebirds. (Illustration by John Megahan. Reproduced by permission.)

Behavior and reproduction: Beach hoppers feed at night to avoid both the daytime heat and being eaten by shorebirds. Adults burrow down to 12 inches (300 millimeters) beneath the surface and stay there during the day. They jump by using the rear of their abdomens and their uropods as a spring.

Adults mate in their burrows from June until November. The male deposits a jellylike mass of sperm on the underside of the female and soon leaves the burrow. The dark blue eggs are brooded inside a pouch made by broad, leaflike appendages on the thorax. Newly hatched juveniles closely resemble the adults.

Beach hoppers and people: Beach hoppers do not impact people or their activities.

Conservation status: The World Conservation Union (IUCN) does not consider beach hoppers to be threatened or endangered. ▪

FOR MORE INFORMATION

Books:

Brusca, R. C., and G. L. Brusca. *Invertebrates.* Second edition. Sunderland, MA: Sinauer Associates, Inc., 2003.

Morris, R. H., D. P. Abbott, and E. C. Haderlie. *Intertidal Invertebrates of California.* Stanford, CA: Stanford University Press, 1980.

Periodicals:

Holsinger, J. R. "The Freshwater Amphipod Crustaceans (Gammaridae) of North America." *Biota of Freshwater Ecosystems,* Identification Manual No. 5, Environmental Protection Agency (1972): 17-24.

Web sites:

Amphipoda (Pericarida, Malacostraca). http://www.crustacea.net/crustace/www/amphipod.htm (accessed on March 22, 2005).

The Biology of Amphipods. http://www.mov.vic.gov.au/crust/amphbiol.html (accessed on March 22, 2005).

Endangered Species Bulletin. "Endemic Amphipods in Our Nation's Capital—Brief Article." http://endangered.fws.gov/esb/2002/01-02/toc.html (accessed on March 22, 2005).

Subterranean Amphipod Database. http://web.odu.edu/sci/biology/amphipod/ (accessed on March 22, 2005).

Class: Maxillipoda
Subclass: Thecostraca
Number of families: 48 families

subclass
CHAPTER

PHYSICAL CHARACTERISTICS

Adult barnacles and their relatives have very unusual bodies compared to other crustaceans. In fact, it is only during the free-swimming larval stages that most species are recognizable as crustaceans at all. The first pair of antennae, or antennules (an-TEN-yuls), of the larvae (LAR-vee) is used for grasping. They help the larvae, or young animals, to attach themselves to a host animal or object, their final home as adults. The bodies of the adults are different because of their sessile (SHE-sihl) or parasitic (PAIR-uh-SIH-tik) lifestyles. Sessile barnacles are unable to move because they are permanently attached to other objects, and the parasitic species spend most of their lives feeding inside the bodies of other animals. Most adult barnacles and their relatives have very small heads, lack eyes, and have abdomens with no appendages underneath. The second pair of antennae is usually absent. Thecostraca (thee-koh-STRAH-kay), is divided into three groups: barnacles and their parasitic relatives, ascothoracids, and the y-larvae.

Barnacles are the only group of sessile crustaceans. However, some species are able to move because they attach themselves to animals or floating objects. Adults have white, pink, red, purple, yellow, or brown bodies and live on their heads, upside down, in cone-shaped shells. In most crustaceans, the carapace (CARE-eh-pes) is tough and shieldlike. The carapace of barnacles is soft, sacklike, and called the mantle (MAN-tuhl). The mantle surrounds the body and gives off a substance that forms the cone-shaped shell. The shell is made up of thick, protective

phylum
class
◇ **subclass**
order
monotypic order
suborder
family

plates that join together in the shape of a round or flat cone. The plates are either distinct or tightly joined (fused) together. Inside the mantle is a multi-purpose space, or chamber, where the mouth and reproductive organs are located. It is also where solid waste is released from the barnacle's body. The eggs are kept in this chamber, and the larvae develop there until they are released into the open sea. Adults have a six-segmented thorax with six pairs of cirri (SIH-ree). Cirri are long, bristly, tentaclelike limbs and are either branched or not. They are used together for breathing and like a net to catch bits of food floating in the water. In acorn barnacles, the shell is attached directly to a solid object, but those of gooseneck barnacles are located on top of a soft, flexible stalk. Barnacles without stalks measure up to 9 inches (230 millimeters) in length and 3.1 inches (80 millimeters) across. Stalked species measure up to 27.5 inches (700 millimeters) in length.

There are two small groups of parasitic crustaceans closely related to barnacles. They burrow into corals or into the shells of mollusks (mussels, clams, snails), or they invade the bodies of decapods and isopods. They do not live inside a shell and measure only a few millimeters in length. In one group, the bodies of the adults are completely enclosed inside a folded carapace. Adult females are much larger than the males. The tiny male lives like a parasite and is permanently attached to the female. In the other group, the adults look almost plantlike. They have rootlike bodies that spread out through the tissues of their hosts to soak up nutrients.

The bodies of ascothoracids are completely surrounded by a folded carapace. Their mouthparts are cone-shaped and used to suck the body fluids from their hosts. The thorax has up to six pairs of cirri, and the tip of the abdomen has a pair of appendages.

As their nickname suggests, the y-larvae are y-shaped. They are very small, measuring less than 0.039 inches (1 millimeter) and are free-swimming. The fact that they have grasping antennules and hooked mouthparts suggests that the adults are probably parasites. However, the y-larvae have never been seen clearly associated with their adults.

GEOGRAPHIC RANGE

Barnacles and their relatives are found worldwide in oceans and estuaries (EHS-chew-AIR-eez), where rivers meet the sea.

HABITAT

All thecostracan larvae and some adult males of ascothoracids swim in open water. Adult barnacles are sessile and will usually attach themselves to rocks. They will also attach to other solid objects like shells, floating wood, wharf pilings, ship bottoms, and floating bottles or other trash. Most barnacles live at or just below the seashore, but some prefer living in deep-sea habitats near hot water geysers known as hydrothermal vents. Still others attach themselves to living animals, such as jellyfishes, crabs, other barnacles, sea turtles, sharks, and whales. The adults of parasitic species related to barnacles burrow into corals, the shells of mollusks, or live inside the bodies of other crustaceans. Most ascothoracids live on or inside the bodies of anemones, sea stars, and their relatives.

DIET

Most barnacles eat algae (AL-jee), bacteria, tiny animals, and bits of other organisms floating in the surrounding water. Some stalked species prey on larger floating animals by capturing them with a single limb, or cirrus (SIH-ruhs). Parasitic thecostracans eat the tissues and fluids of their hosts.

BEHAVIOR AND REPRODUCTION

Most barnacles and their relatives can move about freely while they are larvae. Some ascothoracids still have the ability to swim as adults, attaching themselves to objects only temporarily when they are ready to feed. They attach themselves by the front of their heads using glue that comes from special glands in their antennules.

At low tide, barnacles on rocky shores survive out of water by sealing the plates in their shells to keep themselves moist and protected from high temperatures. The larvae are attracted to chemicals produced by the adults and usually settle in large numbers where there are other living or dead barnacles.

Many barnacles and their relatives are hermaphrodites (her-MAE-fro-daits), where individuals have both male and female reproductive organs. In species with both males and females, the male is often much smaller and permanently attached to the female like a parasite. These males seldom feed and lack internal organs, other than those directly involved with reproduction. However, most barnacles require both males and females to reproduce.

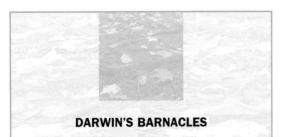

DARWIN'S BARNACLES

Charles Darwin (1809-1882) collected a never-before-seen burrowing barnacle in a conch shell in Chile. In order to classify his discovery properly, Darwin began a careful study of all barnacles, including fossils. In eight years (1846-1854) he wrote four important books on barnacles, representing the first modern studies of the group. Darwin's work with barnacles, earthworms, insect-eating plants, and other organisms helped him to write his most important book, *On The Origin of Species*, in 1859.

The eggs of barnacles and their relatives are brooded inside the chamber in the carapace or mantle. The eggs hatch into free-swimming nauplius (NAH-plee-us) larvae. Nauplius larvae use antennae and mouthparts—the only appendages they have—for swimming. They molt, or shed their external skeletons (exoskeletons), several times before reaching the next larval stage. This stage does not eat, and its body is completely surrounded by a folded carapace.

BARNACLES, THEIR RELATIVES, AND PEOPLE

Native Americans once ate barnacles. Today, the rock barnacle is popular as seafood in parts of South America. Many other barnacles are considered pests. When attached to the bottoms of ships, barnacles can slow their speed by more than one-third. This increases the amount of fuel needed to get from place to place. Much time, money, and effort has been spent on the development of paints that will prevent barnacles from settling on ship bottoms.

CONSERVATION STATUS

Two species of thecostracans—barnacles *Armatobalanus nefrens* and *Balanus aquila*—are listed by the World Conservation Union (IUCN) as Data Deficient. This means there is not enough information to make a judgment about their threat of extinction.

Trypetesa lampas

NO COMMON NAME
Trypetesa lampas

Physical characteristics: *Trypetesa lampas* (abbreviated *T. lampas*) does not have a hard carapace. Females reach 0.78 inches (20 millimeters) in length. Their body is clear or yellowish and covered by a large, folded carapace. There is one pair of small cirri near the mouth and three uniramous (YU-neh-RAY-mus), or unbranched, pairs on the thorax. The tiny, bottle-shaped males have antennae and no other appendages. They measure 0.047 inches (1.2 millimeters).

Geographic range: They are found along the shores of the Pacific and Atlantic oceans north of the Equator.

Habitat: Adult females use the mantle and chemicals to bore into the shells of living or dead snails and hermit crabs.

Adult females use the mantle and chemicals to bore into the shells of living or dead snails and hermit crabs. (Illustration by Jonathan Higgins. Reproduced by permission.)

Diet: Females flex their bodies to suck water carrying food particles inside the mantle.

Behavior and reproduction: Both males and females are required for reproduction. Adult males select and attach themselves to females while they are still in the non-feeding larval stage. Nauplius larvae molt four times before reaching the non-feeding larval stage. This stage has simple eyes and six pairs of thoracic limbs. Each simple eye has one lens and is used to find a suitable place to begin burrowing.

***Trypetesa lampas* and people:** This species does not impact people or their activities.

Conservation status: This species is not considered threatened or endangered. ∎

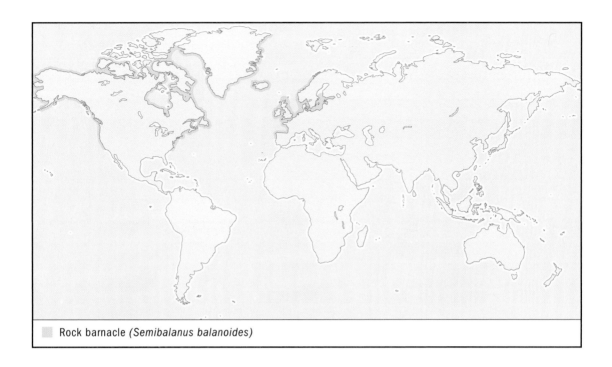

Rock barnacle (*Semibalanus balanoides*)

ROCK BARNACLE
Semibalanus balanoides

Physical characteristics: Rock barnacles measure 0.19 to 0.59 inches (5 to15 millimeters) across. The shell is made up of six gray or white plates that are fused together. Two of the plates form a cover that opens and closes. Through this opening six pairs of biramous (BY-ray-mus), or branched, cirri fan out into the water or can be safely withdrawn inside. Tissue inside this opening is white or pinkish.

Geographic range: Rock barnacles are found in intertidal rocky shores in North America, Europe, and the Arctic.

Habitat: Rock barnacles attach themselves to rocks, pilings, and crabs. They prefer low tide areas sometimes splashed by water.

Diet: They eat bits of food floating in the water.

Behavior and reproduction: Rock barnacles feed only during high tide when the shell is covered by water. Food is collected from the

Rock barnacles attach themselves to rocks, pilings, and crabs. (Dr. Eckart Pott/OKAPIA/Photo Researchers, Inc.)

water by the last three pairs of cirri that form a fan-shaped net. The cirri are extended and withdrawn inside the shell 33 to 37 times a minute as they collect food from the water.

Individuals are hermaphrodites. Eggs are fertilized in the mantle cavity and six thousand to thirteen thousand nauplius larvae develop there. The non-feeding larvae attach themselves to objects using their antennules. Rock barnacles live a total of three to eight years.

Rock barnacles and people: Rock barnacles are studied by scientists interested in learning how animals live and survive in harsh seashore habitats.

Conservation status: This species is not considered threatened or endangered.   ■

FOR MORE INFORMATION

Books:

Anderson, D. T. *Barnacles. Structure, Function, Development and Evolution.* Melbourne, Australia: Chapman and Hall, 1994.

Brusca, R. C., and G. J. Brusca. *Invertebrates.* Second edition. Sunderland, MA: Sinauer Associates Inc., 2003.

Stott, R. *Darwin and the Barnacle: The Story of One Tiny Creature and History's Most Spectacular Scientific Breakthrough.* New York: W. W. Norton & Company, 2003.

Periodicals:

"Earth Almanac. Hot Stuff. Pepper Paint Foils Barnacles." *National Geographic* (May 1994) 185, no. 4.

Starbird, E. A. "Friendless Squatters of the Sea." *National Geographic* (November 1973) 144, no. 5: 623-633.

Web sites:

Barnacles. http://www.old.umassd.edu/public/people/kamaral/thesis/Barnacles.html (accessed on March 21, 2005).

Biology of the Barnacles. http://www.mov.vic.gov.au/crust/barnbiol.html (accessed on March 21, 2005).

Introduction to the Cirripedia—Barnacles and Their Relatives. http://www.ucmp.berkeley.edu/arthropoda/crustacea/maxillopoda/cirripedia.html (accessed on March 21, 2005).

Class: Maxillopoda

Subclass: Tantulocarida

Number of families: 4 families

subclass

CHAPTER

PHYSICAL CHARACTERISTICS

Tantulocaridans (tan-too-loh-KAR-ee-dans) are very strange-looking animals that are external parasites on other deep-sea crustaceans. External parasites spend most of their lives attached to the bodies of their hosts. The larvae (LAR-vee), or young animal form, are very, very small, measuring from 0.00335 to 0.00709 inches (0.0085 to 0.0018 millimeters) in length. The head does not have any appendages, except for a pair of antennae that are present only during one larval stage. The mouthparts are platelike in appearance. The body trunk has six thoracic and two abdominal segments. There are six pairs of thoracic limbs that are used for swimming. The first five pairs are branched, or biramous (BY-ray-mus). The sixth pair is not branched, or uniramous (YU-neh-RAY-mus). The abdomen does not have any appendages underneath, but does have a pair on the very tip.

Adult females come in two distinct forms. Forms that do not mate to reproduce measure up to 0.08 inches (2 millimeters) long and have a small, narrow head with a small projection, or rostrum. They use their suckerlike mouthparts to attach themselves to the external skeletons (exoskeletons) of their hosts. The sacklike thorax is filled with eggs or developing larvae and does not have any limbs. There are no body openings. To escape the sacklike thorax, the larvae must break out through the adult female's body wall.

Females that mate to reproduce are smaller, less than 0.02 inches (0.5 millimeters) in length. Their bodies have two distinct body regions. The head and thorax are tightly joined, or fused, into a single body region called the cephalothorax (SEH-feh-lo-THOR-acks). The cephalothorax has a pair of antennae and a reproductive opening, but does not have any mouthparts. Small numbers of eggs are carried inside the cephalothorax. A five-segmented body follows the cephalothorax. The first two segments of the trunk each have a pair of biramous thoracic limbs that are used for grasping. The fifth and last segment has a pair of long, slender appendages. Adult males are similar in size and appearance to the adult females that mate to reproduce. They have six pairs of biramous limbs used for swimming.

GEOGRAPHIC RANGE

Very little is know about the distribution of these animals because of their small size. They are currently known to live in the North and South Pacific, North and South Atlantic, Arctic, and Antarctic oceans.

HABITAT

Tantulocaridans spend most of their lives attached to other marine crustaceans living on the ocean floor. Their hosts include cumaceans, tanaids, isopods, amphipods, copepods, and ostracods. Some larval stages are also found in mud or sand on the ocean bottom.

DIET

Tantulocaridans are external parasites and feed on the body fluids of their hosts.

BEHAVIOR AND REPRODUCTION

Very little is known about the behavior of tantulocaridans, especially about how they find and attach themselves to their hosts. After leaving their mothers, larvae spend some time burrowing on the sea bottom before attaching themselves to a crustacean living on or near the ocean bottom.

Tantulocaridans have a very strange double life cycle. Part of the life cycle involves sac-shaped females that can produce

FOR TANTULOCARIDANS, LESS IS MORE

Different kinds of parasites often resemble each other. Compared to non-parasites, blood-sucking parasites are usually smaller and have fewer body segments and appendages, if they have appendages at all. Whether the parasite is a tick, louse, or tantulocaridan, small body size reduces its chances of being picked off by an irritated host. And, there is little need to walk, swim, or fly. Once the parasite settles, it's all it can eat, all the time!

larvae without mating. These larvae are released into the sea fully formed and are capable of attaching themselves to a new host. As the larvae develop, they lose all of their thoracic and abdominal segments and become adult females that also reproduce without males. Their now sacklike bodies expand to make room for the eggs and larvae developing inside.

In the life cycle that requires mating, the larvae attach themselves to their host with their mouthparts. As they feed and grow, a sacklike structure begins to grow near the rear of the body. In this sac, the larva will become an adult male or female. Mature adults escape into the sea when the sac breaks open. These males and females have never been observed alive, but it is believed that males are good swimmers and actively search for females. Fertilized eggs are thought to develop inside the expandable cephalothorax of the female.

TANTULOCARIDANS AND PEOPLE

Tantulocaridans do not impact people or their activities.

CONSERVATION STATUS

No tantulocaridans are considered threatened or endangered.

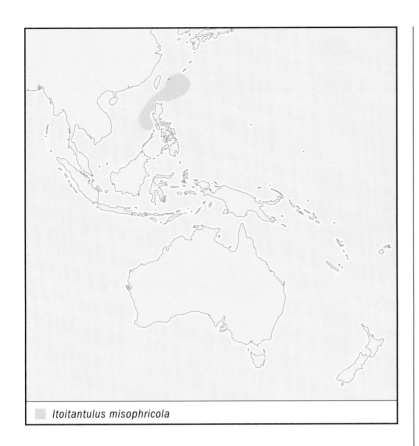

Itoitantulus misophricola

NO COMMON NAME
Itoitantulus misophricola

Physical characteristics: The larvae have long appendages on the tips of their abdomens. The thoracic limbs are used for swimming; the last pair has a long, curved spine on each tip. The sac where adult males or females develop is formed behind the sixth thoracic segment. Males have an unsegmented abdomen with distinct appendages on the tip.

Geographic range: *Itoitantulus misophricola* (abbreviated *I. misophricola*) are found from the southern Japanese island of Okinawa, south to the Philippines.

Habitat: *I. misophricola* are external parasites on copepods living on or near the ocean bottom, at depths of 550 to 6,725 feet (167 to 2,050 meters).

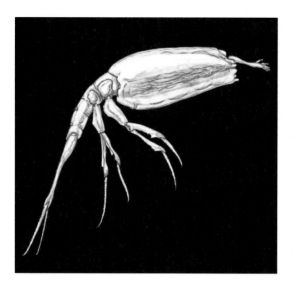

Itoitantulus misophricola *eat the body fluids of certain groups of copepods. (Illustration by Bruce Worden. Reproduced by permission.)*

Diet: *I. misophricola* eat the body fluids of certain groups of copepods.

Behavior and reproduction: Nothing is known about their behavior.

The unusual double life cycle of tantulocaridans was first described in this species.

***Itoitantulus misophricola* and people:** This species does not impact people or their behaviors.

Conservation status: *I. misophricola* is not considered threatened or endangered. ◼

FOR MORE INFORMATION

Periodicals:

Boxshall, G. A., and R. J. Lincoln. "The Life Cycle of the Tantulocarida (Crustacea)." *Philosophical Transactions of the Royal Society of London.* B315 (1987): 267-303.

Huys, R., G. A. Boxshall, and R. J. Lincoln. "The Tantulocaridan Life Cycle: The Circle Closed?" *Journal of Crustacean Biology* 13 (1993): 432-442.

Web sites:

Tantulocarida (Maxillipoda). http://www.crustacea.net/crustace/www/tantuloc.htm (accessed on March 16, 2005).

Class: Maxillopoda
Subclass: Branchiura
Number of families: 1 family

subclass
CHAPTER

PHYSICAL CHARACTERISTICS

Most fish lice are external parasites of freshwater fishes. They live on the outside of the bodies of their hosts and feed on blood and other body fluids. Fish lice are flat, egg-shaped crustaceans and have bodies divided into three regions: head, thorax, and abdomen. A well-developed, shield-like carapace (CARE-eh-pes) covers the head. In some species the carapace covers the sides of the body and legs, and sometimes covers part of the abdomen. The carapace has special organs inside that help the fish louse to digest its food and control the quality of fluids inside the body. The compound eyes are distinct and are not set on stalks. Each compound eye has multiple lenses. Both pairs of antennae are very short and have claws. The claws are used to help them attach to their host. The tubelike mouthparts have jaws, or mandibles, at the tip. The mandibles are used to scrape loose tiny chunks of skin. These bits of tissues, along with body fluids, are sucked into the mouth. A second pair of mandibles, or maxillae (mack-SIH-lee), has spines and claws. There are no maxillipeds (mack-SIH-leh-pehds), or thoracic limbs, that work together with the mouthparts. Instead, all four pairs of branched, or biramous (BY-ray-mus), limbs on the thorax are used for swimming. In males, the third and fourth pairs of limbs are used to transfer sperm to the female during mating. The unsegmented abdomen does not have any appendages underneath. It ends in two, rounded projections, or lobes, separated by a notch.

GEOGRAPHIC RANGE

Fish lice are found in freshwater habitats on all continents.

HABITAT

Fish lice parasitize freshwater fishes. A few species attack fish living along the coast or in estuaries, but they are never found out in the open sea. They are sometimes found on amphibians.

DIET

Fish lice eat the skin and blood of their host.

BEHAVIOR AND REPRODUCTION

Only the behavior of *Argulus* is well known. They use their mandibles to scrape skin into their mouth. They use their needle-like mouthparts to inject chemicals into the host's body. These chemicals may help turn nearby tissues into liquid so that they can be sucked into the mouth.

After taking a meal, mature females leave their hosts to lay eggs. They glue their eggs in rows on hard surfaces and leave them to hatch on their own. The newly hatched larvae (LAR-vee) do not resemble the adults at all. Their antennae, mouthparts, and first two pairs of thoracic limbs are bristly and used for swimming. They grow by molting, or shedding their external skeletons (exoskeletons). After the second molt, fish lice replace the bristles on the antennae with strong claws in preparation for their new lives as parasites. The claws are used to grab on to their first host. As they grow and develop, fish lice will change hosts several times. As the larvae mature, they develop thoracic limbs, sucking mouthparts, and reproductive organs.

Both males and females are required for reproduction. In most species, males transfer their sperm directly to the reproductive organs of the female with their third and fourth pairs of thoracic limbs. In *Dolops*, however, males transfer their sperm inside a packet.

FISH LICE AND PEOPLE

Fish lice are important pests in fish culture facilities. They usually occur in freshwater facilities, but occasionally infest marine fish farms. Aquarium fish may be killed by infestations of fish lice.

CONSERVATION STATUS

No species of fish lice is considered threatened or endangered.

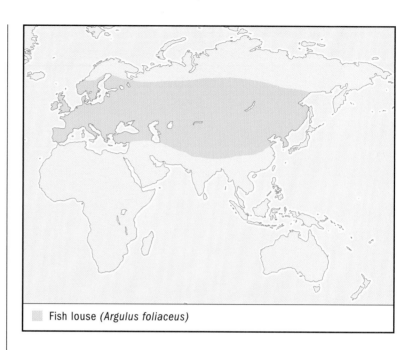

Fish louse (*Argulus foliaceus*)

FISH LOUSE
Argulus foliaceus

Physical characteristics: The abdominal lobes of fish lice are broadly rounded. The notch between the lobes is not very deep and less than half the length of the lobes. The first three pairs of thoracic limbs are dark at their bases. Adult females measure 0.39 inches (10 millimeters) in length, while the males are 0.35 inches (9 millimeters).

Geographic range: They are found in Europe, east to central Asia and Siberia.

Habitat: Fish lice are external parasites on many kinds of freshwater fishes.

Diet: Fish lice eat fish skin and blood.

Behavior and reproduction: After hatching, the larvae swim in open water for two or three days before attaching themselves to a host.

Up to four hundred eggs are laid at a time in two to six rows. The eggs hatch after twenty-five days at temperatures of 59°F

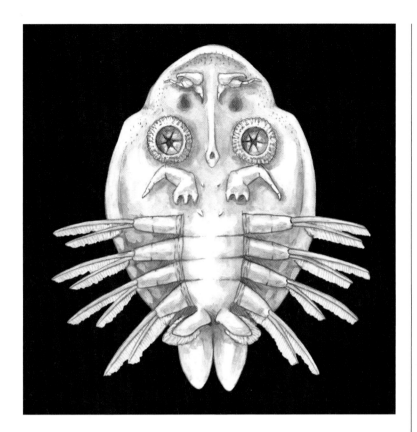

Fish lice are external parasites on many kinds of freshwater fishes. (Illustration by Bruce Worden. Reproduced by permission.)

(15°C). Depending on temperature, the first larval stage lasts about six days, and the animal molts every four to six days until reaching adulthood.

Fish lice and people: They sometimes infest fish hatcheries and aquariums. Their feeding activities spread disease and weaken or kill fish.

Conservation status: Fish lice are not considered threatened or endangered. ■

FOR MORE INFORMATION

Books:

Overstreet, R. M., I. Dyková, and W. E. Hawkins. "Branchiura." In *Microscopic Anatomy of Invertebrates.* Vol. IX, *Crustacea*, edited by F. W. Harrison. New York: J. Wiley and Sons, 1992.

Periodicals:

Gresty, K. A., G. A. Boxshall, and K. Nagasawa. "The Fine Structure and Function of the Cephalic Appendages of the Branchiuran Parasite,

Argulus japonicus Thiele." *Philosophical Transactions of the Royal Society of London* B339 (1993): 119-135.

Web sites:

Arguloidea (Branchiura, Maxillipoda). http://www.crustacea.net/crustace/www/arguloid.htm (accessed on March 16, 2005).

Introduction to Branchiura. Fish Lice! http://www.ucmp.berkeley.edu/arthropoda/crustacea/maxillopoda/branchiura.html (accessed on March 16, 2005).

Class: Maxillopda
Subclass: Mystacocarida
Number of families: 1 family

subclass
CHAPTER

PHYSICAL CHARACTERISTICS

Mystacocarids (my-stah-koh-KAR-ids) are small, wormlike crustaceans that reach up to 0.039 inches (1 millimeter) in length. Nearly one-third of their entire body length is made up of a head that is not covered with a shieldlike carapace (CARE-eh-pes). The eyes are simple and are not set on stalks. Each simple eye has only one lens. The head is sharply narrowed between the pairs of antennae. The first pair of antennae, or antennules (an-TEN-yuhls), is uniramous (YU-neh-RAY-mus), or not branched. The antennules are about half as long as the entire body. The second pair of antennae is branched, or biramous (BY-ray-mus). The jaws, or mandibles, are also biramous, while the second set of mouthparts, or maxillae (mack-SIH-lee), are uniramous. There are long, hairlike structures on the inside margin of the maxillae. The thorax has five segments. The first thoracic segment is not tightly joined, or fused, with the head. It has a pair of biramous limbs called maxillipeds (mack-SIH-leh-pehds). Maxillipeds work together with the mouthparts. Each of the four remaining thoracic segments has a pair of leglike limbs called pereopods (PAIR-ee-oh-pawds). The uniramous pereopods are sometimes used for grasping. The five abdominal segments do not have any appendages underneath. The tip of the abdomen ends in a large taillike segment, or telson. The telson is fused to the last abdominal segment. A well developed bladelike structure is found on either side of the telson.

phylum

class

◇ **subclass**

order

monotypic order

suborder

family

GEOGRAPHIC RANGE

Mystacocarids are found along the coasts of the eastern and western Atlantic, southern South America, western Australia, and the Mediterranean Sea.

HABITAT

Mystacocarids live in the spaces between the grains of sand found along coastal beaches.

DIET

Mystacocarids probably eat algae (AL-jee) and bacteria living on the surfaces of sand grains.

BEHAVIOR AND REPRODUCTION

Mystacocarids use their antennae, mandibles, and slender bodies to burrow through the sand.

Both males and females are required for reproduction, but mating has never been observed by scientists. Females release fertilized eggs into the sand. The hatching larvae (LAR-vee), or young animals, do not resemble the adults. They molt, or shed their external skeletons (exoskeletons), several times, adding body segments and thoracic limbs as they grow.

MYSTACOCARIDS AND PEOPLE

Mystacocarids are of interest to scientists who want to learn more about how crustaceans live and reproduce.

CONSERVATION STATUS

No species of mystacocarids is considered threatened or endangered.

Derocheilocaris typicus

NO COMMON NAME
Derocheilocaris typicus

Physical characteristics: Adults measure less than 0.039 inches (1 millimeter) in length. This species is distinguished by very small differences in the size and shape of their body structures. They also have grooves on the body with edges that resemble teeth. The mouthparts are bristly, and the bladelike structures on the tip of the abdomen are short.

Geographic range: *Derocheilocaris typicus* (abbreviated as *D. typicus*) lives along the Atlantic coast of the United States, from Cape Cod south to southern Florida.

Habitat: This species lives deeply buried in beach sand. They are sometimes found several feet (meters) inland, but still within the zone where the tides keep the sand wet.

Derocheilocaris typicus *use their antennae to crawl between sand grains. (Illustration by Jonathan Higgins. Reproduced by permission.)*

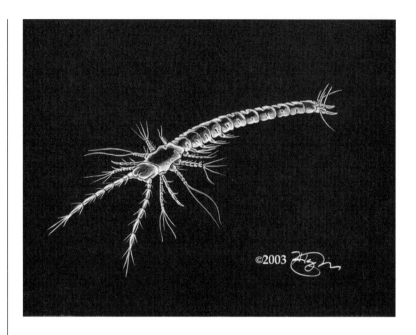

©2003

Diet: They eat small bits of algae and bacteria between or living on the surfaces of sand grains.

Behavior and reproduction: They use their antennae to crawl between sand grains.

Eggs are laid in the sand. The larvae go through seven stages before reaching adulthood. Adults molt once.

***Derocheilocaris typicus* and people:** This was the first mystacocarid ever to be discovered, resulting in the creation of a new order and subclass of crustaceans.

Conservation status: *D. typicus* is not considered endangered or threatened. ▪

FOR MORE INFORMATION

Books:

Brusca, R. C., and J. G. Brusca. *Invertebrates.* Second edition. Sunderland, MA: Sinauer Associates, Inc. 2003.

Periodicals:

Lombardi, J., and E. E. Ruppert. "Functional Morphology of Locomotion in *Derocheilocaris typica* (Crustacea: Mystacocarida)." *Zoomorphology* 100 (1982): 1-10.

Pennak, R. W., and D. J. Zinn. "Mystacocarida, a New Order of Crustacea from Intertidal Beaches in Massachusetts and Connecticut." *Smithsonian Miscellaneous Collections* 103 (1943): 1-11.

Web sites:

Mystacocarida (Maxillopoda). http://www.crustacea.net/crustace/www/mystacoc.htm (accessed on March 17, 2005).

PHYSICAL CHARACTERISTICS

Copepods are usually very small and measure 0.019 to 0.78 inches (0.5 to 20 millimeters) in length. A few free-living species, those that are not parasites, reach 0.7 inches (18 millimeters). Parasitic copepods spend most or all of their lives on or in the bodies of fish and eat their body fluids. Some whale parasites, such as *Pennella balaenopterae*, may grow up to 13 inches (330.2 millimeters).

The copepod body is made up of two regions: the front, or fore body, and the abdomen. Their bodies are distinctly narrowed where these two regions meet. The fore body includes the head and thorax. The head has two pairs of antennae. The first pair of antennae, or antennules (an-TEN-yuls), is not branched, or uniramous (YU-neh-RAY-mus). They are usually very long in most species. The second pair of antennae is either uniramous or biramous (branched). Copepods have a single, simple eye, which have only one lens. Three pairs of appendages make up the mouth, including a pair of biramous jaws, or mandibles.

The first segment of the thorax is tightly joined, or fused to the head. It has a pair of uniramous limbs called maxillipeds (mack-SIH-leh-pehds). The maxillipeds work with the mouthparts. A head shield covers the top of the head and the back of first thoracic segment. The remaining five thoracic segments have four or five pairs of biramous limbs that are used for crawling or swimming. Species living in the open ocean have limbs covered with tiny hairs that prevent them from sinking. Each pair of limbs is joined together at the bases so that they move together. Depending on the group of copepods, the abdomen is either four- or five-segmented. It does not have any appendages underneath. The abdomen ends in a pair of short or long taillike structures. Adult females often have a pair of egg sacs attached to their abdomens.

GEOGRAPHIC RANGE

Copepods are found on every continent, including Antarctica. They also live in all of the world's oceans and seas.

HABITAT

Free-living copepods live in nearly all bodies of water on the planet, including temporary pools and rain puddles. Depending on the species, they are active in open water or live on or in sandy or muddy bottoms. They are often found among plants growing along the seashore. Many species swim near the surface of the ocean, while others are found to depths of 32,814 feet (10,000 meters). A few species are found only in undersea caves, deep-sea coldwater springs, or underwater geysers called hydrothermal vents. Others live in wet sand, mud, or mosses. They are also are found in hot springs and other bodies of freshwater underground and in caves. Some copepods live in extremely salty lakes on land. They have even been found in freshwater lakes on the slopes of the Himalayas at an elevation of 18,175 feet (5,540 meters). About half of all known copepods, many of which are parasites, live on or inside the bodies of sponges, worms, echinoderms, snails, tunicates, fishes, and marine mammals.

DIET

As a group, copepods eat a wide variety of foods. Some species grab tiny organisms, or bits of their tissues, floating in the water. Others are specialists and will eat only tiny algae (AL-jee). Species living on the bottom usually scavenge dead organisms, but some prey on tiny animals. Parasites living on or inside their hosts feed on body tissues and fluids.

BEHAVIOR AND REPRODUCTION

Many free-living copepods gather food from the water by using their antennae and maxillipeds. The swimming movements of these appendages help to create a flow of food-carrying water toward their mouths.

Both male and female copepods are required for reproduction. Males locate females by following their pheromone trails in the water. Pheromones (FEH-re-moans) are chemicals that attract members of the same species. Males place a single sperm packet on the female's abdomen. The sperm escapes the packet, enters the female's body through the opening of her reproductive system, and is stored in special sacs. The fertilized eggs are usually carried in a pair of sacs attached to the abdomen.

The newly hatched nauplius (NAH-plee-us) larva does not resemble the adult. Nauplius larvae do not feed and have only antennae and mouthparts for appendages. They use these appendages for swimming. The nauplius molts, or sheds its external skeleton (exoskeleton), six times before reaching a larval stage that resembles the adult. This stage must molt five times before reaching adulthood. In parasitic species, the development of the nauplius larva is much shorter, if it exists at all.

COPEPODS AND PEOPLE

Copepods are extremely abundant. It is estimated that there are more individual copepods on Earth (1.37×10^{21}) than there are insects. They are a vital link in ocean food chains. They eat floating plants, which are then eaten by all kinds of fish. Many of these fish are harvested from the sea and used as food for people. A few freshwater species that are found in drinking water can spread human parasites known as the guineaworm, *Dracunculus mediensis*. Sealice and other parasitic species are major pests in fish farms. A few species attack marine algae grown as food for people in parts of Asia. But not all of contacts with copepods are bad. Some species are important predators of mosquito larvae. These predatory copepods have been introduced to various parts of the world to stop the spread of deadly malaria, which is carried by the mosquito.

CONSERVATION STATUS

The World Conservation Union (IUCN) lists 108 species of freshwater copepods, all of which are found only in caves or underground springs. Three species are listed as Extinct, or no longer in existence; six are Critically Endangered, or facing extremely high risk of extinction in the wild; 73 are Vulnerable, or facing a high risk of extinction in the wild; six are listed as Lower Risk, or at risk of becoming threatened with extinction in the future, and 20 are listed as Data Deficient, which means there is not enough information to make a judgment about the threat of extinction.

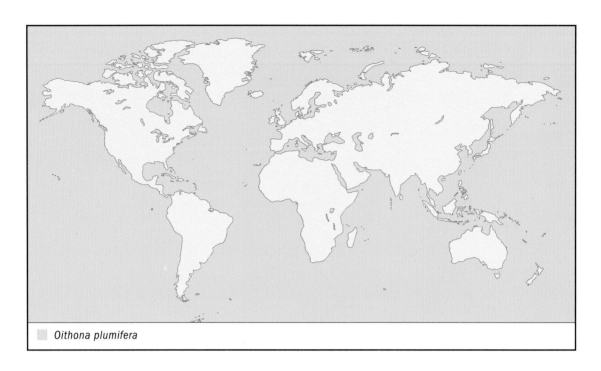

Oithona plumifera

SPECIES ACCOUNTS

NO COMMON NAME
Oithona plumifera

Physical characteristics: Adult females measure 0.039 to 0.059 inches (1 to 1.5 millimeters) in length, while males are 0.029 to 0.039 inches (0.75 to 1 millimeters). The fore body is egg-shaped and has a beaklike projection on the front. The female's antennules have very long hairlike structures, while those of the male are bent. The maxillipeds are well developed. The first four pairs of thoracic limbs are also well developed, but the last pair is small and feathery. Each has a bristle at the base. The abdomen is slender and is nearly equal in length to the fore body.

Geographic range: They are found in all oceans.

Habitat: *Oithona plumifera* live along coastlines and out in the open sea, from the surface down to 328 feet (100 meters).

Diet: They eat bits of tiny plants and animals floating in the water.

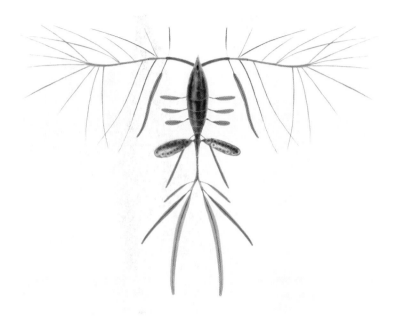

Oithona plumifera *eat bits of tiny plants and animals floating in the water. (Illustration by John Megahan. Reproduced by permission.)*

Behavior and reproduction: Their life cycle consists of six stages of nauplius larvae, followed by five larval stages resembling the adult.

Little is known about their mating behavior. Males and females probably meet in swarms in the water. The male probably grasps the female's fourth pair of thoracic limbs before depositing his sperm packet. The fertilized eggs are stored in a pair of sacs.

***Oithona plumifera* and people:**   *Oithona plumifera* forms an important middle link in the oceanic food web between tiny algae and commercially harvested fishes breeding in estuaries and in coastal waters.

Conservation status: This species is not considered threatened or endangered. ∎

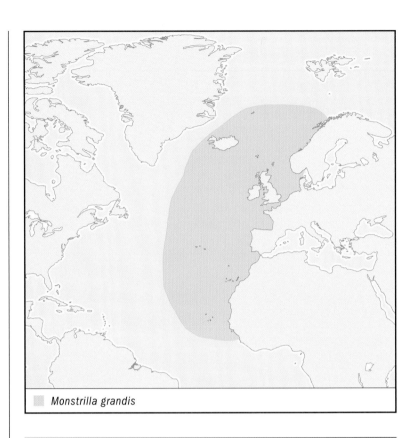

Monstrilla grandis

NO COMMON NAME
Monstrilla grandis

Physical characteristics: Adult females measure 0.147 inches (3.75 millimeters) in length, while males are 0.074 inches (1.9 millimeters). The fore body is long and the mouthparts are absent. The antennules are short in both males and females; those of the males are bent. The first four pairs of thoracic limbs are well developed, but the last pair is small. They are in the shape of two rounded structures, or lobes. The short abdomen has a pair of egg-bearing spines and a pair of large structures on the tip.

Geographic range: This species is found in the Northeastern Atlantic Ocean.

Habitat: The free-living adults live along the coast and are found in the upper layers of water. Parasitic nauplius larvae develop inside the bodies of snails or worms.

Diet: Adults lack mouthparts and do not eat. The nauplius larvae absorb nutrients from their hosts.

Behavior and reproduction: Females carry their eggs on long spines. The eggs hatch into free-living nauplius larvae. The nauplius finds a host and attaches itself with special claws on the antennae and jaws, or mandibles. They eventually burrow through the skin. Once inside, the nauplius becomes sacklike in shape and its appendages rootlike. They use their appendages to soak up nutrients from the host's body. When the last larval stage is reached, the larva leaves the host and molts to become an adult.

Little is known about mating behavior. Males presumably grab females with their antennules and use their swimming limbs to transfer the sperm packet.

***Monstrilla grandis* and people:** This species does not impact people or their activities.

Conservation status: This species is not considered threatened or endangered. ■

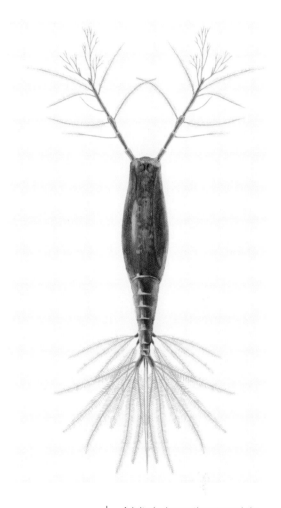

Adults lack mouthparts and do not eat. The nauplius larvae absorb nutrients from their hosts. (Illustration by John Megahan. Reproduced by permission.)

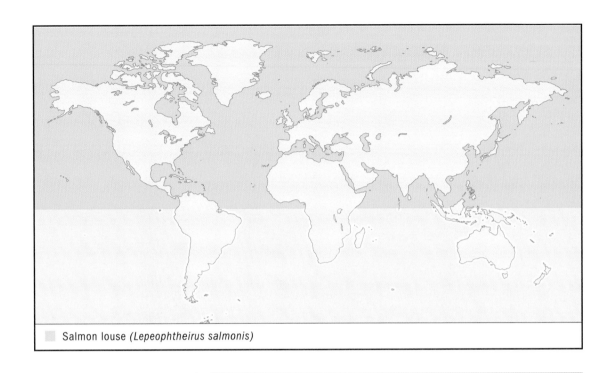

Salmon louse *(Lepeophtheirus salmonis)*

SALMON LOUSE
Lepeophtheirus salmonis

Physical characteristics: Adult females measure 0.27 to 0.49 inches (7 to 12.5 millimeters) in length, while males are 0.17 to 0.26 inches (4.5 to 6.7 millimeters). Their bodies are flat from top to bottom. The antennules of both males and females are short. The clawed antennae and mouthparts are used to grab the skin of their hosts. The mouthparts form a cone-shaped structure. The third pair of thoracic limbs makes an apronlike structure that forms part of a sucker on the fore body. The fourth pair of limbs is uniramous. The abdomen is long and slender.

Geographic range: They are found in the North Atlantic and North Pacific oceans, including Arctic waters.

Habitat: Salmon louse live as external parasites on the bodies of salmon and their relatives living in the sea. They abandon their hosts when they enter freshwaters to reproduce.

Diet: Salmon louse eat the tissue and blood of their host.

Behavior and reproduction: They eat by scraping the salmon skin with the needlelike tips of their mandibles. After a while the wound begins to bleed and they feed on the blood.

The life cycle begins with two free-living nauplius larval stages that do not eat. Each nauplius stage lasts about a day. These are followed by a larval stage that resembles the adult. It is this stage that attacks the salmon host. It can survive up to 10 days without a host. However, its chances of survival are much better if it can find a host in the first 48 hours. Six additional larval stages take place on the host before adulthood is reached. The first four larval stages after the nauplius have a special threadlike structure that helps to keep them firmly attached to the host. The last two larval stages are able to crawl around on the host, just like the adults.

Males locate females while they are in their last larval stage and guard them. Mating only takes place after the female molts and reaches adulthood. Males deposit a pair of sperm packets on the female. Females store the sperm in special sacs inside their bodies until the eggs are laid. They produce several pairs of eggs in strings. Each string has as many as 700 disc-shaped eggs all stacked together.

Salmon louse and people: The feeding activities of salmon lice weakens fishes through the loss of blood and by leaving open wounds that become infected. They are a serious pest in salmon farms in northern Europe and North America, causing losses of up to $30 million per year in Europe alone.

Conservation status: Salmon louse are not considered threatened or endangered. ◼

FOR MORE INFORMATION

Books:

Huys, R., and G.A. Boxshall. *Copepod Evolution.* London: The Ray Society, 1991.

Salmon louse live as external parasites on the bodies of salmon and their relatives. (Illustration by John Megahan. Reproduced by permission.)

Mauchline, J. *The Biology of Calanoid Copepods. Advances in Marine Biology.* New York and London: Academic Press, 1998.

Periodicals:

Reebs, S. "Samples: Fold Three Times and Drink to Prevent Cholera in Rural Bangladesh." *Natural History* 112, no. 4 (May 2003): 16.

Wheeler, M. "Light Element: In the Nose of Jaws. Some Parasitic Copepods Have Seized on a Unique Piece of Real Estate." *Discover* 19, no. 3 (March 1998).

Caloyianis, N. "Greenland Sharks." *National Geographic* 194, no. 3 (September 1998): 60-71.

Web sites:

Calanoida (Copepoda, Maxillipoda). http://www.crustacea.net/crustace/www/calanoid.htm (accessed on March 22, 2005).

subclass

CHAPTER

PHYSICAL CHARACTERISTICS

The bodies of mussel shrimp are completely surrounded by a folded, shieldlike carapace (CARE-eh-pes) that resembles an upside down taco. Depending on the species, the carapace may be smooth, bumpy, pitted, bristly, or spiked. The front of the carapace may or may not have a beaklike projection. The two halves of the carapace are not the same size and one side fits snugly inside the other. They have fewer body segments and appendages than other crustaceans. Most species are 0.08 inches (2 millimeters) or less, but some "giant" species measure 1.26 inches (32 millimeters). Ostracods resemble clam shrimp, but their shells do not have growth rings.

The compound eyes are not set on stalks, if they have eyes at all. Each compound eye has multiple lenses. There are two pairs of antennae and three pairs of mouthparts. The first pair of antennae, the antennules (an-TEN-yuls), is uniramous (YU-neh-RAY-mus), or not branched. The second pair of antennae is branched, or biramous (BY-ray-mus). Adults use their feathery antennae, and sometimes the antennules, for swimming. The thorax and abdomen usually do not have segments and look very similar to each other. There are one to three pairs of biramous limbs. Depending on the species, these limbs are used for walking or cleaning. The tip of the abdomen has a pair of slender or platelike appendages.

GEOGRAPHIC RANGE

Mussel shrimp are found in all oceans and on all continents.

HABITAT

Most species live on the bottom, or near bottom. Some attach themselves to other organisms living on or near the bottom, including other species of crustaceans. One species lives in the gills of fish. Some live in open water, while others are found in very wet moss and leaf litter on land. Some ocean-dwelling species live at depths of 22,965 feet (7,000 meters).

DIET

Most mussel shrimp eat bits of plant material, although some species prey on small animals or scavenge their dead bodies.

BEHAVIOR AND REPRODUCTION

Mussel shrimp have different ways of getting around. Species living on the bottom open their carapace, extend the antennae and limbs, and walk with a rocking motion. Open water species keep their carapaces closed, with just their antennae and limbs poking out. They swim by rowing their appendages through the water.

Both males and females are required for reproduction. Eggs are released into the water or brooded inside the carapace until they hatch. The young hatch as nauplius (NAH-plee-us) larvae (LAR-vee) with folded carapaces covering their bodies. Nauplius larvae have antennae and mouthparts for appendages and use them for walking or swimming. They molt, or shed their external skeletons (exoskeletons), five to eight times before reaching adulthood, adding more appendages with each molt. Mussel shrimp usually live for one year or less.

MUSSEL SHRIMP AND PEOPLE

Scientists use fossil ostracods to help them understand conditions in ancient habitats. Fossils are impressions left by species that died and settled on the mud bottoms of ancient seas. Over millions of years the mud hardens into stone.

CONSERVATION STATUS

No mussel shrimp are considered threatened or endangered by the World Conservation Union (IUCN). However, species living on listed species of freshwater crayfish and isopods could become threatened if their hosts disappear.

Vargula hilgendorfii

NO COMMON NAME
Vargula hilgendorfii

Physical characteristics: This ostracod measures 0.12 inches (3 millimeters) in length. It has a beaklike projection on the front of the smooth, round, clear carapace. The black eyes are visible through the carapace. The carapace has large notches through which the antennae stick out. The appendages at the tip of the abdomen are very large and visible between the folded halves of the carapace.

Geographic range: They are found along the Pacific coast of central Japan.

Habitat: This species is very common in shallow waters with sandy bottoms.

Diet: In captivity they will attack worms, scavenge dead fish, or eat fish food.

Behavior and reproduction: *Vargula hilgendorfii* remain buried just under the surface of the sand during the day. At night they use their

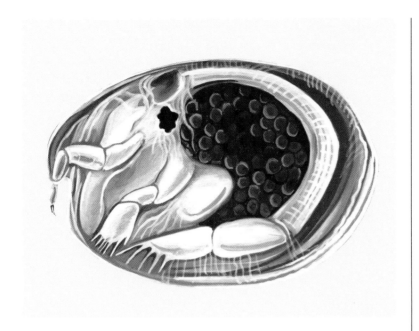

antennae to move across the bottom or swim over the bottom. When threatened they will use the large appendages on the tip of the abdomen to push themselves into the sand. They also use these structures to lift themselves quickly up from the sand and into the water.

Males hold females for about 30 to 60 minutes before mating actually begins. Males transfer a packet of sperm to the female's reproductive organs. Females brood their eggs under the carapace. The larvae molt five times before reaching adulthood. Young larvae are capable of crawling, digging, and swimming.

***Vargula hilgendorfii* and people:** They are eaten by some fish that are caught and used as food for people.

Conservation status: This species is not considered threatened or endangered by the World Conservation Union (IUCN). ∎

FOR MORE INFORMATION

Books:

Benson, R. H., et al. *Treatise on Invertebrate Paleontology, Part Q, Arthropoda 3.* Lawrence, KS: Geological Society of America and University of Kansas Press, 1961.

Periodicals:

Vannier, J., and K. Abe. "Functional Morphology and Behavior of *Vargula hilgendorfii* (Ostracoda: Myodocopida) from Japan, and Discussion of Its Crustacean Ectoparasites: Preliminary Results from Video Recordings." *Journal of Crustacean Biology* 13 (1993): 51-76.

Web sites:

Crustacea, the Higher Taxa. Ostracoda (Maxillipoda. http://www.crustacea .net/crustace/www/ostracod.htm (accessed on March 18, 2005).

IRGO. The International Research Group on Ostracoda. Ostracoda. http://www.uh.edu/rmaddock/IRGO/ostracoda.html (accessed on March 18, 2005).

Recent British Intertidal Ostracoda. http://www.staff.ncl.ac.uk/ ian.boomer/gallery/modern-IT-ostracods.htm (accessed on March 18, 2005).

C H A P T E R

PHYSICAL CHARACTERISTICS

As their common name suggests, many adult pentastomids (pen-tah-STOH-mids) have long, wormlike bodies in the shape of a tongue. They measure up to 5.9 inches (150 millimeters) in length. The head has a small mouth underneath with a hook on each side. The hooks can be withdrawn inside the head. Their long, fluid-filled bodies are ringed, but not segmented. The soft external skeleton (exoskeleton) is whitish or clear. Because they live inside their food and are surrounded by everything they need, tongue worms do not have or need circulatory, respiratory, or excretory systems. They move like a maggot (fly larva), inching along by contracting their muscles and shifting body fluids inside to force the body forward or backward. Adult females are much larger than males and are usually filled with hundreds of thousands to millions of eggs.

GEOGRAPHIC RANGE

Tongue worms are found on all continents, but most species are found in the warmer tropics and subtropics.

HABITAT

Adult tongue worms live in respiratory systems of vertebrates (birds, reptiles, and mammals). The larvae (LAR-vee) of tongue worms develop in the tissues and organs of hosts different from those of the adults. Larval hosts include arthropods, birds, reptiles, and mammals.

■ **phylum**
class
subclass
order
monotypic order
suborder
family

ARE TONGUE WORMS REALLY CRABBY?

For many years, tongue worms were not considered arthropods at all and were placed in a phylum near velvet worms and water bears. Recent studies, based on the structures of the genetic material, sperm, and larvae of tongue worms, show they are crustaceans. They might be related to fish lice, but not all scientists agree. They have been on Earth for 500 million years, long before their modern vertebrate hosts. Ancient fishlike animals may have been their original hosts.

DIET

Both the adults and the larvae of tongue worms are internal parasites. Internal parasites spend most their lives inside other animals, where they eat their tissues and fluids. Most species feed on blood, but tongue worms eat the tissues and linings inside the nose and its sinuses (SIGH-nes-ehs). Sinuses are openings, or channels, inside the head that are connected to the nose.

BEHAVIOR AND REPRODUCTION

Tongue worms usually need to complete their life cycle in more than one host. Larval hosts are called intermediate hosts, while the hosts of adults are called definitive hosts. An intermediate host accidentally swallows the eggs as they eat. The larvae hatch and infect the tissues and organs of the intermediate host. They molt, or shed their exoskeletons, several times before reaching the infective stage of their life cycle. The infective stage is a dormant, or resting, stage, and the larvae are surrounded by a non-living, protective covering called a cyst (sist). The larvae break out of the cyst when another animal, the definitive host, eats the intermediate host and its cysts. In most species, the larvae first burrow into the lining of the intestines or stomach of their definitive host. Later, they move into the body cavity before tunneling into the lung.

Both males and females are required for reproduction. Mating occurs when the males and females are about the same size. Females store the sperm in their bodies. Mated females increase in size as their bodies fill up with developing eggs. Hundreds of thousands to millions of eggs are produced and released continuously. Eggs released in the lungs are coughed up by the definitive host, swallowed, and then passed out of the body with the solid waste. The eggs of species that live in the nose and its sinuses are sneezed out or swallowed and passed out of the body with the solid waste.

TONGUE WORMS AND PEOPLE

Five species of tongue worms are known to infect people. In four of these, people are only an accidental intermediate host.

Human infection with these species is usually the result of eating uncooked snake meat. However, both the larvae and adults of *Linguatula serrata* can infect humans.

CONSERVATION STATUS

No species of tongue worms are considered threatened or endangered.

TONGUE WORM
Linguatula serrata

Physical characteristics: Tongue worms are long, tongue-shaped worms. The males are 0.71 to 0.79 inches (18 to 20 millimeters) in length, while the females are 3.15 to 4.72 inches (80 to 120 millimeters).

Geographic range: They are found worldwide, especially in warm tropical regions. Because they are found throughout the world, no distribution map is provided.

Habitat: Adult tongue worms live in the noses of dogs, foxes, coyotes, wolves, and cats (definitive hosts). They rarely infect people. The larvae infest the tissues and organs of rabbits, horses, goats, and sheep (intermediate hosts).

Diet: Adults eat the tissues and secretions lining the nasal passages and sinuses. The larvae feed on blood and lymph (limf) of the hosts. Lymph is a yellowish body fluid filled with white blood cells.

Behavior and reproduction: Both males and females are required for mating. Males only mate with females that are close to their own size. The bodies of females may contain up to five hundred thousand eggs at a time and can produce several million eggs in their lifetime. Fertilized eggs are sneezed out or swallowed and passed from the body with solid waste. Intermediate hosts, such as rodents, cattle, sheep, and goats, accidentally swallow the eggs with their food. The eggs hatch into four-legged larvae that travel through blood vessels into the lungs and the digestive organs. The larvae must molt six to eight times before they become infective cysts. Definitive hosts, dogs and their relatives, eat the infested flesh. When swallowed, the larvae go directly into the air passages and sinuses associated with the nose inside the head. There they develop into adults.

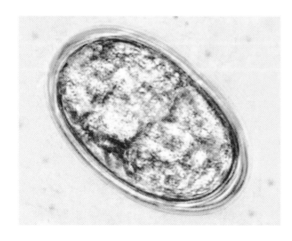

Tongue worms live in the noses of dogs, foxes, coyotes, wolves, and cats. (Illustration by The Gale Group.)

Tongue worms and people: People living in the Middle East, India, Africa, southeast Asia, and the East Indies are sometimes infected with the larvae. Infections are usually the result of eating raw glands of cattle, sheep, and goats that have the larvae. These glands are considered a special treat in these parts of the world. People may not be aware that they have an infestation or suffer from irritation in their nose and throat. Deaths have been reported due to blocked air passages. Larval infestations also occur when the eggs are accidentally swallowed. There is no cure for infestations in dogs or humans, but most single infestations disappear after a year.

Conservation status: Tongue worms are not considered threatened or endangered by the World Conservation Union (IUCN). ■

FOR MORE INFORMATION

Books:

Mehlhorn, H. *Parasitology in Focus.* Berlin: Springer Verlag, 1988.

Periodicals:

Martin, J. W., and G. E. Davis. "An Updated Classification of the Recent Crustacea." *Science Series, Natural History Museum of Los Angeles County* 39 (2001): 1-124.

Riley, J. "The Biology of Pentastomids." *Advances in Parasitology* 25 (1986): 46-128.

Web sites:

Arthropod Oddments. http://www.kendall-bioresearch.co.uk/arthrpod .htm#penta (accessed on March 18, 2005).

External Parasitic Diseases of Dogs and Cats. http://www.ivis.org/ special_books/carter/carter7/chapter_frm.asp?LA=1 (accessed on March 18, 2005).

APLACOPHORANS

Aplacophora

Class: Aplacophora

Number of families: 30 families

PHYSICAL CHARACTERISTICS

Aplacophorans (ah-plak-oh-FOR-ans) are mollusks and are related to clams, mussels, octopuses, and squids. Their worm-shaped bodies range from long and slender to almost ball-shaped and measure between 0.039 and 3.9 inches (1 to 100 millimeters) or more in length. A thick sheet of skin, or mantle, covers their bodies. The mantle makes up the shells, or valves, in most mollusks. However, aplacophorans are the only mollusks that do not have any valves. Instead, their mantles produce sharp, needlelike projections or small, scaly plates that are imbedded in the mantle over the back. These projections and scales make most aplacophorans look shiny. Like the valves of other mollusks, these projections and plates are hard and made up of a mineral called calcium carbonate. The surface of the mantles themselves are smooth, rough, bumpy, or spiny.

The head is poorly developed, and there are no eyes or tentacles. At the back of the mouth of most species is a rough structure called the radula (RAY-jeh-leh). The radula is covered with lots of rows of small teeth. The edges of the teeth are sawlike and made up of even smaller teeth called denticles (DEHN-te-kelz). The radula is used to scrape bits of food off rocks and other hard surfaces. In most mollusks, the radula is ribbonlike in shape but not in aplacophorans. Their radulas are part of their gut. There is a bundle of nerves, or ganglion, inside the head that is attached to a nerve chord that runs along their underside. The body cavity is small. The circulatory system is open, and the blood is not always contained inside blood vessels. There are no kidneylike organs, and there is either one or a pair of reproductive organs.

They do not have a well-developed muscular foot like other mollusks. They move slowly, either with the help of tiny bristles on their bodies called cilia (SIH-lee-uh) or on a track of mucus produced by a groove underneath their bodies. The mucus smoothes the way for the aplacophoran as it glides over the track. At the end of the body is a cavity that has the openings to the reproductive organs and the anus. The anus is the opening at the end of the digestive system where solid waste leaves the body. Breathing organs may or may not be present.

GEOGRAPHIC RANGE

Aplacophorans are found in all oceans.

RADIAL VERSUS BILATERAL

Aplacophorans were first discovered by a Swedish naturalist in 1841. At first they were thought to be related sea cucumbers (Echinodermata). Not until 1875 were they properly recognized as mollusks. Echinoderms have radial symmetry. This means that their bodies are arranged around an imaginary line, or axis, through the center of their bodies; there are no distinct left or right sides. Mollusks, however, have bilateral symmetry. Their bodies always have a left side and a right side.

HABITAT

They are found at depths ranging from 16 to 17,390 feet (5 to 5,300 meters). One group of aplocophorans lives on hydroids, corals, or on the ocean bottom. The other group burrows into the ocean bottom and lives in their tunnels upside down.

DIET

Some species prey on sea anemones, corals, hydroids, sea fans, and their relatives, as well as other organisms. Others are scavengers and swallow sand and mud that contain bits of food.

BEHAVIOR AND REPRODUCTION

Very little is known about the behavior of aplacophorans.

Aplocophorans are either male, female, or hermaphrodites. Hermaphrodites are individual animals that have both male and female reproductive organs at the same time. Depending on the species, the eggs are fertilized in the water or inside the female's body.

APLACOPHORANS AND PEOPLE

Aplacophorans are used by scientists to study the origins of all mollusks.

CONSERVATION STATUS

Aplacophorans are not considered threatened or endangered.

Spiomenia spiculata

NO COMMON NAME
Spiomenia spiculata

Physical characteristics: The curved body is widest at the middle and becomes slightly narrower toward the rear. They are covered with long spines. The longest spines are at the rear of the body. The radula has twenty-two to twenty-five teeth. Each tooth has twenty-two or twenty-three denticles.

Geographic range: They are found in the West European Basin of the Atlantic Ocean.

Habitat: They live on the sea bottom at depths of 6,560 to 13,120 feet (2,000 to 4,000 meters).

Diet: *Spiomenia spiculata* eat diatoms and possibly sponges.

Spiomenia spiculata *is of interest to scientists studying mollusks. (Illustration by Bruce Worden. Reproduced by permission.)*

Behavior and reproduction: Very little is known about their behavior or reproduction, other than that they are hermaphrodites.

***Spiomenia spiculata* and people:** *Spiomenia spiculata* is of interest to scientists studying mollusks.

Conservation status: *Spiomenia spiculata* is not considered threatened or endangered. ■

FOR MORE INFORMATION

Books:

Brusca, Richard C., and Gary J. Brusca. *Invertebrates.* Sunderland, MA: Sinauer Associates, 2003.

Periodicals:

Arnofsky, Pamela. "*Spiomenia spiculata,* Gen. et sp. nov (Aplacophora: Neomeniomorpha) Collected from the Deep Water of the West European Basin." *The Veliger* 43, no. 2 (2000): 110-117.

Web sites:

"Class Aplacophora." http://animaldiversity.ummz.umich.edu/site/accounts/information/Aplacophora.html (accessed on March 30, 2005).

"Shelled Marine Mollusks of Temperate Australia. Interactive Information and Identification." http://www.danceweb.com.au/marine/data/majgrps.htm#top (accessed on March 30, 2005).

Welcome to the Aplacophora Homepage. http://www.whoi.edu/science/B/aplacophora/ (accessed on March 30, 2005).

Class: Monoplacophora
Number of families: 1 family

class
CHAPTER

phylum
● **class**
subclass
order
monotypic order
suborder
family

PHYSICAL CHARACTERISTICS

Monoplacophorans (mon-oh-plak-oh-FOR-ans) look like limpets, but their single round shell, or valve, is bilaterally symmetrical. This means that the valve has a distinct left side and a distinct right side. The point of the valve is located in the middle, just over the front edge. Depending on the species, the caplike valve varies from flat and shieldlike to a short, squat cone. The valve is mostly thin but becomes slightly thicker toward the edges. They measure 0.25 to 1.25 inches (3 to 30 millimeters) in length.

The head is small but distinct. There are no eyes, and the only tentacles are found next to the mouth. Behind the mouth is a round, muscular foot. The foot is located on the end of a short column and is not very strong. It is surrounded by a small groove called the mantle cavity. The mantle cavity has five or six pairs of gills used for breathing and separates the foot from the fleshy mantle. The mantle produces the mineral calcium carbonate that makes up the valve. There are three to seven pairs of kidneylike organs. Males and females have a pair of reproductive organs. The anus is located opposite the head at the end of the digestive system. The anus is the opening where solid waste leaves the body.

GEOGRAPHIC RANGE

They are found in the South Atlantic Ocean, Gulf of Aden, and several places in the eastern Pacific Ocean.

MONOPLACOPHORANS IN THE FLESH

Monoplacophorans were once only known from fossils. These stone impressions preserved only the details of the hard valves of these ancient species, not their soft bodies. In 1952, a Danish expedition named "Galathea" dredged up ten living specimens from the deep waters off the Pacific coast of Mexico. Their never-seen-before fleshy bodies revealed the similarities of monoplacophorans to chitons and snails. The new species was given the name *Neopilina galathea*. *Neopilina* comes from the Greek *neos*, or new, and *pilion*, or little cap.

HABITAT

Monoplacophorans live on deep-sea bottoms at depths between 624 to 22,980 feet (190 to 7,000 meters). They are found attached to rocks and solid objects.

DIET

Monoplacophorans feed on bits of plants, animals, and other organisms.

BEHAVIOR AND REPRODUCTION

Nothing is known about their behavior.

Both males and females are required for reproduction. There are not any differences on the outside of their bodies to distinguish males and females. The eggs are thought to be fertilized in water, outside of the female's body.

MONOPLACOPHORANS AND PEOPLE

Scientist studying the origins of mollusks or how animals adapt to deep-sea life use monoplacophorans as research subjects.

CONSERVATION STATUS

No monoplacophorans are considered threatened or endangered.

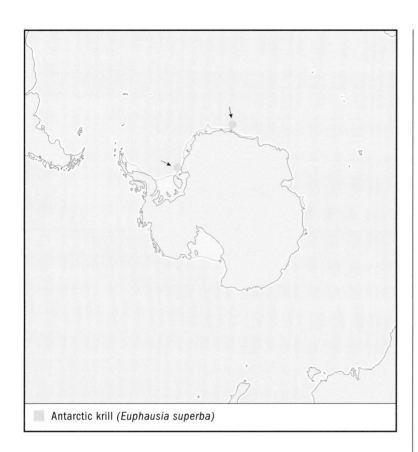

Antarctic krill *(Euphausia superba)*

NO COMMON NAME
Laevipilina antarctica

Physical characteristics: The transparent valve is small, thin, and somewhat flat. The point on the valve is shaped like a nipple. The surface of the valve near the point is fairly smooth but becomes more ridged toward the margins. The tentacles are short, swollen at their tips, and have approximately seven short and thick appendages. The mantle cavity has five pairs of gills. The foot measures 0.06 by 0.04 inches (1.5 by 0.9 millimeters) across when it is not expanded.

Geographic range: They are found in the Weddell and Lazarev Seas, off the coast of Antarctica.

Habitat: They live attached to rocks and old shells on sea bottoms at depths of 690 to 2,100 feet (210 to 644 meters).

Laevipilina antarctica *are found in the Weddell and Lazarev Seas, off the coast of Antarctica. (Illustration by Bruce Worden. Reproduced by permission.)*

Diet: They scrape up bits of minerals, plants, animals, and other organisms that settle on the sea bottom.

Behavior and reproduction: Nothing is known about their behavior or reproduction.

***Laevipilina antarctica* and people:** They are studied by scientists.

Conservation status: *Laevipilina antarctica* is not considered threatened or endangered. ■

FOR MORE INFORMATION

Books:

Brusca, Richard C., and Gary J. Brusca. *Invertebrates.* Sunderland, MA: Sinauer Associates, 2003.

Periodicals:

Warén, A., and S. Hain. "*Laevipilina antarctica* and *Micropilina arntzi:* Two New Monoplacophorans from the Antarctic." *The Veliger* 35 (1992): 165-176.

Web sites:

"Class Monoplacophora." http://animaldiversity.ummz.umich.edu/site/accounts/information/Monoplacophora.html (accessed on March 30, 2005).

"Class Monoplacophora." *FactMonster* http://www.factmonster.com/ce6/sci/A0859721.html (accessed on March 30, 2005).

"Monoplacophora." http://www.biologydaily.com/biology/Monoplacophora (accessed on March 30, 2005).

"Shelled Marine Mollusks of Temperate Australia. Interactive Information and Identification." http://www.danceweb.com.au/marine/data/majgrps.htm#mono (accessed on March 30, 2005).

"*Neopilina*. A living fossil." http://www.weichtiere.at/Mollusks/Andere/neopilina.html (accessed on March 30, 2005).

Class: Polyplacophora
Number of families: 10 families

class

CHAPTER

PHYSICAL CHARACTERISTICS

Chitons (KI-tons) are flattened mollusks that are egg-shaped in outline. They have eight distinct and overlapping shell plates, or valves, across their backs. The valves are layered, with each layer made up of mostly calcium carbonate. Each valve is usually shaped like a butterfly. A ring of tissue surrounds or sometimes covers the entire body. This tissue is the margin of the mantle. As in other mollusks, the mantle produces the valves. Because the chiton mantle is stiff and surrounds the body, it is referred to as a girdle. Depending on the species, the surface of the chiton's body may be covered with scales, bristles, or small spines.

The underside of the body is made up of a broad, muscular foot. On the sides of the body, the foot and girdle are separated by a special groove. Inside the groove are gills that help the chiton to breathe underwater. Oxygen-carrying water enters the grooves near the head, flows through the gills, and exits at the rear of the body. As the water exits this system, it carries away waste products released from the anus. The anus is the opening at the end of the digestive tract through which solid waste leaves the body. The water also flushes away liquid waste produced by the chiton's two large kidneylike organs. These kidney-like organs remove waste from the blood found inside the body cavity.

The adult chiton head is not distinct and does not have any eyes or tentacles. The mouthparts are made up of the radula. The radula is a long, beltlike structure with seventeen bands of curved teeth. The teeth are very hard. In some species, the teeth are covered with a material that contains iron.

GEOGRAPHIC RANGE

Chitons are found along seashores worldwide but are most common in cooler waters.

HABITAT

Chitons live on hard surfaces, especially rocks. They are found from the seashore to depths of more than 13,123 feet (4,000 meters).

DIET

Chitons eat many kinds of algae (AL-jee). *Placiphorella velata* preys on worms and small crustaceans.

BEHAVIOR AND REPRODUCTION

Most chitons feed by scraping food off rocks with their radula. Others eat large species of algae, such as kelp. Predatory species use a special flap on the mantle near their head to capture small animals. Most species usually feed at night. Species living along the shore remain in one place when exposed to the air by low tides.

Chitons have few defenses. If pulled off their rocks, some species will roll up like a pillbug. This motion also helps them to right themselves. Some species will return to the same spot on a rock after they forage for food, while others continue to move on as they feed.

Both male and female chitons are usually required for reproduction. Males always release their sperm into the sea. The sperm is carried on the ocean currents to the eggs. Depending on the species, females either release their eggs singly or in strings into the water or keep them inside the special groove that separates the girdle and muscular foot. Eggs fertilized in the water usually develop into free-swimming, unsegmented larvae (LAR-vee) covered with tiny, hair-like structures called cilia (SIH-lee-uh). Eggs that develop inside the groove remain with the adult female until they become well-developed young chitons.

WHERE IS THE BEST PLACE TO FIND CHITONS?

Roughly half of the approximately one thousand species of chitons live near coastlines. And, more kinds of chitons live along the eastern shores of the Pacific Ocean than anywhere else. About one-fifth of all the world's species live on or near the coastline that runs from Alaska south to Southern California.

CHITONS AND PEOPLE

Native Americans living along the Pacific Coast of North America used to eat the gumboot chiton, *Cryptochiton stelleri*. The remains of their valves are commonly found in their ancient trash heaps.

CONSERVATION STATUS

No species of chiton is considered threatened or endangered.

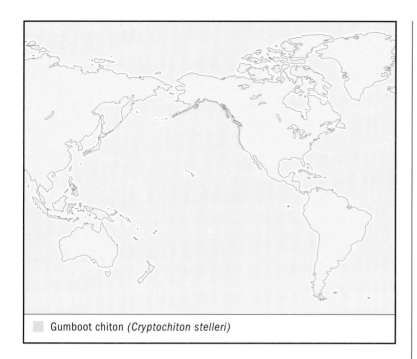

Gumboot chiton *(Cryptochiton stelleri)*

GUMBOOT CHITON
Cryptochiton stelleri

Physical characteristics:　This is the largest chiton in the world, measuring up to 13 inches (330 millimeters) in length and 5 inches (130 millimeters) across. It resembles a brick-red meatloaf. Its large size and color distinguish this species from other chitons. The leathery and reddish mantle wraps around the entire body and hides all of the valves. It is covered with bundles of tiny spines.

Geographic range:　Gumboot chitons are found from the Aleutian Islands in Alaska, south to San Miguel and San Nicolas Islands off the coast of southern California. They are also found in northern Hokkaido Island, Japan, and the Kurile Islands in Kamchatka, Russia.

Habitat:　This species lives on rocky shorelines and soft bottoms in protected habitats near deep channels at depths of 70 feet (21.3 meters).

Diet:　They eat several kinds of algae, including giant kelp, sea lettuce, and red algae.

This is the largest chiton in the world, measuring up to 13 inches (330 millimeters) in length and 5 inches (130 millimeters) across. (Al Lowry/Photo Researchers, Inc.)

Behavior and reproduction: This species grows very slowly and lives as long as twenty years. They have a weak grip and often fall from their rocks at low tide. They do not live in groups and move very slowly. Captured individuals have remained within 65.6 feet (20 meters) of their release point, even after two years.

California populations reproduce between March and May. The reddish eggs are laid in jelly-like spiral strings measuring up to 3.3 feet (1 meter) in length. The strings are broken up into smaller pieces by ocean waves. The eggs hatch about five days after they are fertilized. The free-swimming larval stage lasts about twenty hours. Then they settle to the bottom and develop into young chitons.

Gumboot chitons and people: This species was eaten by Native Americans living along the Pacific Coast of North America.

Conservation status: Gumboot chitons are not considered threatened or endangered. ■

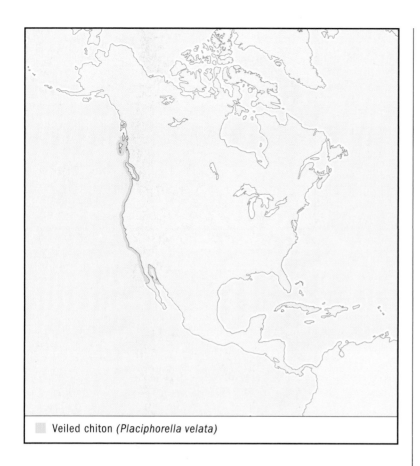

Veiled chiton (*Placiphorella velata*)

VEILED CHITON
Placiphorella velata

Physical characteristics: This species is distinguished by the girdle around the margins of shell valves, which is greatly expanded toward the front to form a "head flap." The girdle is red and green underneath. The body is up to 1.9 inches (5 centimeters) long, with brown to red shell valves that are short and wide and variously mottled and streaked with green, beige, white, and brown.

Geographic range: Although uncommon, the veiled chiton is found from Forrester Island (Alaska) to Isla Cedros (Baja California) and the upper Gulf of California.

Although uncommon, the veiled chiton is found from Forrester Island (Alaska) to Isla Cedros (Baja California) and the upper Gulf of California. (© Phillip Colla/SeaPics.com)

Habitat: This species lives in rocky depressions and crevices or under stones. They are found from the lower levels of shorelines affected by tidal action to a depth of 50 feet (15.2 meters).

Diet: They scrape algae off rocks or capture small worms and crustaceans.

Behavior and reproduction: This species belongs to the only group of predatory chitons. Like other chitons, this species moves very slowly, but it uses a special flap on the girdle near the head to capture small animals.

California populations reproduce in September.

Veiled chitons and people: This species is not known to impact people or their activities.

Conservation status: Veiled chitons are not considered threatened or endangered. ■

FOR MORE INFORMATION

Books:

Meinkoth, N. A. *The Audubon Society Field Guide to North American Seashore Creatures.* New York: Alfred A. Knopf, 1992.

Pearse, V., J. Pearse, M. Buchsbaum, and R. Buchsbaum. *Living Invertebrates.* Boston, MA: Blackwell Scientific Publications, 1997.

Slieker, F. J. *Chitons of the World.* Ancona, Italy: L'Informatore, 2000.

Web sites:

Worldwide Chitons! http://biology.fullerton.edu/deernisse/chitons/ (accessed on April 27, 2005).

Welcome to Chitons.com. http://home.inreach.com/burghart/chitons-welcome.htm (accessed on April 27, 2005).

Class: Gastropoda

Number of families: about 355
families

class

phylum

● **class**

subclass

order

monotypic order

suborder

family

PHYSICAL CHARACTERISTICS

The most conspicuous feature of many gastropods is the shell. Although sometimes flattened and caplike, most shells are cone-shaped shelters into which they can completely withdraw their bodies. The single, lopsided shells are usually made up of spiraled tubes called whorls (worlz). The shells are lopsided because whorls form below one another, instead of around each other. In spite of the fact that they are lopsided, the shell is carried over the back so that its weight is evenly balanced over the body. But not all gastropods have lopsided shells. In sea snails, known as cowries, the last whorl completely covers all the others and appears to be symmetrical. The left and right sides of symmetrical objects are the same size and shape, giving them a balanced, rather than lopsided, look. Young limpets have a distinctly lopsided and coiled shell, but as they develop into adults, the shell becomes smooth and symmetrical, resembling a Chinese hat.

The whorls form around a central line, or axis. Inside the shell, the whorls turn around a central column of shell called the columella (kol-yuh-MEL-uh). The smallest whorls are the oldest and were made while the gastropod was still in the larval stage. The last and largest whorl is the newest and ends at the opening of the shell, where the head and foot stick out. The spiraled stack of whorls above the opening is called the spire. If the whorls develop counterclockwise, the shell is said to be left-handed, while clockwise whorls are right-handed. To determine if a shell is left- or right-handed, stand the shell up so that the spire is pointed up and the opening faces toward you. If the shell opens to the right of the spire, it is said to be right-handed; if the opening is on the left, it is left-handed. Most gastropods have right-handed shells, while some species are left-handed. A few species have individuals that are either right- or left-handed. Some marine and land snails have a flat, horny disc above the back of their foot called the operculum (o-PUHR-kye-lem). The operculum is usually made of the same tough material that covers the outside of the shell. When the head and foot are withdrawn into the shell, the operculum follows to form a tight cover over the shell's opening.

In species with shieldlike shells, such as keyhole limpets and abalones, there is a notch of one or more holes in the shell that allow a current of oxygen-carrying water to reach the body and eggs, sperm, and wastes to be carried away. These animals live on rocks in the pounding surf, and their low shells and muscular feet help to keep them from being knocked off and washed away by the tides.

Gastropod shells, if present at all, come in a wide array of colors, patterns, and surface sculptures. The surface of the shell is sometimes pearly or has a highly polished, porcelainlike quality. A thin or thick covering usually protects the outer part of the shell. The shells of cowries lack this protective coating and are instead covered by the mantle. In sea slugs, the shell is small, thin, and found either inside or outside the body, if there is a shell at all. The mantle is the fleshy organ located between the body and the shell. It makes the shell by producing a hard mineral called calcium carbonate.

Like other mollusks, the bodies of gastropods are soft and fleshy. The bodies of sea slugs are often brilliantly colored and patterned and sometimes covered with fleshy, stinging outgrowths. In snails, the head and foot are withdrawn into the shell by a powerful muscle that is attached inside to the columella. The heads of all gastropods are more distinctive than in most other mollusks and may or may not have eyes and one or two pairs of tentacles. The mouthparts include a radula (RAE-jeh-leh). The radula is a tonguelike structure with rows of extremely hard teeth that are used to scrape food off rocks or pull and tear at flesh. The muscular foot has been changed in some groups to help with swimming or burrowing. The mantle forms a cavity that lies in front or to the right of the muscular foot. Inside the mantle cavity is a comblike gill used for breathing. The digestive tract is u-shaped. Both it and the nervous system are twisted. Gasropods have one or two kidney-like organs that filter out wastes from the blood. These organs, along with the anus, open into the mantle cavity above or near the head. The anus is the opening at the end of the digestive tract where solid wastes leave the body.

GEOGRAPHIC RANGE

Gastropods are found on all continents and in all oceans.

HABITAT

Gastropods live in a wide variety of habitats in the ocean, on land, and in bodies of fresh water.

DIET

Gastropods eat many kinds of foods. Some species filter out bits of plants, animals, and other organisms floating in the water. Many scrape algae (AL-jee) or crustlike animals off rocks in tide pools and elsewhere on the ocean bottom. Others prey on all kinds of freshwater or marine animals. Most species living on land eat both living and dead plants. Some land snails prey on earthworms or other snails.

BEHAVIOR AND REPRODUCTION

Like most animals, gastropods must feed, fight, flee, and mate. To do all this they have developed many different behaviors. Most species sense their world through the presence of certain kinds of chemicals produced by their foods and other members of their own species. Aquatic species regularly move up and down in the water at certain times of the day in search of food and mates. Depending on the species, they may become active during the day or at night, whenever they are least likely to be attacked by predators.

Gastropods usually require both males and females to reproduce, although some species are hermaphroditic (her-MAE-fro-DIH-tik). Hermaphroditic individuals either have the reproductive organs of both sexes at the same time or start out as males and later become females. In most species, the males transfer sperm, or packets of sperm, directly into the female's reproductive system. The sperm is stored in a special sac. Fertilization takes place only when the eggs are laid. The eggs are laid or released individually or in groups. The eggs of species living in water usually hatch into larvae (LAR-vee) known as veligers (VEL-ih-jerz). The veliger has a special, round feeding organ lined with hairlike cilia (SIH-lee-uh) that it also uses for swimming. It also has a foot, shell, and other adult features. During this stage a single, powerful muscle, usually permanently twists the body and shell, if present. In some snails, including those living on land, the veliger stage takes place inside the egg, which then hatches into a tiny version of the adult.

GASTROPODS AND PEOPLE

For centuries, gastropod shells, especially cowries, have been used as money. The flesh of some gastropods, especially the muscular foot, is often considered a very tasty treat. People also use the shells of some gastropods to create works of art, as well as bowls, fishhooks, buttons, beads, and other forms of jewelry. Shell collecting has been popular for centuries, with some species commanding high prices.

CONSERVATION STATUS

One thousand one hundred eighty-two (1,182) species of gastropods are listed by the World Conservation Union (IUCN) as threatened or endangered.

GASTROPODS DO THE TWIST

Gastropods are the only animals that twist as they develop. The mantle and body of the veliger rotates 90° to 180° in relation to the foot. This rotation twists the digestive tract into a u-shape and turns part of the nervous system into an imperfect figure eight. The twisting of the body and its developing shell is referred to as torsion (TOR-shen). Torsion in gastropods is caused by the uneven pull of a single muscle inside the body.

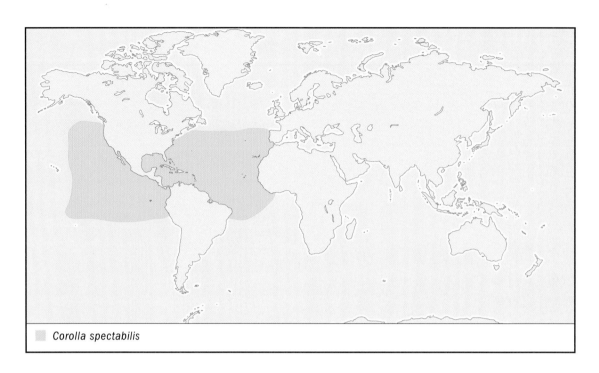

Corolla spectabilis

NO COMMON NAME
Corolla spectabilis

Physical characteristics: The body of this small, jellylike species is transparent. The dark contents of its digestive tract are clearly visible from the outside. It does not have a shell. Large, winglike plates stick out from the sides of the body. Adults measure up to 3 inches (80 millimeters) long, while the wing plates span 6 inches (160 millimeters) across.

Geographic range: This species is found in the Atlantic and Pacific Oceans, between the latitudes of 40° North and 5° South.

Habitat: This species is found near the surface of the open sea.

Diet: *Corolla spectabilis* eats tiny animals floating in the water.

Behavior and reproduction: *Corolla spectabilis* sometimes live in large numbers at the water's surface. Food is captured with sheets of a sticky material made by special glands along the edges of the wings. When frightened they can swim away very quickly.

The species is hermaphroditic. Adults mature as males and then later become females. Their mating behavior is unknown. Eggs are produced in long, sticky strings measuring up to 1.6 feet (0.5 meters) long.

Corolla spectabilis and people: This species is not known to impact people or their activities.

Conservation status: This species is not considered threatened or endangered. ▪

Roman snail (*Helix pomatia*)

ROMAN SNAIL
Helix pomatia

Physical characteristics: This species is the largest snail in Europe. Its ball-like shell is creamy white with spirals of brown bands. It measures up to 2 inches (50 millimeters) across. The body is gray with paler bumps.

Geographic range: Originally from Central and Southern Europe, this species now also lives in the United Kingdom, Scandinavia, and Spain.

Habitat: They live in woods, hedges, and weeds up to elevations of 6,500 feet (2,000 meters).

Diet: This species eats living plants.

The roman snail is the largest snail in Europe. (Illustration by Patricia Ferrer. Reproduced by permission.)

Behavior and reproduction: Roman snails hibernate in shallow holes during the winter. They have the ability to forage as far as 150 to 300 feet (50 to 100 meters) and still find their way back.

Males and females have elaborate courtship behavior lasting several hours. Batches of up to forty eggs are laid in the ground during the spring and summer. They take from three to five weeks to hatch. Snails reach adulthood in three or four years and live up to ten years.

Roman snails and people: They are eaten by people, especially in France, but are considered pests on grapes grown to make wine.

Conservation status: Roman snails are not considered threatened or endangered. ∎

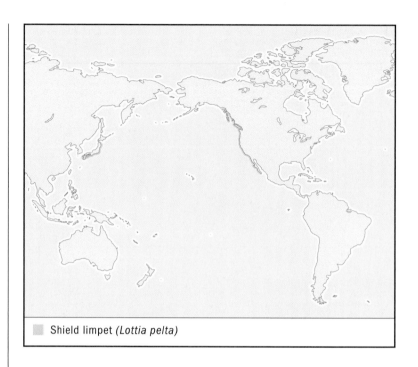

Shield limpet (*Lottia pelta*)

SHIELD LIMPET
Lottia pelta

Physical characteristics: The surface of the hatlike shell has fine growth rings and ribs radiating out from the center like spokes on a wheel, with a high point slightly toward the front. The color varies from blue black to light brown, with or without white markings. Adult shells reach up to 2.3 inches (60 millimeters) across.

Geographic range: They are found in the Northern Pacific Ocean, from Honshu, Japan, across to Baja California, Mexico.

Habitat: They live along rocky coastlines, in the middle of the area affected by high and low tides.

Diet: Shiled limpets eat a variety of kinds of algae.

Behavior and reproduction: This species is active at night. The color and surface texture of individual shells gradually change as the limpet moves onto different surfaces.

Males and females larger than 0.39 inches (10 millimeters) reproduce in spring. Smaller individuals, as well as those living in the water just beyond the tide action, reproduce throughout the year. Eggs and sperm are released into the water where fertilization takes place.

Shield limpets and people: This species was once an important food source for ancient peoples living along the coast.

Conservation status: Shield limpets are not considered threatened or endangered. ■

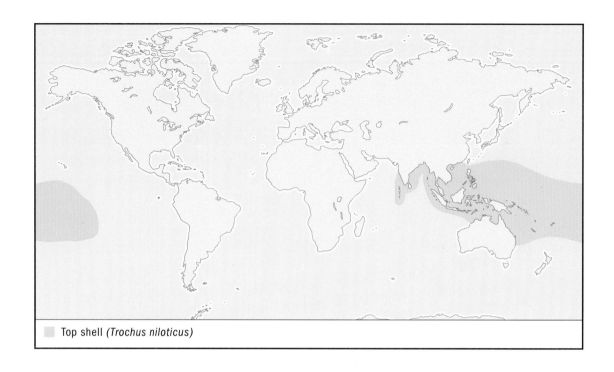

Top shell (*Trochus niloticus*)

TOP SHELL
Trochus niloticus

Physical characteristics: This species has a large, cone-shaped shell with a wide base measuring 1.6 to 3.9 inches (40 to 100 millimeters) in height. The shell is marked with wavy, purplish pink lines These markings are sometimes covered by crustlike growths of algae.

Geographic range: This species is found in the warm, tropical waters of the Indo-Pacific.

Habitat: They live on coral reefs and in lagoons.

Diet: This species eats threadlike algae and diatoms.

Behavior and reproduction: Top shells are active at night.

Eggs and sperm are united in the water, where the produced larvae spend only a brief period of time.

Top shells and people: The flesh is eaten, and the shells are used for decoration.

Conservation status: Top shells are not considered threatened or endangered. ▪

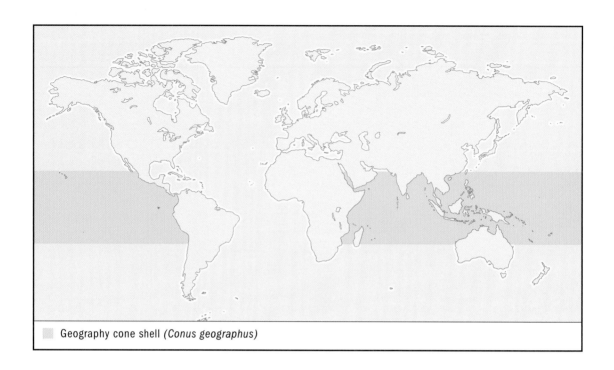

Geography cone shell *(Conus geographus)*

GEOGRAPHY CONE SHELL
Conus geographus

Physical characteristics: The shell spire is flat with knobby whorls. The shell opening is long and slightly expanded toward the front. The outer surface is marked with light, gold brown markings.

Geographic range: This species is found in the warm, tropical waters of the Indo-Pacific.

Habitat: They live around coral reefs, in sand, and on chunks of broken reefs.

Diet: They eat fishes, worms, and other snails.

Behavior and reproduction: They hunt at night. The radula has a few poison-injecting teeth that are used like harpoons and shot from the end of a long, trunklike proboscis. Fishes and other prey are hooked by the teeth and then pulled in.

The eggs are fertilized inside the female's body.

Grzimek's Student Animal Life Resource

Geography cone shells and people: The venom from their bite is very toxic and can be fatal.

Conservation status: Geography cone shells are not considered threatened or endangered. ■

FOR MORE INFORMATION

Books:

Brusca, Richard C., and Gary J. Brusca. *Invertebrates.* Sunderland, MA: Sinauer Associates, 2003.

Gordon, D. G. *Field Guide to the Slug.* Seattle, WA: Sasquatch Books, 1994.

Meinkoth, N. A. *National Audubon Society Field Guide to North American Sea Shore Creatures.* New York: Alfred A. Knopf, 1981.

Periodicals:

Davidson, T. "Tree Snails. Gems of the Everglades." *National Geographic* (March 1967): 372-387.

Hamner, W. M. "Blue-water Plankton." *National Geographic* (October 1974): 530-545.

Web sites:

"Abalone." http://seafood.ucdavis.edu/pubs/abalone.htm (accessed on May 2, 2005).

"Class Gastropoda (Gastropods, Slugs, and Snails)." http://animaldiversity.ummz.umich.edu/site/accounts/information/Gastropoda.html (accessed on May 2, 2005).

"Gastropods." http://www.mesa.edu.au/friends/seashores/gastropods.html (accessed on May 2, 2005).

Hardy's Internet Guide to Marine Gastropods. http://www.gastropods.com/ (accessed on May 2, 2005).

BIVALVES
Bivalvia

Class: Bivalvia

Number of families: 105 families

class

CHAPTER

phylum

class

subclass

order

monotypic order

suborder

family

PHYSICAL CHARACTERISTICS

Bivalves have bodies that are flattened from side to side and completely surrounded by two shells called valves. Each valve is made up of a hard mineral called calcium carbonate and is joined to the other by a hinge on the back. Interlocking teeth or sockets form the hinge on the valves, which are then held together by an elastic ligament or fiberlike tissue made up mostly of protein. Powerful muscles contract ligaments to keep the valves closed and relax to open them. The bulge near the hinge is called the umbo and is the oldest part of the shell. The ridges that form around the umbo trace the growth of the valve. The valves are usually similar to one another in size, shape, color, and texture. The outer surface is usually plain, but some species have distinctive colors and patterns.

Inside the valves is the body surrounded by the mantle. The mantle makes the calcium carbonate that forms the valves. In some bivalves, the rear edge of the mantle forms special tubelike openings called siphons (SAI-fens), which take in water carrying bits of food and expel waste, eggs, and sperm into the water. The mantle holds digestive and reproductive organs and a muscular foot. The inside lining of the stomach is tough enough to grind up food. The foot can stretch outward and attach the bivalve to rocks, wood, and other hard surfaces. The very small head lacks the eyes, tentacles, and radula found in most other mollusks. The radula (RAE-jeh-leh) is part of the mouth that is thick or ribbonlike and has rows of teeth. Light-sensitive organs called eye spots may be found on other parts of the body.

GEOGRAPHIC RANGE

Bivalves are found worldwide in freshwater and ocean habitats.

HABITAT

All bivalves need fresh or sea water to breathe, reproduce, and feed. Ocean-dwelling species are found from the seashore to deep-sea habitats. However, the Australian *Enigmonia* lives on mangrove leaves or seawalls beyond high tide and gets its moisture from sea spray. Most species live on the bottom or burrow into mud and sand. Others attach themselves to rocks, wood, and other solid objects. A few burrow into rock and wood or live on the bodies of other animals.

DIET

Most bivalves eat bits of plants and animals floating in the water. A few species collect food from the bottom. Others absorb nutrients directly into their bodies or capture small crustaceans and worms by grabbing them with a special intake siphon.

BEHAVIOR AND REPRODUCTION

Most bivalves stay in the same place for much of their lives, but others are able to move around. Burrowers move up and down through mud and sand by extending their foot. Then they expand the tip of their foot to anchor themselves and pull their shelled bodies up or down in the burrow. Others "swim" through the water by clapping their valves together.

Bivalves usually require both males and females to reproduce, although some species individuals either have the organs of both sexes or start out as males and later become females. Bivalve eggs and sperm are usually released into the water, where fertilization takes place. The eggs hatch into veligers (VEL-ih-jerz), or young, that live among and eat other plankton. Plankton is made up of microscopic plants and animals that drift about on ocean currents. Eventually, the veligers settle on rocks, wood, or the ocean bottom and begin to develop their valves.

HOW THE GEODUCK GOT ITS NAME

The geoduck (gooey-duck) is the common name for the clam *Panopea abrupta*. It burrows in the sandy beaches along the North American shore of the Pacific Ocean from Alaska to California. The Nisqaully tribe of southern Puget Sound hunted and ate this clam and called it *gweduc*, which means "dig deep." The first European settlers in the region changed the name to gooeyduck or goeduck. In time, through countless misspellings, the bivalve became known as a geoduck.

BIVALVES AND PEOPLE

Clams, mussels, oysters, and scallops are raised commercially in the ocean for food. Oysters are sources of natural pearls and mother-of-pearl shell. For more than fifty years, cultured pearls have increased in both quantity and quality through advanced techniques in oyster culturing perfected by the Japanese.

Some bivalves are considered pests. They may concentrate bacteria, viruses, harmful chemicals and other pollutants in their bodies and can cause sickness and spread disease when eaten by humans. Shipworms burrow into and damage or destroy wooden structures, such as boats and piers. In the United States, introduced freshwater zebra mussels clog pipes of water treatment plants and irrigation systems, which cost millions to repair.

CONSERVATION STATUS

Habitat pollution and alteration are the greatest threat to freshwater bivalves, but the introduction of exotic species, such as zebra mussels, can also be disastrous. Nearly one hundred species of freshwater pearl mussels in Eastern North America are already extinct. Most of the remaining species are protected and officially listed by the government as either threatened or endangered. Over two hundred bivalve species are listed by the World Conservation Union (IUCN). Only eight, all giant clams, live in the ocean.

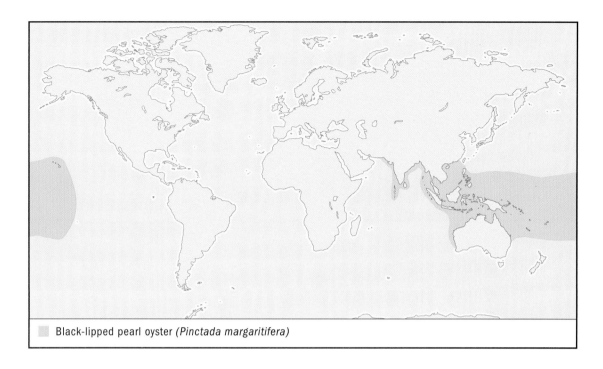

Black-lipped pearl oyster (*Pinctada margaritifera*)

BLACK-LIPPED PEARL OYSTER
Pinctada margaritifera

Physical characteristics: Outside blackish valves with white to green spots are round and flat. The inner valve surfaces can be blue, gray, green, pink, and yellow. The valves measure 6 to 10 inches (150 to 250 millimeters) across. The mantle is orange, while the foot is gray or black.

Geographic range: This species naturally occurs in the Indian Ocean and the western to central Pacific, including the Hawaiian Islands. It is also raised commercially in French Polynesia, Cook Islands, Gilbert Islands, Marshall Islands, Solomon Islands, southern China, northern and western Australia, Seychelles, and the Sudan.

Habitat: Black-lipped pearl oysters live at depths of 3 to 130 feet (1 to 40 meters) attached to hard surfaces in and around coral reefs. This species prefers calm, clear waters often poor in nutrients.

Diet: They eat bits of plant and animal plankton.

Behavior and reproduction: Foreign particles or parasites stuck between the valve and the body are encased in hard, shiny layers of calcium carbonate forming a pearl.

Hermaphroditic adults first develop into males, then females. Eggs and sperm released into the water are fertilized there.

Black-lipped pearl oysters and people: This species is the most important source of mother-of-pearl used for carvings and inlays, as well as Tahitian black pearls.

Conservation status: Black-lipped pearl oysters are not considered threatened or endangered. ■

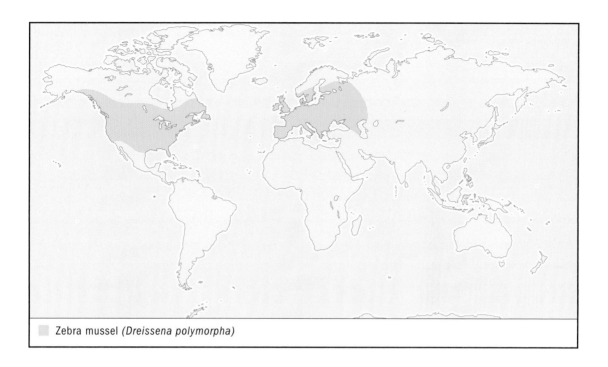

Zebra mussel (Dreissena polymorpha)

ZEBRA MUSSEL
Dreissena polymorpha

Physical characteristics: The valves are narrowly triangular in shape and pointed at the front end. At the rear, the valves are smooth and appear swollen. They are alternately banded with dark brown and cream, suggesting a "zebra" pattern. Mature adults have valves about 2 inches (50 millimeters) long.

Geographic range: This species was first known from the Black and Caspian Seas. It has since been introduced into the canals and inland waterways of Western Europe. In the past twenty years it has also become established in the Great Lakes, on the Mississippi River, and in other major river systems in the United States.

Habitat: Zebra mussels lives on the bottom and attaches to rocks, wood, boats, and other hard surfaces at depths down to 195 feet (60 meters). Populations may contain one hundred thousand individuals per square yard (meter).

Diet: They eat plankton.

Behavior and reproduction: Smaller mussels can detach themselves and move around, but larger individuals cannot. This species is introduced to new bodies of water by ships releasing water containing mussel larvae.

Both males and females are required for reproduction. A single female can release as many as forty thousand to one million eggs into the water each season. The veligers live among plankton, but eventually settle on hard surfaces after eighteen to twenty-eight days. Total life span is about two years.

Zebra mussels and people: Introduction of this species into waterways in Europe and North America has clogged the pipes of power plants and irrigation systems. They also threaten native bivalve populations by eating all of the available food and taking up living space.

Conservation status: Zebra mussels are not considered threatened or endangered. ■

Coquina clam (*Donax variabilis*)

COQUINA CLAM
Donax variabilis

Physical characteristics: The triangular valves are sculptured with ridges radiating out from center and come in white, yellow, orange, pink, purple, and blue. The inside surface of the valves is not pearly and is usually purple. The margins of the valves are finely toothed. Mature individuals grow up to 1 inch (25 millimeters) long.

Geographic range: They are found along the Eastern coast of North America from Chesapeake Bay to Florida and around the Gulf of Mexico to Yucatan.

Habitat: They burrow in sandy beaches that have wave action.

Coquina clams are found along the Eastern coast of North America from Chesapeake Bay to Florida and around the Gulf of Mexico to Yucatan. (© Harry Rogers/Photo Researchers, Inc.)

Diet: Coquina clams eat tiny plants and animals floating in the water.

Behavior and reproduction: They use their muscular foot to rebury themselves after being exposed by the waves and move up and down in the sand and along the beach.

Both males and females are required for reproduction. Eggs and sperm are released into the water, where fertilization takes place. They live up to two years.

Coquina clams and people: They are eaten in "coquina broth," and their shells are used for decorating gardens.

Conservation status: Coquina clams are not considered threatened or endangered.   ■

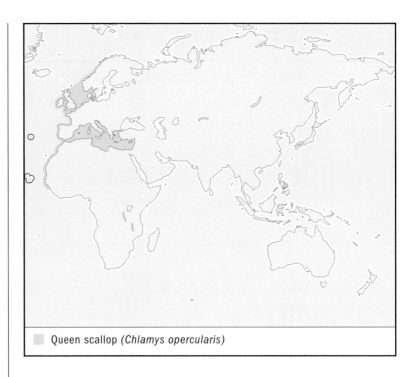

Queen scallop (Chlamys opercularis)

QUEEN SCALLOP
Aequipecten opercularis or *Chlamys opercularis*

Physical characteristics: The valves are flat and round and have about 20 ribs extending out from the umbo. On either side of the umbo is a pair of small, winglike extensions that are slightly unequal in size. The colors of the outer surface are variable, spotted or solid, and can be white, red, or orange. The right valve is lighter in color than the left. The inside of each valve is white. The margin of the mantle has lots of sensitive tentacles with eyes.

Geographic range: They are found in the Mediterranean Sea and eastern Atlantic coast from Norway to the Cape Verde Islands, the Azores and the North Sea. They are also raised on experimental farms in Spain, France, and the United Kingdom.

Habitat: Queen scallops live on all bottoms, except those covered with rocks, at depths down to 1,312 feet (400 meters), but are most common at about 130 feet (40 meters).

Diet: They eat tiny plants and animals floating in the water.

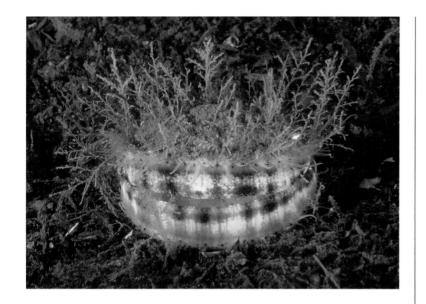

Behavior and reproduction: They escape danger by "swimming."

Individuals have the reproductive organs of both males and females at the same time. Eggs and sperm are released into the water, where fertilization takes place.

Queen scallops and people: People eat the entire body or just the muscle that closes the valves. The valves are sometimes worn as jewelry.

Conservation status: The species is not considered threatened or endangered.   ■

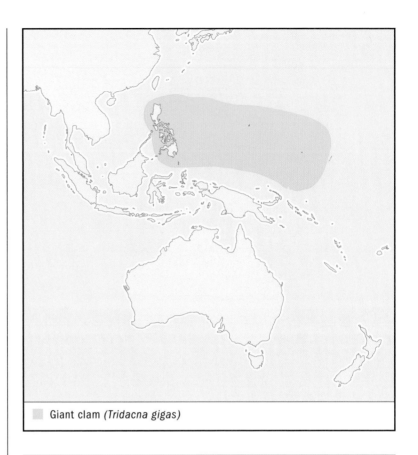

Giant clam (*Tridacna gigas*)

GIANT CLAM
Tridacna gigas

Physical characteristics: This largest of all living bivalves measures up to 53.9 inches (1,369 millimeters) long and weighs up to 579.5 pounds (262.8 kilograms). The whitish valves are thick, heavy, and have four to six distinct folds. The inside surfaces of the valves are white and smooth. The mantle is brightly colored, ranging from yellowish brown to olive green with shiny blue green spots. The openings to the siphons are quite distinctive.

Geographic range: They are found in the Southwestern Pacific from Philippines to Micronesia.

Habitat: Giant clams live at depths of 6 to 66 feet (2 to 20 meters) on coral reefs, partially buried in sand or rubble.

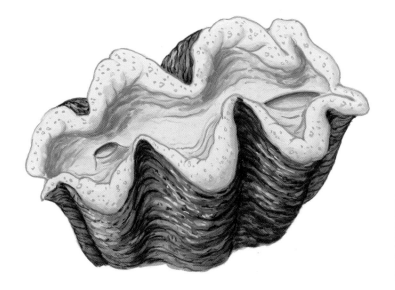

This largest of all living bivalves measures up to 53.9 inches (1,369 millimeters) long and weighs up to 579.5 pounds (262.8 kilograms). (Illustration by Barbara Duperron. Reproduced by permission.)

Diet: Giant clams rely on the nutrients made by algae that live only in the tissues of the clam's mantle. Giant clams supplement this diet with tiny bits of plants and animals floating in the water.

Behavior and reproduction: Adults move about coral reefs with their valves hinge-down. The valves remain open unless the clam is threatened. Larger individuals cannot completely close their valves.

Giant clams develop first as males and later become females. Eggs and sperm are released into the water, where they are fertilized. The life span is unknown but is estimated to range from decades to one hundred years.

Giant clams and people: People living on Pacific Islands harvest giant clams and eat the muscle that closes the valves. Giant clam shells have long been used to make mallets, hoes, scrapers, and wash basins. They are also raised to sell to people that keep them in salt water aquariums.

Conservation status: Giant clams are considered Vulnerable by the IUCN, which means they face a high risk of extinction in the wild. ■

FOR MORE INFORMATION

Books:

Brusca, Richard C., and Gary J. Brusca. *Invertebrates.* Sunderland, MA: Sinauer Associates, 2003.

Gordon, D. G. *Field Guide to the Geoduck. The Secret Life of the World's Biggest Burrowing Clam—from Northern California to Southeast Alaska.* Seattle, WA: Sasquatch Books, 1996.

Gordon, D. G., N. E. Blanton, and T. Y. Nosho. *Heaven on the Half Shell. The Story of the Northwest's Love Affair with the Oyster.* Portland, OR: West Winds Press, 2001.

Nalepa, Thomas F., and Donald W. Schloesser, eds. *Zebra Mussels: Biology, Impacts, and Control.* Boca Raton, FL: Lewis Publishers, 1993.

Rehder, H. A. *National Audubon Society Field Guide to North American Seashells.* New York: Alfred A. Knopf, 1997.

Periodicals:

Doubilet, D. "Black Pearls of French Polynesia." *National Geographic* (June 1997): 30-37.

Zahl, P. A. "The Magic Lure of Seashells." *National Geographic* (March 1969): 386-429.

Web sites:

"Class Bivalvia (Bivalves and Clams)" http://animaldiversity.ummz .umich.edu/site/accounts/information/Bivalvia.html (accessed on May 1, 2005).

Welcome to the Zebra Mussell Page. http://nas.er.usgs.gov/taxgroup/ mollusks/zebramussel/ (accessed on May 1, 2005).

PHYSICAL CHARACTERISTICS

The tubelike shells of scaphopods (SKAF-oh-pods) measure up to 7.8 inches (200 millimeters) in length. They are long, tusk-shaped, and open at both ends. The broadest end of the shell is considered the front. A muscular foot and slender feeding tentacles reach out from the front opening. The mouthparts are made up of a radula (RAE-jeh-leh) that is short, thick, and has five extremely hard teeth. The opening at the narrow end, or at the rear of the shell, is where oxygen-carrying water flows in and waste, eggs, or sperm flow out. The shell is usually white, but in some species the shells are green or have red or yellow bands. The shells of other species are clear, and the internal reproductive organs are sometimes clearly visible.

GEOGRAPHIC RANGE

Tusk shells are found in cool and warm water oceans worldwide, from seashores to depths down to about 23,000 feet (7,000 meters).

HABITAT

Tusk shells are found only in soft, muddy ocean bottoms where they burrow to search for food.

DIET

Tusk shells eat microscopic organisms, especially foraminiferans (fo-re-mi-NIH-fer-ehns), single-celled organisms that have a nucleus. The nucleus is a structure that contains the genetic

phylum
class
subclass
order
monotypic order
suborder
family

information. Other species feed on tiny crustaceans, as well as clams and their relatives.

BEHAVIOR AND REPRODUCTION

All tusk shells burrow into soft ocean bottoms. Some species completely bury themselves, as much as 16 inches (400 millimeters). Others are shallow burrowers and leave the tips of their shells sticking out of the mud.

Most species require males and females to reproduce. Only a few species are hermaphrodites, with individuals having both male and female reproductive organs. Eggs and sperm are released into the water, where fertilization takes place. The eggs hatch into free-swimming larvae (LAR-vee) that resemble the immature stages of other mollusks.

TUSK SHELLS AND PEOPLE

Tusk shells were used as money by Native Americans in the Pacific Northwest and circulated throughout western Canada south to California. Tusk shells were also worn as displays of wealth. Today they are sold to shell collectors and made into jewelry. The eggs of tusk shells, especially those of *Antalis entalis* are used to study the early development of fertilized eggs.

CONSERVATION STATUS

No species of scaphopod is considered threatened or endangered.

Tusk shell (*Antalis entalis*)

TUSK SHELL
Antalis entalis

Physical characteristics: The shell is smooth and white and sometimes has faint, lengthwise ribs toward the narrow rear.

Geographic range: Tusk shells live in the northeastern Atlantic, from Ireland to the Canary Islands; another population lives in the northwestern Atlantic, from Nova Scotia to Cape Cod.

Habitat: They burrow in soft ocean bottoms at depths down to about 6,600 feet (2,000 meters).

Diet: Tusk shells eat all kinds of microscopic organisms, but prefer foraminiferans.

Behavior and reproduction: They burrow into soft ocean bottoms, leaving only the tips of their shells exposed. Males and females are

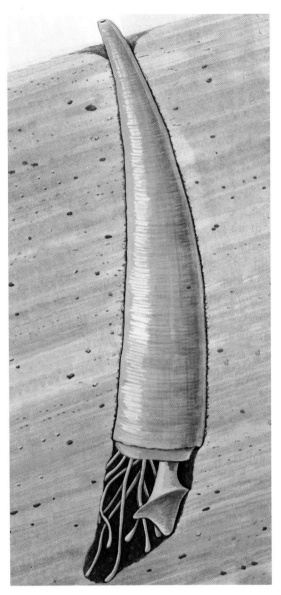

Tusk shells were used as money by Native Americans in the Pacific Northwest and circulated throughout western Canada south to California. Tusk shells were also worn as displays of wealth. Today they are sold to shell collectors and made into jewelry. (Illustration by Dan Erickson. Reproduced by permission.)

required for reproduction. Both eggs and sperm are released into the water, where fertilization and development take place.

Tusk shells and people: This species is not known to impact people or their activities.

Conservation status: Tusk shells are not considered threatened or endangered. ∎

FOR MORE INFORMATION

Books:

Brusca, Richard C., and Gary J. Brusca. *Invertebrates*. Sunderland, MA: Sinauer Associates, 2003.

Periodicals:

Reynolds, P. D. "The Scaphopoda." *Advances in Marine Biology* (2002): 137-236.

Web sites:

"Class Scaphopoda (tusk shells)." http:// animaldiversity.ummz.umich.edu/site/accounts/ information/Scaphopoda.html (accessed on April 27, 2005).

"Introduction to the Scaphopoda." http://www.ucmp .berkeley.edu/mollusca/scaphs/scaphopoda.html (accessed on April 27, 2005).

"Preface to the Class Scaphopoda." http://www.fish .washington.edu/naturemapping/mollusks/scap/ 8scap_int.html (accessed on April 27, 2005).

The Scaphopod Page. http://academics.hamilton .edu/biology/preynold/Scaphopoda/ (accessed on April 27, 2005).

NAUTILIDS, OCTOPODS, CUTTLEFISHES, SQUIDS, AND RELATIVES
Cephalopoda

Class: Cephalopoda

Number of families: About 45 families

phylum
● class
subclass
order
monotypic order
suborder
family

PHYSICAL CHARACTERISTICS

The bodies of all cephalopods (SEF-oh-lo-pahd) remain firm thanks to a system of muscles that maintain fluid pressure inside. Their bodies are more or less divided into three regions: the armlike tentacles surrounding the mouth; the head that has a pair of large, distinctive eyes, one on each side; and the body, or mantle, sometimes with a pair of fins on the sides. Some species, like nautiluses, have sixty tentacles arranged in two rings around the mouth, while others have a single ring of eight tentacles. Of these species, some have a pair of additional tentaclelike appendages and appear as though they have ten tentacles. The head has beaklike mouthparts and a scraping or drilllike radula (RAE-jeh-leh). The radula is a tonguelike organ covered with rows of very hard teeth. Inside the head is a highly complex brain. Inside the head and mantle of cephalopods is a highly developed nervous system, although it is less developed in the nautiluses.

The mantles of the smallest adult cephalopods measure only 0.23 to 0.31 inches (6 to 8 millimeters) in length, while the mantle length of giant squids (*Architeuthis* may reach 71 inches (1.8 meters). These giants are believed to weigh up to 661.3 pounds (300 kilograms). Several kinds of squid and at least two species of octopuses grow larger than an adult human.

Many cephalopods have the ability to change their colors rapidly. They do this with several different kinds of color-producing organs in their skin that are controlled by the nervous system. Together these organs can create different colors and patterns in an instant. Some species have light-producing organs. These organs either produce blue green light by mixing chemicals together or rely on special bacteria that live inside chambers associated with the ink sac. The ink sac produces a thick inky fluid that is squirted into the water and helps them to hide from predators.

GEOGRAPHIC RANGE

Cephalopods are found in all of the world's oceans.

HABITAT

Cephalopods are found in tide pools, on sea bottoms, and swimming in open water. They live at depths of 16,400 feet (5,000 meters) or more.

DIET

Most cephalopods prey on fishes, crustaceans, and mollusks, including other cephalopods. However, nautiluses and their relatives scavenge dead animals.

BEHAVIOR AND REPRODUCTION

Cephalopods have large brains, well-developed eyes, and complex behaviors. Some species, such as octopuses, lead solitary lives, while others, like cuttlefish, live in small to very large groups called schools. Some cuttlefishes or squids get together only to find a mate and reproduce. Many species live at depths of 1,310 to 3,280 feet (400 to 1,000 meters) during the day and swim closer to the surface at night to feed, but the activity patterns of most are unknown. Most cephalopods do not guard or defend territories. Some species will change their colors as a means of camouflage or to startle predators. Many squids and octopuses have special glands for making a defensive inklike fluid that is squirted in the water to confuse their enemies.

Both males and females are required for reproduction, but the mating behaviors of most cephalopods remain unknown. Although nautiluses reproduce many times throughout their lives, most cephalopods do so only once. The time for reproduction in these species may be either very brief or extended over a long period of time. In some species, the male simply grabs the female and places a packet of sperm in a specific place on or inside her body. Others engage in elaborate courtship behaviors that involve lots of touching just before they mate.

Depending on the species, females produce dozens to hundreds of thousands of eggs at a time. One or more layers of a special, protective coating surround each egg. The eggs are usually laid in masses, either on the ocean bottom, in between rocks, or inside seashells, while others release them into the open water. Only some kinds of octopuses and squids care for their eggs until they hatch.

The eggs take a few days to several months to hatch. The hatchlings of some species look and live like the adults and simply grow larger as they develop. Others look nothing like the adults and spend the early part of their lives as plankton. Planktonic plants, animals, and other organisms live in open water and float about on ocean currents. Eventually, the young planktonic cephalopods settle to the ocean bottom, where they develop to more closely resemble the adults in both form and habit.

DEEP-SEA BATTLES

It has long been known that sperm whales eat giant squids. Whalers would find parts of these enormous cephalopods in the bellies of their catch, especially the tentacles and their beaklike mouthparts. The bodies of the whales sometimes bore the sucker patterns inflicted by the long tentacles of the squid. Win or lose, these battle scars prove that giant squids certainly do not go down without a fight.

CEPHALOPODS AND PEOPLE

For hundreds of years, cephalopods have appeared in the art and literature of many human cultures around the world. Today they are sometimes featured in science fiction books and films as "sea monsters." Stories of giant squids washed up on the beach or captured in fishing nets sometimes dominate the news.

In 2000, about 4.0 million tons (3.6 million metric tons) of cephalopods were harvested, equaling about 4.2% of the world's total marine catch. Around the world, many people consider carefully prepared squids, cuttlefishes, and octopuses as tasty meals. Fishermen commonly use cephalopods as bait to catch very desirable species of marine fish for the dinner table.

Cephalopods are of unusual interest to scientists because they have well-developed brains and eyes, but they do not have backbones. They represent one of the most highly developed of all animals but are not related to fishes, birds, mammals, or other animals with backbones. The nerve tissues of giant squids have helped scientists to understand the basic functioning of the human nervous system. In fact, the study of cephalopod bodies is helping medical doctors to understand other aspects of human bodies.

Sometimes octopuses are considered pests because they enter traps set to capture mollusks such as whelks or lobsters. Once inside, they eat the catch. On rare occasions, cephalopods can be directly harmful to humans. Their bites, especially those of some octopuses, are painful to divers and sometimes deadly because of their toxic secretions. Schools of the large Humboldt squid have been known to attack scuba divers and fishermen who have fallen into the water.

CONSERVATION STATUS

No species of cephalopods are considered threatened or endangered.

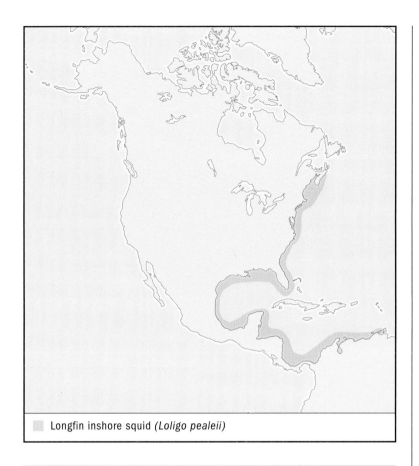

Longfin inshore squid (*Loligo pealeii*)

LONGFIN INSHORE SQUID
Loligo pealeii

Physical characteristics: The mantle is of variable color with brown, red, purplish, and yellow speckles. It is cylinder-shaped, tapered toward the rear, and measures about 17 inches (430 millimeters) long, and 3.62 inches (92 millimeters) wide. The head has a large pair of eyes that are covered by a clear membrane. The eight tentacles are about half the length of the mantle, while the pair of tentaclelike appendages is about two-thirds its length. The triangular fins on each side of the rear end are each about half the length of the mantle.

Geographic range: This species is found in the Western Atlantic continental shelf and upper slope waters from Nova Scotia to Venezuela, including the Gulf of Mexico and the Caribbean Sea.

Females lay their eggs in jelly-covered, fingerlike strands attached to solid surfaces at depths down to 820 feet (250 meters). The strands are often bunched together in large masses and are called "sea mops."
(Andrew J. Martinez/Photo Researchers, Inc.)

Habitat: They live near the ocean surface and in shallow waters in summer, but move to depths of 92 to 1,200 feet (28 to 366 meters) in winter. Adults live on the ocean bottom during the day and swim toward the surface at night.

Diet: They eat crustaceans, fishes, and other squids.

Behavior and reproduction: They migrate north and closer to the shore in summer to reproduce, returning to deeper, more southerly water in fall and winter.

Females lay their eggs in jelly-covered, fingerlike strands attached to solid surfaces at depths down to 820 feet (250 meters). The strands are often bunched together in large masses and are called "sea mops." The hatchlings do not resemble the adults and are planktonic.

Longfin inshore squid and people: They are harvested as food for humans and are also used as study animals by scientists looking at animal behavior and the workings of the nervous system.

Conservation status: The longfin inshore squid is not considered threatened or endangered. ■

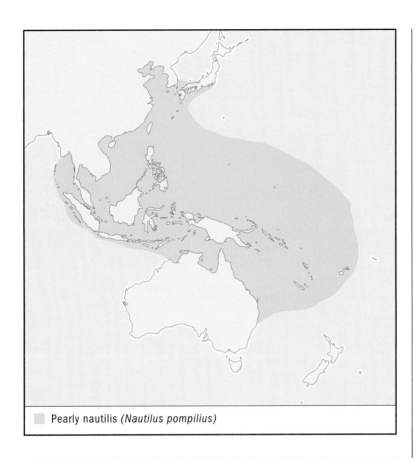

Pearly nautilis (*Nautilus pompilius*)

PEARLY NAUTILUS
Nautilus pompilius

Physical characteristics: The pearly nautilus lives inside a coiled, snaillike shell that has a distinctive flame-striped color pattern. The shell is divided internally into a series of chambers.

Geographic range: This species is found in the Indo-West Pacific.

Habitat: They prefer to live in habitats with a hard ocean bottom, especially among coral reefs. They swim down to depths of about 2,460 feet (750 meters).

Diet: The nautilus eats bottom-dwelling animals, as well as dead or decaying animal flesh.

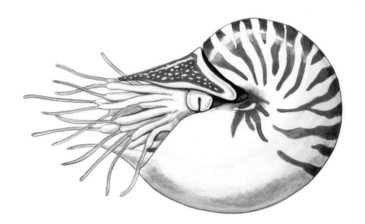

Behavior and reproduction: They are active mostly at night.

Like other nautiluses, they reproduce repeatedly throughout their adult lives. Females protect their eggs by covering them with irregular shaped coverings. The egg mass is then attached to hard surfaces.

Pearly nautiluses and people: This species is harvested for food. Collectors also value their shells.

Conservation status: The pearly nautilus is not considered threatened or endangered. ■

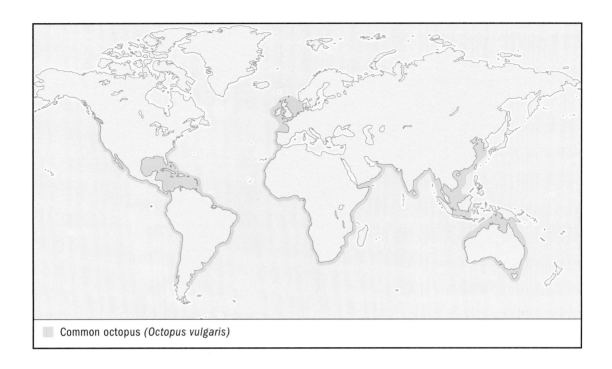

Common octopus *(Octopus vulgaris)*

COMMON OCTOPUS
Octopus vulgaris

Physical characteristics: The mantle plus the longest tentacle is about 120 inches (3 meters) long. The ball-shaped mantle is variable in color but usually reddish brown. The skin is smooth but may temporarily have bumps of different sizes and shapes. The thick, armlike tentacles are four times the length of the mantle and have two alternating rows of suckers. The head is nearly as wide as the mantle and has a pair of distinctive eyes.

Geographic range: They are found worldwide in both cool and warm waters.

Habitat: They live on the ocean bottom among rocks, coral reefs, and seagrass beds, from the seashore down to depths of 656 feet (200 meters).

Diet: They eat mostly crabs, lobsters, clams, and snails.

Common octopuses are harvested as food and are used as study animals by scientists interested in animal behavior. (Illustration by Barbara Duperron. Reproduced by permission.)

Behavior and reproduction: These animals appear to be quite intelligent, and their complex behaviors are well-known to scientists.

Adults reproduce twice a year, in spring and fall. Females lay between 120,000 and 400,000 eggs in strings and deposit them among rocks and corals in shallow waters. The hatchlings are planktonic.

Common octopuses and people: They are harvested as food and are used as study animals by scientists interested in animal behavior.

Conservation status: The common octopus is not considered threatened or endangered. ■

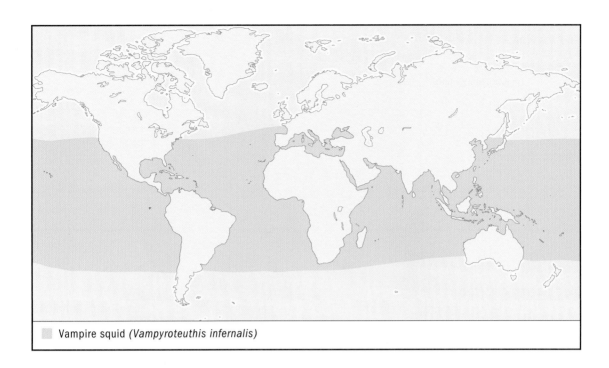

Vampire squid (*Vampyroteuthis infernalis*)

VAMPIRE SQUID
Vampyroteuthis infernalis

Physical characteristics: This squid's skin has many light-producing organs. There are large, circular light-producing organs just behind the fins on the mantle. The tentaclelike arms are covered by tiny, hairlike structures called cirri (SIH-ree). The arms have suckers only on the outer halves.

Geographic range: This species is found in all cool and warm water oceans.

Habitat: Vampire squids live in open waters at depths of 1,965 to 4,920 feet (600 to 1,500 meters).

Diet: They probably eat jellylike animals carried about on ocean currents.

Behavior and reproduction: These fast-swimming animals resemble an umbrella or a bell shape as they move through the water with

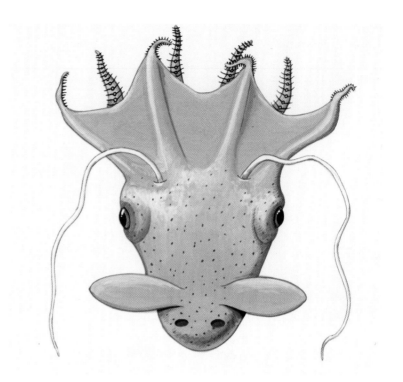

This species is commonly seen on television programs featuring deep-sea animals. (Illustration by Barbara Duperron. Reproduced by permission.)

their webbed arms extended forward. They create complex flashing displays with their light-producing organs.

Vampire squids and people: This species is commonly seen on television programs featuring deep-sea animals.

They hatch with one pair of fins, but then develop a second pair closer to the front of the body. For a short period the vampire squid has two pairs of fins. The first pair soon disappears. Except for the fins, young vampire squid resemble the adults.

Conservation status: The vampire squid is not considered threatened or endangered. ■

FOR MORE INFORMATION

Books:

Okutani, T. *Cuttlefish and Squids of the World in Color.* Tokyo: National Cooperative Association of Squid Processors, 1995.

Periodicals:

Bavendam, F. "Eye to Eye with the Giant Octopus." *National Geographic* (March 1991): 86-97.

Bavendam, F. "The Giant Cuttlefish. Chameleon of the Reef." *National Geographic* (September 1995):94-107.

Clarke, M. R., ed. "The Role of Cephalopods in the World's Oceans." *Philosophical Transactions of the Royal Society, London* (1996): 977-1112.

Faulkner, D. "The Chambered Nautilus." *National Geographic* (January 1976): 38-41.

Voss, G. L. "Squids: Jet-powered Torpedos of the Deep." *National Geographic* (March 1967): 386-411.

Web sites:

"Cephalopoda Cuvier 1797. Octopuses, Squids, Nautiluses, etc." http://tolweb.org/tree?group=Cephalopoda (accessed on April 29, 2005).

"Class Cephalopoda (Octopuses and Squids)." http://animaldiversity .ummz.umich.edu/site/accounts/information/Cephalopoda.html (accessed on April 29, 2005).

The Cephalopod Page. http://is.dal.ca/ceph/TCP/index.html (accessed on April 29, 2005).

In Search of Giant Squid. http://seawifs.gsfc.nasa.gov/squid.html (accessed on April 29, 2005).

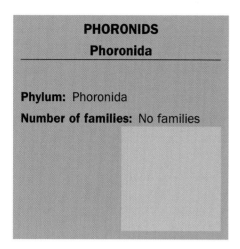

PHORONIDS

Phoronida

Phylum: Phoronida
Number of families: No families

phylum

CHAPTER

■ **phylum**

class

subclass

order

monotypic order

suborder

family

PHYSICAL CHARACTERISTICS

Phoronids (for-OH-nihds) are long, thin, wormlike animals that live inside slender tubes that they make with their own bodies. When relaxed, adults normally measure up to 18 inches (450 millimeters), but some phoronids can extend their bodies nearly five times that length. Their body thickness measures 0.006 to 0.2 inches (0.15 to 5 millimeters). There is no distinct head. The slitlike mouth is covered by a flap of skin and is found between the horseshoe-shaped, tentacle-bearing ridges that make up the lophophore (LO-fo-for). The tentacles of the lophophore help phoronids to breathe, eat, and protect themselves. The ends of the horseshoe-shaped ridges are coiled like springs. The slender body trunk is swollen, or bulb-shaped, at the end. This region of the body contains most of the internal organs.

Inside they have a body cavity and a u-shaped digestive system. The nervous system includes a nerve center between the mouth and the anus. The anus is located at the end of the digestive system and is where solid waste leaves the body. At the base of the lophophore is a ringlike nerve structure. Phoronids have blood that circulates inside a system of tubes, or vessels. They have a pair of kidneylike organs that not only remove wastes from the blood, they also work as part of the reproductive system.

GEOGRAPHIC RANGE

Phoronids are found in all oceans and seas, except the Antarctic Ocean.

HABITAT

Adult phoronids live along coastlines, from the zones that are affected by the tides, rarely going deeper than 180 feet (54 meters). A few species have been found at depths of approximately 1,310 feet (400 meters). They live inside flexible, layered, parchmentlike tubes. Some species live alone, buried straight up and down in sand, mud, or fine gravel. Others live in large groups, their tangled tubes often covering rocks and shells. They are free to leave their tubes and make another one somewhere else. One species intertwines its tube with that of a tube-living sea anenome. Some species do not make a tube. They bore into rock and live inside the tunnel.

DIET

Phoronids eat algae (AL-jee), small animal larvae (LAR-vee), and other plankton floating in the water.

BEHAVIOR AND REPRODUCTION

Phoronids have extremely flexible bodies. They will quickly direct their lophophores to take full advantage of food-carrying ocean currents. Tiny bristles, or cilia (SIH-lee-uh), on their lophophores help carry bits of food trapped by sticky mucous on the tentacles down special grooves all the way to the mouth. They are also quick to respond to danger and will withdraw inside their tubes when they are threatened. If injured by a predator, phoronids can regenerate lost or damaged body parts in just a few days.

Phoronids reproduce in different ways. Sometimes both males and females are required to reproduce. In other species, individuals may have both male and female reproductive organs at the same time. This way, every phoronid is a potential mate. Phoronids can also reproduce without eggs and sperm at all. Instead, individuals simply divide their bodies, breaking off at the middle into halves. Each half quickly develops into a complete animal.

Reproduction usually takes place from spring through fall. In most species, eggs and sperm are released, and fertilization

WHEN THE COWS COME HOME

The name *Phoronida* comes from the Latin *Phoronis*, the last name of the mythological Io. Zeus, the king of gods, turned Io into a cow because he wanted to hide her from his wife. Io Phoronis wandered the Earth for many years, until she was returned to her original body. Phoronids were first discovered and known for many years only as larvae. It was only much later that they were associated with their tube-building adults.

usually takes place in the water. In a few species, the males produce sperm packets and transfer them directly to the female. Fertilization takes place inside the female's body cavity. The eggs develop in special tissues in the lophophore or inside the body cavity. The newly hatched larvae of all phoronids swim freely and live with other plankton. After about twenty days they settle to the bottom. In less than thirty minutes, they can transform into slender, young phoronids ready to burrow into their surroundings.

PHORONIDS AND PEOPLE

Phoronids do not impact people or their activities.

CONSERVATION STATUS

No species is considered threatened or endangered.

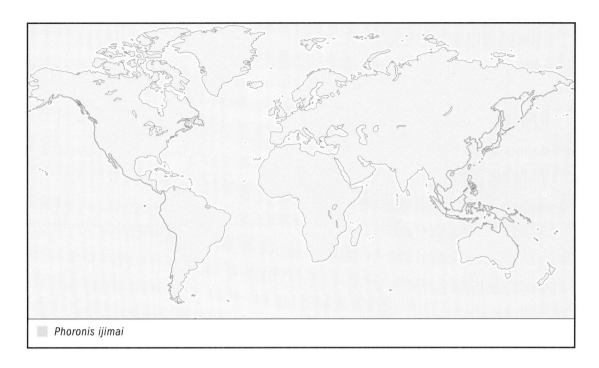

Phoronis ijimai

NO COMMON NAME
Phoronis ijimai

Physical characteristics: Fully stretched out, these flesh-colored or clear-bodied phoronids may reach a length of 5 inches (120 millimeters) and are 0.02 to 0.08 inches (0.5 to 2 millimeters) thick. The lophophore sometimes is clear and has white spots. The lophophore is horseshoe-shaped, or coiled with a single spiral, and has as many as 230 tentacles. Each tentacle is 0.08 to 0.2 inches (2 to 5 millimeters) long.

Geographic range: This species is found in the eastern and western Pacific Ocean and the northwestern Atlantic Ocean.

Habitat: This species lives along coastlines, in zones affected by tides down to depths of approximately 33 feet (10 meters). They are found in groups of intertwined tubes covering rocks, wood, and other hard surfaces. They sometimes burrow in rock, algae, coral, and the shells of mollusks (mussels, clams, snails, and their relatives).

Diet: They capture plankton with their sticky tentacles.

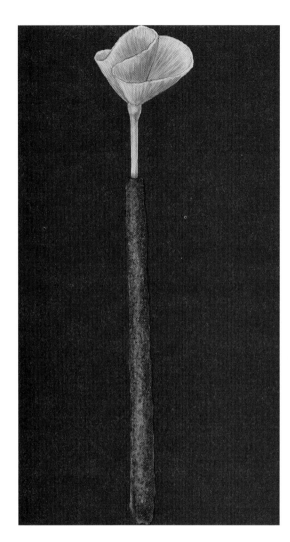

Fully stretched out, these flesh-colored or clear-bodied phoronids may reach a length of 5 inches (120 millimeters). (Illustration by Bruce Worden. Reproduced by permission.)

Behavior and reproduction: They protect themselves by quickly withdrawing inside their tubes. Injured animals can replace damaged or lost body parts in just a few days.

This species has both male and female reproductive organs. The fertilized eggs are brooded in two groups on the tentacles. Fully grown larvae are approximately 0.03 inches (0.8 millimeters) long. Adults also reproduce by dividing their bodies in two.

Phoronis ijimai and people: This species is not known to impact people or their activities.

Conservation status: *Phoronis ijimai* is not considered threatened or endangered. ◼

FOR MORE INFORMATION

Periodicals:

Emig, C. C. "The Biology of Phoronida." *Advances in Marine Biology* (1982): 1-89.

Garey, J. R., and A. Schmidt-Rhaesa. "The essential role of "minor" phyla in molecular studies of animal evolution." *American Zoologist* 38, no. 6 (December): 907-917.

Web sites:

Introduction to the Phoronida. http://www.ucmp .berkeley.edu/brachiopoda/phoronida.html (accessed on March 28, 2005).

Phoronid@2005. http://www.com.univ-mrs.fr/DIMAR/Phoro/ (accessed on March 28, 2005).

"Phoronida. Horseshoe Worms." http://www.angelfire.com/mo2/ animals1/phylum/phoronida.html (accessed on March 28, 2005).

"The Phoronida." http://www.ldeo.columbia.edu/edu/dees/ees/life/ slides/phyla/phoronida.html (accessed on March 28, 2005).

Phylum: Ectoprocta

Number of families: about 160
families

phylum
CHAPTER

PHYSICAL CHARACTERISTICS

Ectoprocts are similar in appearance to corals, seaweeds, and sponges. They live in sessile (SEH-sill) colonies that resemble jellylike masses, crusts, cups, or plantlike structures. Sessile organisms are attached to one place and cannot move. A colony is any group of organisms that lives together. A single colony may be less than 0.039 inches (1 millimeter) high or grow as tall as 3.28 feet (1 meter). Depending on the species, the outer covering of the entire ectoproct colony is either jellylike or made of chitin ((KYE-tehn). Chitin is the tough, flexible material that makes up most of the external skeletons (exoskeletons) of arthropods (insects, spiders, and their relatives). Some ectoproct colonies are covered with a bony or calcified (KAEL-sih-faid) covering. Calcified coverings are made up mostly of minerals called calcium salts.

Individual animals are called zooids (zu-ihdz). Most zooids are so small that they must be studied through a microscope. Each zooid has a circular or u-shaped lophophore (LO-fo-for) surrounding a mouthlike opening. Lophophores have sticky tentacles covered in tiny bristles, or cilia (SIH-lee-uh). They help ectoprocts to breathe, eat, and protect themselves. Inside, they each have a body cavity, a single nerve bundle, and a u-shaped digestive system. In some colonies, all of the zooids are similar in appearance, but in others, there may be several different kinds. For example, some zooids spend most of their time eating. Others exist only to reproduce or to provide extra support for the calcified skeleton. In some colonies, a network

phylum

class

subclass

order

monotypic order

suborder

family

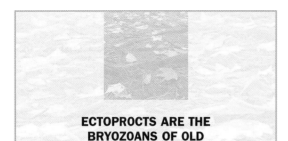

ECTOPROCTS ARE THE BRYOZOANS OF OLD

The colonies of many ectoproct species are plantlike in appearance. They were once given the name of moss animals and placed in the phylum Bryozoa. The name Bryozoa comes from the Greek words *bryon*, meaning moss, and *zoön*, or animal. Like many mosses, ectoprocts grow in mats or clumps.

of tubes connects the zooids to each other so they can share digested food.

GEOGRAPHIC RANGE

Freshwater ectoprocts are found on every continent, including Antarctica. Marine species live in every ocean.

HABITAT

Freshwater species are found in shallow, still waters. They attach themselves to the sides or undersides of rocks, wood, plants, and trash. Marine ectoprocts live in shallow waters near the coastline to deep-sea bottoms at depths of 26,900 feet (8,200 meters). They are also found on the surfaces of solid objects, including rocks, seashells, seaweed, and wood.

DIET

Both freshwater and marine ectoprocts eat anything, as long as it is small. Most of their food is made up of tiny bits of plants and animals floating in the water and small, living organisms.

BEHAVIOR AND REPRODUCTION

The life cycle of ectoprocts includes sexual (SEK-shu-uhl) and asexual (ay-SEK-shu-uhl) reproduction. Sexual reproduction involves males and females producing sperm and eggs. In some groups of ectoprocts, each zooid is a hermaphrodite (her-MAE-fro-dait). Some hermaphrodites have the reproductive organs of both males and females at the same time, while others produce eggs or sperm at different times of their life. Some ectoproct colonies have zooids that do nothing else but produce eggs and sperm. Sperm is released into the water to fertilize eggs that are attached in some way to parts of the colony. In some groups the fertilized eggs develop in special sacs or inside the body cavities of feeding zooids. The newly hatched larvae (LAR-vee) are independent at first. They swim for several hours before they settle and attach to a solid object.

Asexual reproduction does not require males or females. Instead, ectoprocts reproduce by budding or breaking off parts of the colony. Each broken piece is capable of developing into a new colony. In some species, these pieces are equipped with special flotation devices that help them to float away and settle in new habitats. Some ectoprocts can only form new colonies by budding.

ECTOPROCTS AND PEOPLE

Freshwater ectoprocts are sometimes a problem when they attach themselves to the insides of water pipes and filters. They can block the flow of water to irrigate fields or prevent filters from removing particles and other organisms from drinking water. Some marine species produce chemicals that are used for medicine and other research purposes.

CONSERVATION STATUS

No species of ectoprocts is considered threatened or endangered.

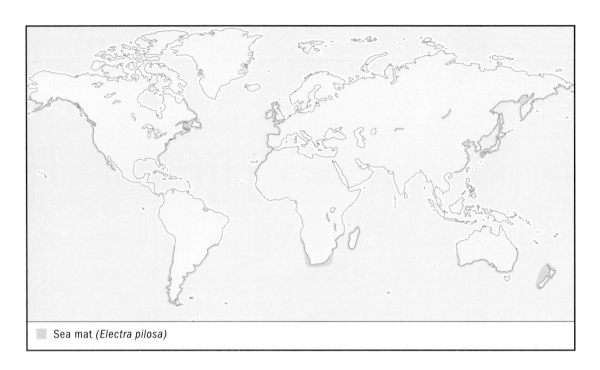

Sea mat (*Electra pilosa*)

SPECIES ACCOUNT

SEA MAT
Electra pilosa

Physical characteristics: Sea mats form star-shaped or wide sheets of calcified crusts on seaweeds, rocks, and shells. The zooids are longer than they are wide and are sometimes egg-shaped. They have four to twelve spines, giving the colony a "hairy" look.

Geographic range: They are found all around the world in oceans with waters that are not too cold or warm.

Habitat: Sea mats live in shallow marine waters down to approximately 164 feet (5 meters). Their colonies are attached to small species of marine algae (AL-jee) and on the shells of mussels and other mollusks.

Diet: They eat bits of algae floating in the water.

Behavior and reproduction: Very little is known about the behavior of sea mats.

They reproduce asexually by budding. Sexual reproduction involves fertilized eggs released into the water where they hatch into larvae.

Sea mats and people: This species does not impact people or their activities.

Conservation status: Sea mats are not considered threatened or endangered.

FOR MORE INFORMATION

Books:

Brusca, Richard C., and Gary J. Brusca. *Invertebrates.* Sunderland, MA: Sinauer Associates, 2003.

Smith, Douglas G. *Pennak's Freshwater Invertebrates of the United States: Porifera to Crustacea.* New York: Wiley and Sons, 2001.

Periodicals:

McKinney, F. K. "Feeding and Associated Colonial Morphology in Marine Bryozoans." *Reviews in Aquatic Sciences* (1989): 255-280.

Web sites:

The Bryozoa. http://www.nhm.ac.uk/hosted_sites/iba/pages/bryozoa .html (accessed on March 29, 2005).

Bryozoa Home Page. http://www.civgeo.rmit.edu.au/bryozoa/default.html (accessed on March 29, 2005).

International Bryozoology Association. http://petralia.civgeo.rmit.edu.au/bryozoa/iba.html (accessed on March 29, 2005).

What Is a Bryozoan? http://www.sms.si.edu/irlspec/IntroBryozoa.htm (accessed on March 29, 2005).

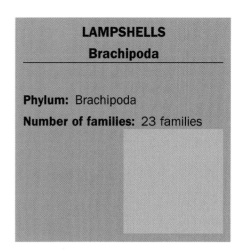

LAMPSHELLS
Brachipoda

Phylum: Brachipoda
Number of families: 23 families

phylum
CHAPTER

PHYSICAL CHARACTERISTICS

Lampshells live as individual animals. Their bodies are completely enclosed, above and below, by a pair of shells. Each shell is called a valve. The phylum is divided into two distinct groups, or classes. In class Inarticulata, the valves are not hinged together. Instead, muscles keep them together. In the Articulata, a special tooth-and-socket hinge joins the valves. The valves of individual lampshells are usually different sizes. The largest valves measure 0.039 to 3.54 inches (1 to 90 millimeters) across, and the outer surface is smooth, pitted, or spiny.

Nearly all lampshells are sessile (SEH-sill). Sessile animals attach themselves to surfaces and cannot move. Lampshells attach themselves to solid surfaces by a soft, flexible stalk, called a pedicel (PEH-dih-sel). The pedicel is part of the body wall and is connected to the lower valve. A few species with pedicels either do not attach themselves to anything or anchor themselves in loose sand so they can still move around. Species without pedicels glue themselves directly to objects.

Lampshells have crownlike ridges with sticky tentacles that surround the mouth. The lophophore (LO-fo-for) is used to help them to breathe, feed, and protect themselves. It is also used to remove body waste from inside the valves. The lophophores are circular, u-, or spiral-shaped. The body wall has special tissues that form the mantle lobes. The mantle lobes make the valves. They have an internal body cavity. The digestive system is u-shaped and may or may not have an anus. The nervous system includes two groups of nerve cells, one in

phylum

class

subclass

order

monotypic order

suborder

family

front of, the other behind the mouth. A ring of nerves surrounds the upper portion of the digestive system, with nerves leading into each of the tentacles of the lophophore. The open circulatory system carries clear blood. The blood in open circulatory systems does not always stay inside of tubes, or vessels. Kidneylike organs help to remove waste from body fluids. They are also used to release eggs or sperm into the water.

GEOGRAPHIC RANGE

Lampshells are found in all oceans.

HABITAT

Lampshells live on the bottom of oceans with cold, moderate, or warm waters. They either attach themselves to hard objects or bury themselves in mud or sand. They are found along seashores to depths of 17,410 feet (5,300 meters).

DIET

Lampshells eat bits of plants, animals, and other organisms floating in the water. The sticky tentacles collect food from water flowing past the body in between the valves.

BEHAVIOR AND REPRODUCTION

Some species live in burrows in soft, sandy or muddy sea bottoms. When threatened, they close their valves and quickly pull themselves into the burrow by using the muscles in their pedicels. Some species live out in the open. They attach themselves to rocks with their very muscular pedicels and can pull themselves down toward the bottom if they are disturbed. Lampshells without pedicels attach their lower valves directly to hard, flat surfaces and usually live in groups.

Most species of lampshells require both males and females for reproduction. Eggs and sperm are released from the kidneylike organs into the water where fertilization takes place. Only in a few species do the eggs develop inside the valves. The newly hatched larvae (LAR-vee) have rows of bristlelike cilia (SIH-lee-uh) on their bodies. They swim, have distinct body regions, and may or may not resemble adults. Once they settle on the bottom, the larvae begin to make their own valves. Most species live less than two years, but some are known to live for six to ten years.

LAMPSHELLS AND PEOPLE

Some inarticulate lampshells are eaten by people living on islands in the eastern Pacific, from Japan to New Caledonia. Articulate lampshells are used by scientists to understand the fossil record. Fossils are impressions of ancient organisms left in mud that have become stone after million of years. These fossils also help us to understand how life has changed, or evolved, over millions of years.

CONSERVATION STATUS

No species is considered threatened or endangered.

LAMPSHELLS MUST COMPETE FOR FOOD AND SPACE

As a group, lampshells are very ancient animals, at least 600 million years old. More than 12,000 different kinds of fossil species are known. They reached their peak just over 300 million years ago, when they were one of the most abundant life forms. Since then, their numbers have declined. Some scientists think this is partly because they cannot compete with clams and scallops living in the same habitats.

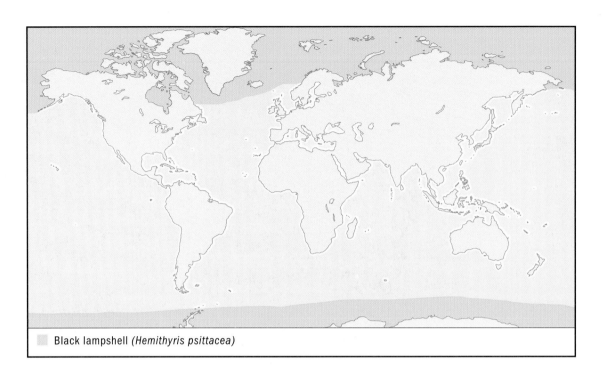

Black lampshell (*Hemithyris psittacea*)

SPECIES ACCOUNT

BLACK LAMPSHELL
Hemithyris psittacea

Physical characteristics: The hinged valves of adult black lampshells are small to medium in size, with a maximum width of 1.38 inches (35 millimeters). The brownish purple valves are thick and bulging. The lower valve has a long, curved beaklike projection. The lophophore has two spirals and an external support. There are two pairs of kidneylike organs. The pedicel is short. The digestive system is curved and does not have an anus.

Geographic range: They are found all around the North Pole, mostly in the Pacific and Atlantic Oceans.

Habitat: Black lampshells live in warm and cold waters near seashores, between depths of about 33 to 4,265 feet (10 to 1,300 meters).

Diet: They eat bits of plants, animals, and nutrients floating in the water.

Behavior and reproduction: These animals attach themselves to hard surfaces with their pedicels. The rear of each mantle lobe has special tissues that produce eggs or sperm.

Black lampshells and people: This species does not impact people or their activities.

Conservation status: Black lampshells are not considered threatened or endangered. ■

FOR MORE INFORMATION

Books:

Audubon Society Encyclopedia of Animal Life. New York: Clarkson N. Potter, 1982.

Brunton, C., L. Howard, M. Robin, M. Cocks, and S. L. Long, eds. *Brachiopods Past and Present.* London and New York: Taylor and Francis, 2001.

Brusca, R. C., and G. J. Brusca. *Invertebrates.* Sunderland, MA: Sinauer Associates, 2003.

Periodicals:

Gee, H. "Lophophorates prove likewise variable." *Nature* (1995): 493.

Morris, S. C. "Nailing the lophophorates." *Nature* (1995): 365-366.

Web sites:

BrachNet. Brachiopoda and Brachiopodologists. http://paleopolis .rediris.es/BrachNet/ (accessed on March 29, 2005).

Species List by Biome

CONIFEROUS FOREST
Common pillbug
Common shiny woodlouse
Roman snail
Tongue worm

CONTINENTAL MARGIN
Common octopus
Giant tiger prawn
Green bonellia
Gumboot chiton
Hutchinsoniella macracantha
Longfin inshore squid
Nannosquilla decemspinosa
Norwegian tubeworm
Peacock mantis shrimp
Pearly nautilus
Phoronis ijimai
Queen scallop
Red king crab
Sand isopod
Sea mat
Sipunculus nudus
Skeleton shrimp
Speleonectes gironensis
Tusk shell
Veiled chiton

DECIDUOUS FOREST
Common pillbug
Common shiny woodlouse
Gippsland giant worm
River worm
Roman snail
Tongue worm

DESERT
Common pillbug
Tongue worm

GRASSLAND
Common pillbug
Common shiny woodlouse
Gippsland giant worm
Roman snail
Tongue worm

LAKE AND POND
Anaspides tasmaniae
Antrobathynella stammeri
Common water flea
Fish louse
Longtail tadpole shrimp
Mysis relicta
North American medicinal
  leech
Red swamp crayfish
Zebra mussel

OCEAN
Amphionides reynaudii
Antarctic krill
Apseudes intermedius
Black lampshell
Black-lipped pearl oyster
Common octopus
Corolla spectabilis
Cyclaspis longicaudata
Dahlella caldariensis
Fire worm
Geography cone shell
Giant clam
Giant red mysid
Honeycomb worm
Hydrothermal vent worm
Itoitantulus misophricola
Laevipilina antarctica
Monstrilla grandis
Myzostoma cirriferum
North Pacific krill
Oithona plumifera
Pearly nautilus
Queen scallop
Red king crab
Salmon louse
Sand isopod
Sipunculus nudus
Sperm whale lice
Spiomenia spiculata

Top shell
Tubeworm
Tusk shell
Vampire squid

RAINFOREST
Epiperipatus biolleyi
Tongue worm

RIVER AND STREAM
Anaspides tasmaniae
Antrobathynella stammeri
Common water flea
Fish louse
North American medicinal
  leech
Red swamp crayfish
River worm

Spelaeogriphus lepidops
Thermosbaena mirabilis
Zebra mussel

SEASHORE
Beach hopper
Common octopus
Coquina clam
Derocheilocaris typicus
Fire worm
Giant tiger prawn
Gumboot chiton
Harlequin shrimp
Honeycomb worm
Mictocaris halope
Phoronis ijimai
Queen scallop
Rock barnacle

Sand fiddler crab
Sand isopod
Shield limpet
Sipunculus nudus
Stygiomysis cokei
Trypetesa lampas
Vargula hilgendorfii
Veiled chiton

TUNDRA
Giant yellow water bear

WETLAND
Common water flea
Giant Amazonian leech
North American medicinal
  leech
Red swamp crayfish

Species List by Geographic Range

ALBANIA
Common octopus
Common pillbug
Common shiny woodlouse
Common water flea
Fish louse
Green bonellia
Mysis relicta
Red swamp crayfish
Rock barnacle
Roman snail
Zebra mussel

ALGERIA
Common octopus
Green bonellia
Red swamp crayfish

ANDORRA
Common pillbug
Common shiny woodlouse
Common water flea
Fish louse
Mysis relicta
Red swamp crayfish
Zebra mussel

ANGOLA
Common octopus

Fire worm
Red swamp crayfish
Tongue worm

ANTIGUA AND BARBUDA
Common octopus
Fire worm
Longfin inshore squid
Longtail tadpole shrimp
Tongue worm

ARCTIC
Giant yellow water bear
Rock barnacle

ARCTIC OCEAN
Amphionides reynaudii
Black lampshell
Gumboot chiton
Red king crab
Rock barnacle
Salmon louse
Sperm whale lice
Veiled chiton

ARGENTINA
Common octopus

Longtail tadpole shrimp
Red swamp crayfish

ARMENIA
Common octopus
Red swamp crayfish
Zebra mussel

ATLANTIC OCEAN
Amphionides reynaudii
Antarctic krill
Apseudes intermedius
Black lampshell
Common octopus
Corolla spectabilis
Cyclaspis longicaudata
Derocheilocaris typicus
Giant red mysid
Green bonellia
Harlequin shrimp
Honeycomb worm
Hutchinsoniella macracantha
Hydrothermal vent worm
Laevipilina antarctica
Longfin inshore squid
Mictocaris halope
Monstrilla grandis
Myzostoma cirriferum
Norwegian tubeworm

Oithona plumifera
Phoronis ijimai
Queen scallop
Red king crab
Salmon louse
Sand fiddler crab
Sand isopod
Sea mat
Sipunculus nudus
Speleonectes gironensis
Sperm whale lice
Spiomenia spiculata
Tubeworm
Tusk shell
Trypetesa lampas
Vampire squid

AUSTRALIA

Anaspides tasmaniae
Common octopus
Fire worm
Gippsland giant worm
Giant tiger prawn
Harlequin shrimp
Tongue worm

AUSTRIA

Antrobathynella stammeri
Common pillbug
Common shiny woodlouse
Common water flea
Fish louse
Mysis relicta
Red swamp crayfish
Roman snail
Zebra mussel

BAHAMAS

Common octopus
Fire worm
Longfin inshore squid
Longtail tadpole shrimp
Tongue worm

BAHRAIN

Common octopus

Fire worm
Red swamp crayfish
Tongue worm

BANGLADESH

Common octopus
Fire worm
Red swamp crayfish
Pearly nautilus
Tongue worm

BARBADOS

Common octopus
Fire worm
Longfin inshore squid
Longtail tadpole shrimp
Tongue worm

BELARUS

Common pillbug
Common shiny woodlouse
Common water flea
Fish louse
Mysis relicta
Red swamp crayfish
Zebra mussel

BELGIUM

Antrobathynella stammeri
Common octopus
Common pillbug
Common shiny woodlouse
Common water flea
Fish louse
Honeycomb worm
Mysis relicta
Red swamp crayfish
Rock barnacle
Roman snail
Trypetesa lampas
Zebra mussel

BELIZE

Common octopus

Fire worm
Longtail tadpole shrimp
Tongue worm

BENIN

Common octopus
Fire worm
Red swamp crayfish
Tongue worm

BERMUDA

Common octopus
Fire worm
Longfin inshore squid
Longtail tadpole shrimp
Mictocaris halope
Tongue worm

BOLIVIA

Longtail tadpole shrimp
Red swamp crayfish

BOSNIA AND HERZEGOVINA

Common octopus
Common pillbug
Common shiny woodlouse
Common water flea
Fish louse
Green bonellia
Mysis relicta
Red swamp crayfish
Rock barnacle
Zebra mussel

BOTSWANA

Red swamp crayfish

BRAZIL

Common octopus
Fire worm
Giant Amazonian leech
Longtail tadpole shrimp

Red swamp crayfish
Tongue worm

BRUNEI

Common octopus
Fire worm
Giant tiger prawn
Harlequin shrimp
Pearly nautilus
Red swamp crayfish
Tongue worm

BULGARIA

Common octopus
Common pillbug
Common shiny woodlouse
Common water flea
Fish louse
Mysis relicta
Red swamp crayfish
Rock barnacle
Zebra mussel

BURKINA FASO

Red swamp crayfish

BURUNDI

Red swamp crayfish

CAMBODIA

Common octopus
Fire worm
Pearly nautilus
Red swamp crayfish
Tongue worm

CAMEROON

Common octopus
Fire worm
Red swamp crayfish
Tongue worm

CANADA

Beach hopper

Common octopus
Common pillbug
Common shiny woodlouse
Common water flea
Longfin inshore squid
Longtail tadpole shrimp
Mysis relicta
North American medicinal
  leech
Phoronis ijimai
Red king crab
Red swamp crayfish
Rock barnacle
Sand isopod
Trypetesa lampas
Tusk shell

CAPE VERDE

Common octopus
Fire worm
Queen scallop
Red swamp crayfish
Tongue worm

CENTRAL AFRICAN REPUBLIC

Red swamp crayfish

CHAD

Red swamp crayfish

CHILE

Common octopus
Longtail tadpole shrimp
Red swamp crayfish

CHINA

Common octopus
Fire worm
Pearly nautilus
Red swamp crayfish
Tongue worm

COLOMBIA

Common octopus
Fire worm

Giant Amazonian leech
Giant yellow water bear
Longfin inshore squid
Longtail tadpole shrimp
Red swamp crayfish
Tongue worm

COMOROS

Common octopus
Fire worm
Red swamp crayfish
Tongue worm

COSTA RICA

Common octopus
Epiperipatus biolleyi
Fire worm
Longfin inshore squid
Longtail tadpole shrimp
Red swamp crayfish
Tongue worm

CROATIA

Antrobathynella stammeri
Common pillbug
Common shiny woodlouse
Common water flea
Fish louse
Green bonellia
Mysis relicta
Red swamp crayfish
Roman snail
Zebra mussel

CUBA

Common octopus
Fire worm
Longfin inshore squid
Longtail tadpole shrimp
Speleonectes gironensis
Tongue worm

CYPRUS

Common octopus

Fire worm
Red swamp crayfish
Roman snail
Tongue worm
Zebra mussel

CZECH REPUBLIC
Antrobathynella stammeri
Common pillbug
Common shiny woodlouse
Common water flea
Fish louse
Mysis relicta
Red swamp crayfish
Roman snail
Zebra mussel

DEMOCRATIC REPUBLIC OF THE CONGO
Red swamp crayfish

DENMARK
Common pillbug
Common shiny woodlouse
Common water flea
Fish louse
Mysis relicta
Red swamp crayfish
Rock barnacle
Roman snail
Trypetesa lampas
Zebra mussel

DJIBOUTI
Common octopus
Fire worm
Giant tiger prawn
Green bonellia
Harlequin shrimp
Red swamp crayfish
Tongue worm

DOMINICA
Common octopus

Fire worm
Longfin inshore squid
Longtail tadpole shrimp
Red swamp crayfish
Tongue worm

DOMINICAN REPUBLIC
Common octopus
Fire worm
Longfin inshore squid
Longtail tadpole shrimp
Red swamp crayfish
Tongue worm

ECUADOR
Common octopus
Fire worm
Longtail tadpole shrimp
Red swamp crayfish
Tongue worm

EGYPT
Common octopus
Fire worm
Giant tiger prawn
Green bonellia
Harlequin shrimp
Red swamp crayfish
Tongue worm

EL SALVADOR
Common octopus
Fire worm
Longfin inshore squid
Longtail tadpole shrimp
Red swamp crayfish
Tongue worm

EQUATORIAL GUINEA
Common octopus
Fire worm
Red swamp crayfish
Tongue worm

ERITREA
Common octopus
Fire worm
Giant tiger prawn
Green bonellia
Harlequin shrimp
Red swamp crayfish
Tongue worm

ESTONIA
Common octopus
Common pillbug
Common shiny woodlouse
Common water flea
Fish louse
Mysis relicta
Red swamp crayfish
Rock barnacle
Roman snail
Trypetesa lampas
Zebra mussel

ETHIOPIA
Red swamp crayfish

FIJI
Common octopus
Fire worm
Red swamp crayfish
Tongue worm

FINLAND
Common octopus
Common pillbug
Common shiny woodlouse
Common water flea
Fish louse
Mysis relicta
Red swamp crayfish
Rock barnacle
Roman snail
Trypetesa lampas
Zebra mussel

FRANCE
Common octopus

Common pillbug
Common shiny woodlouse
Common water flea
Fish louse
Green bonellia
Honeycomb worm
Mysis relicta
Queen scallop
Red swamp crayfish
Rock barnacle
Roman snail
Trypetesa lampas
Zebra mussel

FRENCH GUIANA
Common octopus
Fire worm
Giant Amazonian leech
Longfin inshore squid
Longtail tadpole shrimp
Red swamp crayfish
Tongue worm

GABON
Common octopus
Fire worm
Red swamp crayfish
Tongue worm

GAMBIA
Common octopus
Fire worm
Red swamp crayfish
Tongue worm

GEORGIA
Common octopus
Fire worm
Red swamp crayfish
Tongue worm
Zebra mussel

GERMANY
Antrobathynella stammeri

Common octopus
Common pillbug
Common shiny woodlouse
Common water flea
Fish louse
Mysis relicta
Red swamp crayfish
Rock barnacle
Roman snail
Trypetesa lampas
Zebra mussel

GHANA
Common octopus
Fire worm
Red swamp crayfish
Tongue worm

GREECE
Common octopus
Common pillbug
Common shiny woodlouse
Common water flea
Fish louse
Green bonellia
Mysis relicta
Red swamp crayfish
Rock barnacle
Roman snail
Zebra mussel

GRENADA
Common octopus
Fire worm
Longfin inshore squid
Longtail tadpole shrimp
Red swamp crayfish
Tongue worm

GUATEMALA
Common octopus
Fire worm
Longfin inshore squid
Longtail tadpole shrimp

Red swamp crayfish
Tongue worm

GUINEA
Common octopus
Fire worm
Red swamp crayfish
Tongue worm

GUINEA-BISSAU
Common octopus
Fire worm
Red swamp crayfish
Tongue worm

GUYANA
Common octopus
Fire worm
Giant Amazonian leech
Longfin inshore squid
Longtail tadpole shrimp
Red swamp crayfish
Tongue worm

HAITI
Common octopus
Fire worm
Longfin inshore squid
Longtail tadpole shrimp
Tongue worm

HONDURAS
Common octopus
Fire worm
Longfin inshore squid
Longtail tadpole shrimp
Red swamp crayfish
Tongue worm

HUNGARY
Antrobathynella stammeri
Common pillbug
Common shiny woodlouse

Common water flea
Fish louse
Mysis relicta
Red swamp crayfish
Roman snail
Zebra mussel

ICELAND
Common octopus
Common pillbug
Common shiny woodlouse
Common water flea
Mysis relicta
Rock barnacle

INDIA
Common octopus
Fire worm
Giant tiger prawn
Pearly nautilus
Red swamp crayfish
Tongue worm

INDIAN OCEAN
Amphionides reynaudii
Antarctic krill
Black-lipped pearl oyster
Common octopus
Geography cone shell
Giant red mysid
Giant tiger prawn
Green bonellia
Laevipilina antarctica
Oithona plumifera
Peacock mantis shrimp
Pearly nautilus
Sea mat
Sipunculus nudus
Sperm whale lice
Top shell
Vampire squid

INDONESIA
Common octopus

Fire worm
Giant tiger prawn
Green bonellia
Harlequin shrimp
Pearly nautilus
Red swamp crayfish
Tongue worm

IRAN
Common octopus
Fire worm
Tongue worm

IRAQ
Common octopus
Fire worm
Tongue worm

IRELAND
Antrobathynella stammeri
Common octopus
Common pillbug
Common shiny woodlouse
Common water flea
Honeycomb worm
Mysis relicta
Red swamp crayfish
Rock barnacle
Trypetesa lampas
Tusk shell

ISRAEL
Common octopus
Fire worm
Tongue worm

ITALY
Common octopus
Common pillbug
Common shiny woodlouse
Common water flea
Fish louse
Green bonellia

Mysis relicta
Red swamp crayfish
Rock barnacle
Roman snail

IVORY COAST
Common octopus
Fire worm
Red swamp crayfish
Tongue worm

JAMAICA
Common octopus
Fire worm
Longtail tadpole shrimp
Tongue worm

JAPAN
Common octopus
Fire worm
Giant tiger prawn
Gumboot chiton
Itoitantulus misophricola
Longtail tadpole shrimp
Pearly nautilus
Phoronis ijimai
Red king crab
Red swamp crayfish
Shield limpet
Tongue worm
Vargula hilgendorfii

JORDAN
Common octopus
Fire worm
Tongue worm

KENYA
Common octopus
Fire worm
Tongue worm

KIRIBATI
Common octopus

Fire worm
Tongue worm

KUWAIT
Common octopus
Fire worm
Tongue worm

LAOS
Common octopus
Fire worm
Red swamp crayfish
Tongue worm

LATVIA
Common octopus
Common pillbug
Common shiny woodlouse
Common water flea
Fish louse
Mysis relicta
Red swamp crayfish
Rock barnacle
Trypetesa lampas
Zebra mussel

LEBANON
Common octopus
Fire worm
Red swamp crayfish
Tongue worm

LESOTHO
Red swamp crayfish

LESSER ANTILLES
Common octopus
Longtail tadpole shrimp
Red swamp crayfish

LIBERIA
Common octopus

Fire worm
Red swamp crayfish
Tongue worm

LIBYA
Common octopus
Green bonellia
Red swamp crayfish

LIECHTENSTEIN
Antrobathynella stammeri
Common pillbug
Common shiny woodlouse
Common water flea
Fish louse
Mysis relicta
Red swamp crayfish
Roman snail
Zebra mussel

LITHUANIA
Common octopus
Common pillbug
Common shiny woodlouse
Common water flea
Fish louse
Mysis relicta
Red swamp crayfish
Rock barnacle
Trypetesa lampas
Zebra mussel

LUXEMBOURG
Antrobathynella stammeri
Common pillbug
Common shiny woodlouse
Common water flea
Fish louse
Mysis relicta
Red swamp crayfish
Roman snail
Zebra mussel

MACEDONIA
Common octopus

Common pillbug
Common shiny woodlouse
Common water flea
Green bonellia
Mysis relicta
Red swamp crayfish
Rock barnacle

MADAGASCAR
Common octopus
Fire worm
Red swamp crayfish
Tongue worm

MALAWI
Red swamp crayfish

MALAYSIA
Common octopus
Fire worm
Giant tiger prawn
Green bonellia
Harlequin shrimp
Pearly nautilus
Red swamp crayfish
Tongue worm

MALDIVES
Common octopus
Fire worm
Red swamp crayfish
Tongue worm

MALI
Red swamp crayfish

MALTA
Common pillbug
Common shiny woodlouse
Common water flea
Fish louse
Mysis relicta
Red swamp crayfish
Rock barnacle
Zebra mussel

MARIANA ISLANDS
Common octopus

MARSHALL ISLANDS
Common octopus
Fire worm
Tongue worm

MAURITANIA
Common octopus
Fire worm
Red swamp crayfish
Tongue worm

MAURITIUS
Common octopus
Fire worm
Red swamp crayfish
Tongue worm

MEDITERRANEAN SEA
Amphionides reynaudii
Apseudes intermedius
Common octopus
Green bonellia
Honeycomb worm
Myzostoma cirriferum
Oithona plumifera
Queen scallop
Sea mat
Sipunculus nudus
Sperm whale lice
Tubeworm
Vampire squid

MEXICO
Common octopus
Common pillbug
Common shiny woodlouse
Common water flea
Coquina clam
Fire worm
Longfin inshore squid

Longtail tadpole shrimp
Mysis relicta
Red swamp crayfish
Rock barnacle
Shield limpet
Stygiomysis cokei
Tongue worm
Veiled chiton

MICRONESIA
Common octopus
Fire worm
Red swamp crayfish
Tongue worm

MOLDOVA
Common octopus
Common pillbug
Common shiny woodlouse
Common water flea
Fish louse
Mysis relicta
Red swamp crayfish
Rock barnacle

MONACO
Common octopus
Common pillbug
Common shiny woodlouse
Common water flea
Fish louse
Green bonellia
Mysis relicta
Red swamp crayfish
Rock barnacle
Roman snail
Zebra mussel

MONGOLIA
Common octopus

MOROCCO
Common octopus

Green bonellia
Honeycomb worm
Red swamp crayfish
Trypetesa lampas

MOZAMBIQUE
Common octopus
Fire worm
Red swamp crayfish
Tongue worm

MYANMAR
Common octopus
Fire worm
Red swamp crayfish
Tongue worm

NAMIBIA
Common octopus
Pearly nautilus
Red swamp crayfish

NAURU
Common octopus
Fire worm
Red swamp crayfish
Tongue worm

NEPAL
Giant yellow water bear

NETHERLANDS
Common octopus
Common pillbug
Common shiny woodlouse
Common water flea
Fish louse
Mysis relicta
Red swamp crayfish
Rock barnacle
Roman snail
Trypetesa lampas
Zebra mussel

NEW ZEALAND
Common octopus
Fire worm
Tongue worm

NICARAGUA
Common octopus
Fire worm
Longtail tadpole shrimp
Red swamp crayfish
Tongue worm

NIGER
Red swamp crayfish

NIGERIA
Common octopus
Fire worm
Red swamp crayfish
Tongue worm

NORTH KOREA
Common octopus
Fire worm
Red swamp crayfish
Tongue worm

NORWAY
Common octopus
Common pillbug
Common shiny woodlouse
Common water flea
Fish louse
Mysis relicta
Norwegian tubeworm
Queen scallop
Red king crab
Red swamp crayfish
Rock barnacle
Roman snail
Trypetesa lampas
Zebra mussel

OMAN
Common octopus

Fire worm
Giant tiger prawn
Harlequin shrimp
Tongue worm

PACIFIC OCEAN
Amphionides reynaudii
Antarctic krill
Beach hopper
Black lampshell
Black-lipped pearl oyster
Common octopus
Corolla spectabilis
Dahlella caldariensis
Geography cone shell
Giant clam
Giant red mysid
Giant tiger prawn
Green bonellia
Gumboot chiton
Harlequin shrimp
Hydrothermal vent worm
Itoitantulus misophricola
Laevipilina antarctica
Nannosquilla decemspinosa
North Pacific krill
Oithona plumifera
Peacock mantis shrimp
Pearly nautilus
Phoronis ijimai
Red king crab
Salmon louse
Sea mat
Shield limpet
Sipunculus nudus
Skeleton shrimp
Sperm whale lice
Stygiomysis cokei
Top shell
Vampire squid
Vargula hilgendorfii
Veiled chiton

PAKISTAN
Common octopus

Fire worm
Tongue worm

PALAU
Common octopus
Fire worm
Tongue worm

PANAMA
Common octopus
Fire worm
Harlequin shrimp
Longfin inshore squid
Longtail tadpole shrimp
Nannosquilla decemspinosa
Red swamp crayfish
Tongue worm

PAPUA NEW GUINEA
Common octopus
Fire worm
Tongue worm

PARAGUAY
Longtail tadpole shrimp
Red swamp crayfish

PERU
Common octopus
Fire worm
Longtail tadpole shrimp
Red swamp crayfish
Tongue worm

PHILIPPINES
Common octopus
Fire worm
Giant tiger prawn
Green bonellia
Pearly nautilus
Phoronis ijimai
Red swamp crayfish
Tongue worm

POLAND
Antrobathynella stammeri
Common octopus
Common pillbug
Common shiny woodlouse
Common water flea
Fish louse
Mysis relicta
Red swamp crayfish
Rock barnacle
Trypetesa lampas
Zebra mussel

PORTUGAL
Common octopus
Common pillbug
Common shiny woodlouse
Common water flea
Fish louse
Honeycomb worm
Mysis relicta
Red swamp crayfish
Rock barnacle
Trypetesa lampas
Zebra mussel

PUERTO RICO
Common octopus
Fire worm
Longfin inshore squid
Longtail tadpole shrimp
Tongue worm

QATAR
Common octopus
Fire worm
Tongue worm

REPUBLIC OF THE CONGO
Common octopus
Fire worm
Red swamp crayfish
Tongue worm

ROMANIA
Antrobathynella stammeri
Common octopus
Common pillbug
Common shiny woodlouse
Common water flea
Fish louse
Mysis relicta
Red swamp crayfish
Rock barnacle
Roman snail
Zebra mussel

RUSSIA
Common octopus
Common pillbug
Common shiny woodlouse
Common water flea
Fire worm
Fish louse
Gumboot chiton
Mysis relicta
Red swamp crayfish
Rock barnacle
Tongue worm
Trypetesa lampas
Zebra mussel

RWANDA
Red swamp crayfish

ST. KITTS-NEVIS
Longfin inshore squid
Longtail tadpole shrimp

ST. LUCIA
Common octopus
Longfin inshore squid
Longtail tadpole shrimp

ST. VINCENT/ GRENADINES
Common octopus

Longfin inshore squid
Longtail tadpole shrimp

SAMOA
Common octopus
Fire worm
Tongue worm

SAN MARINO
Common octopus
Common pillbug
Common shiny woodlouse
Common water flea
Fish louse
Mysis relicta
Rock barnacle

SÃO TOMÉ AND PRÍNCIPE
Common octopus
Fire worm
Red swamp crayfish
Tongue worm

SAUDI ARABIA
Common octopus
Fire worm
Giant tiger prawn
Green bonellia
Harlequin shrimp
Tongue worm

SENEGAL
Common octopus
Fire worm
Red swamp crayfish
Tongue worm

SERBIA AND MONTENEGRO
Common pillbug
Common shiny woodlouse
Common water flea

Fish louse
Mysis relicta
Red swamp crayfish
Roman snail
Zebra mussel

SEYCHELLES
Common octopus
Fire worm
Red swamp crayfish
Tongue worm

SIERRA LEONE
Common octopus
Fire worm
Tongue worm

SINGAPORE
Common octopus
Fire worm
Harlequin shrimp
Tongue worm

SLOVAKIA
Antrobathynella stammeri
Fish louse
Red swamp crayfish
Roman snail
Zebra mussel

SLOVENIA
Antrobathynella stammeri
Fish louse
Green bonellia
Red swamp crayfish
Roman snail
Zebra mussel

SOLOMON ISLANDS
Common octopus
Fire worm
Red swamp crayfish
Tongue worm

SOMALIA
Common octopus
Fire worm
Giant tiger prawn
Harlequin shrimp
Red swamp crayfish
Tongue worm

SOUTH AFRICA
Common octopus
Red swamp crayfish
Spelaeogriphus lepidops

SOUTH KOREA
Common octopus
Fire worm
Pearly nautilus
Tongue worm

SPAIN
Common octopus
Common pillbug
Common shiny woodlouse
Common water flea
Fish louse
Green bonellia
Honeycomb worm
Mysis relicta
Queen scallop
Red swamp crayfish
Rock barnacle
Roman snail
Trypetesa lampas
Zebra mussel

SRI LANKA
Common octopus
Fire worm
Giant tiger prawn
Harlequin shrimp
Red swamp crayfish
Tongue worm

SUDAN
Green bonellia
Red swamp crayfish

SURINAME
Common octopus
Fire worm
Giant Amazonian leech
Longfin inshore squid
Longtail tadpole shrimp
Red swamp crayfish
Tongue worm

SWAZILAND
Red swamp crayfish

SWEDEN
Common octopus
Common pillbug
Common shiny woodlouse
Common water flea
Fish louse
Giant yellow water bear
Mysis relicta
Red swamp crayfish
Rock barnacle
Roman snail
Trypetesa lampas
Zebra mussel

SWITZERLAND
Common pillbug
Common shiny woodlouse
Common water flea
Fish louse
Mysis relicta
Red swamp crayfish
Roman snail
Zebra mussel

SYRIA
Common octopus
Fire worm

Red swamp crayfish
Tongue worm

TAIWAN
Common octopus
Fire worm
Red swamp crayfish
Tongue worm

TANZANIA
Common octopus
Fire worm
Red swamp crayfish
Tongue worm

THAILAND
Common octopus
Fire worm
Pearly nautilus
Red swamp crayfish
Tongue worm

TIMOR-LESTE
Common octopus

TOGO
Common octopus
Fire worm
Tongue worm

TONGA
Common octopus
Fire worm
Tongue worm

TRINIDAD AND TOBAGO
Common octopus
Fire worm
Longfin inshore squid
Longtail tadpole shrimp
Tongue worm

TUNISIA
Common octopus

Green bonellia
Red swamp crayfish
Thermosbaena mirabilis

TURKEY
Common octopus
Common pillbug
Common shiny woodlouse
Common water flea
Fire worm
Fish louse
Giant yellow water bear
Green bonellia
Mysis relicta
Red swamp crayfish
Rock barnacle
Tongue worm

TUVALU
Common octopus
Fire worm
Tongue worm

UGANDA
Red swamp crayfish

UKRAINE
Common pillbug
Common shiny woodlouse
Common water flea
Mysis relicta

UNITED ARAB EMIRATES
Common octopus
Fire worm
Tongue worm

UNITED KINGDOM
Antrobathynella stammeri
Common octopus
Common pillbug

Common shiny woodlouse
Common water flea
Honeycomb worm
Mysis relicta
Queen scallop
Rock barnacle
Roman snail
Trypetesa lampas

UNITED STATES
Beach hopper
Common octopus
Common pillbug
Common shiny woodlouse
Common water flea
Coquina clam
Derocheilocaris typicus
Fire worm
Gumboot chiton
Hutchinsoniella macracantha
Longfin inshore squid
Longtail tadpole shrimp
Mysis relicta
North American medicinal
  leech
Phoronis ijimai
Red swamp crayfish
River worm
Rock barnacle
Sand fiddler crab
Sand isopod
Skeleton shrimp
Tongue worm
Trypetesa lampas
Tusk shell
Veiled chiton
Zebra mussel

URUGUAY
Common octopus
Longtail tadpole shrimp
Red swamp crayfish

VANUATU
Common octopus

Fire worm
Tongue worm

VENEZUELA
Common octopus
Fire worm
Giant Amazonian leech
Longfin inshore squid
Longtail tadpole shrimp
Red swamp crayfish
Tongue worm

VIETNAM
Common octopus
Fire worm
Pearly nautilus
Red swamp crayfish
Tongue worm

YEMEN
Common octopus
Fire worm
Giant tiger prawn

Green bonellia
Harlequin shrimp
Red swamp crayfish
Tongue worm

ZAMBIA
Red swamp crayfish

ZIMBABWE
Red swamp crayfish

Index

Italic type indicates volume number; **boldface** type indicates entries and their pages; (ill.) indicates illustrations.